A HISTORY OF PETTS WOOD

PETER WAYMARK

Millennium Edition

Peter Waymark

4.11.00

PETTS WOOD & DISTRICT RESIDENTS ASSOCIATION

Published by Petts Wood and District Residents' Association

ISBN 0-9509198-2-9

CONTENTS

Peter Pett and Sovereign of the Seas, *the three-decker, three-master warship launched in 1637 (see page 11). Painting by Sir Peter Lely (National Maritime Museum)*

Petts Wood families celebrate VE Day, May 1945, with a street party in Diameter Road. Disused prisoner of war huts are in the background. The picture was lent by Vincent Spears, the smallest of the boys at the table in the centre of the picture and still living in Petts Wood 55 years later.

1. PROLOGUE

Sixty million years ago Petts Wood lay at the bottom of a freshwater lake. That we know from fossils found in the excavations for the Safeway supermarket building by Petts Wood Station in March 1979. The land where Petts Wood stands had been there for millions of years before, submerged by seas which dropped deposits of rocks, including chalk, on it and then withdrew. But you would have to dig down 100 feet or more to find the chalk today.

The freshwater lake of Eocene (Tertiary) times, with its fossil snails (Viviparus lentus) and mussels (Union subparallela) found in the Woolwich Beds, marks the beginning of the rocks which most Petts Wood gardeners are familiar with: the Blackheath Pebble Beds. At this time most of Britain was land, and the sea was out to the east where the North Sea is today. But the deposition of the Blackheath Pebble Beds, sandy soil with pebbles of flint and quartzite, marks the return of the sea from the east. This sea deepened to about 100 fathoms and fine material, London Clay, covers most of the west of Petts Wood and is cut by the Sevenoaks railway line, while the Blackheath Pebble Beds (with the Woolwich Beds underneath and outcropping on the eastern fringe) provide the woodlands and the base for Petts Wood east.

Later in Tertiary times dramatic mountain-building movements formed the Alps and our comparatively gentle hills probably owe something of their shape to these movements. In Quaternary times which followed, the climate became much colder and although no ice caps sat on Petts Wood, the subsoil is likely to have been frozen for some feet down.

The unearthing of flint tools and other artefacts is evidence that the area was inhabited by man in the Paleolithic or Old Stone Age period. Hand axes from about 200,000 years ago have been found at Green Street Green. Other hand axes, discovered during building works at Ramsden in the 1950s, probably date from 100,000 years ago.

As the ice sheets covering Britain diminished, man started living on the edge of lakes and on river banks. The abundance of flints was one magnet to settlement in the area and another was the valley of the Cray. New types of tools came into use, including small flint blades mounted to form the barbs to spears, harpoons and arrows, as well as other forms of flint work. Examples of tools from the Mesolithic or Middle Stone Ages, around 10,000 to 6,000 years ago, have been found at Priory Gardens in Orpington and at Fordcroft, near the junction of Poverest Road and Cray Avenue.

Around 4,500 BC the first ideas about farming were adopted from the Continent, leading to the introduction of domesticated plants and animals. New sources of stone and flint were exploited for making tools and ground stone axes are a common object from this period found in the area.

During the Bronze Age, from around 2,000 BC, metal gradually replaced flint and stone. Two examples of bronze metal work have been found in Petts Wood. In 1967 a flat axe from the early Bronze Age was turned up by Mr J. Dahn in his garden in Grosvenor Road while removing fruit bushes. Measuring 15 cms long

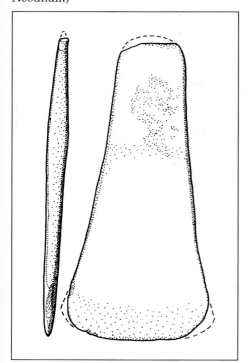

Early Bronze age axe found in a Petts Wood garden in 1967 (© Stuart Needham)

The Roman bath house excavated at Fordcroft, at the bottom of Poverest Road, in the 1970s. The drawing, above, is an artist's impression of the exterior by Christina Clark. The photograph, left, shows part of the surviving floor.

and 7.4 cms across the cutting edge, the axe had a ruddy brown surface with areas of dull dark green. Hafted like an Indian tomahawk, the axe could have been used for felling smallish trees.

In the 1950s Mr H. F. Marfleet of Crossway discovered the cutting edge of a socketed axe in his allotment by the railway just north of Petts Wood Station. The axe belonged to the later Bronze Age, making it perhaps 3,000 years old, and was probably used as a woodworking tool. It can be seen in Maidstone Museum.

As bronze had replaced flint and stone, so bronze was superseded by iron. The most notable Iron Age site in the area is the hill fort known as Caesar's Camp at Holwood, Keston. Roman conquest and settlement date from AD 43 when an army under Aulius Plautius landed near Richborough, north of Sandwich, and quickly swept westwards over the Orpington and Bromley area. There was considerable settlement in the Kent valleys, among them the Darenth, where the villa at Lullingstone is one of the earliest and finest testaments to Roman culture, and its tributary, the Cray.

The remains of a Roman bath house, built after 270 AD, were excavated at Fordcroft during the 1970s. It was probably part of a small settlement situated at the head of navigation of the River Cray. Fragments of glassware and pottery, as well as jewellery, have been found on the site and it is likely people lived there for some hundreds of years. The Fordcroft settlement was probably a local rural centre, providing services and crafts for the surrounding population. A cremation cemetery discovered in May Avenue, St Mary Cray, was almost certainly associated with this settlement.

A Roman farmstead was discovered at Ramsden in the 1950s during preparation of the land for the estate and school. Among the remains found on the site were corn drying kilns, storage pits and a well. From pottery it has been established that the farmstead belongs to the early Roman period.

The other important Roman settlement found in the area is the villa in Crofton Road between the former council offices and Orpington Station. Although villa has come to denote a residence, its Roman meaning embraced not only a large country house but the surrounding estate and farm. Offering a fine view over the valley, the hillside site may have been used before the Romans came. The house was substantial, with more than 20 rooms, and had underfloor heating, tessellated floors and plastered interior walls, some with painted designs. It was inhabited from about AD 140 to AD 400 and was the centre of a farming estate which could have covered between 300 and 500 acres.

Part of the remains were destroyed when the railway was built in the 1860s and there was further destruction with the building of the council offices. A car park planned by Bromley Council in the late 1980s for the extended Civic Hall would have obliterated the entire site, but the scheme was modified to allow a full excavation by the Kent Archaeological Rescue Unit. Twelve large rooms were revealed, with clear evidence of the tiled floors and heating ducts. The site was put under a purpose-built cover and opened to the public in 1993.

With the departure of the Roman administration in the early 5th century, the Cray valley was occupied by the Saxons from northern Europe. On the edge of

Excavations at Crofton Roman Villa, 1988, showing part of the tessellated floor (Local Studies and Archives Department, Bromley Central Library)

the Roman site at Fordcroft an Anglo-Saxon cemetery has been found and 80 burials uncovered. Weapons and jewellery buried with the bodies suggest that the cemetery was used from about AD 450 to about AD 550. A small Saxon dwelling has been excavated on the side of the river, at Kent Road, St Mary Cray, and the church of All Saints at Orpington is of Saxon origin.

The Domesday survey of land ownership in England 20 years after the Norman conquest of 1066 has entries for Orpington and Crofton but throws no light on who may have been the landowners in Petts Wood. The first hard evidence of human settlement in what became residential Petts Wood is the existence of the manor of Town Court in the 13th century. We shall pick this up in Chapter 5.

2. THE REMARKABLE PETTS

In their huge and impressively researched volume, *The History of Chislehurst*, published in 1899, E. A. Webb, G. W. Miller and J. Beckwith suggest that Petts Wood was named after a former owner, who may have been Pett, Pette or Pitt and possibly descended from Thomas de Puteo whose name, meaning pit, appears in the records of local property purchases around 1260. Surprisingly, perhaps, they make no mention of the shipbuilding Petts, who are now generally thought to have given the wood its name.

However, writing nearly 30 years later, when the wood had just been bought for the National Trust, the same George W. Miller was much more definite. He identified William Pett, a shipbuilder for Queen Elizabeth I, as the owner of the wood and claimed that there was still standing a dead tree 'which was the last survivor of Pett's oaks'. Miller went on: 'The greatest interest the wood holds for me is the thought that its former timbers went to the building of England's wooden walls that haply voyaged with Drake and with Blake in the days when our country was gradually gaining its supremacy on the seas.'

Miller may have been embroidering a little for the only evidence of a connection between the Petts and the wood is the will of William, made in 1577, which refers to 'my landes lyeing within the parishe of Chislehurst in the County of Kent and the tenements appurteyning to the same, also the lease of a coppy wood called Hawkeswoode, with the three hundred oaks growing upon the same, in the parishe of Chislehurst.'

From this it is reasonable to assume that the Petts took a lease on the wood to secure timber for their ships. Chislehurst was only a few miles from Deptford and Woolwich, two of the principal shipyards, although we can imagine the felled oaks making a long and tedious journey on horse-drawn carts along the rough tracks that passed as roads. It is nice to think, as some writers have suggested, that oaks from the wood were used in Drake's *Golden Hind* and other famous ships but there is no evidence for this. Similarly speculative is the notion that Petts Wood oak helped to form the barrier of floating logs strung across the Thames to protect London from the Spanish Armada.

Extract from the will of William Pett, dated 1577, establishing the link between the family and the woods (see text) (Public Record Office)

The family's connection with ships probably goes back to the early 15th century for, writing in 1639, Thomas Heywood observed that men of the name of Pett had been officers and architects of the Royal Navy for 'the space of two hundred years and upwards'. One of the first to achieve national prominence was Peter Pett, who was building ships at Deptford during the reign of Henry VIII (1509-47) and was later appointed master shipwright to Edward VI and Elizabeth. During this time he is said to have had an important part in building most of the ships for the navy. In 1583 he was granted a coat of arms depicting 'between three orgresses sable, a lion passant guardant of the field'. Four years later Pett, and Matthew Baker, who was associated with him in the works at Dover, accused Sir John Hawkins, treasurer of the navy, of malpractices in connection with the repair of the Queen's ships. The charges were apparently brought out of pique and were unsubstantiated: but the affair seems not to have hurt Pett, who remained in office until his death in September 1589.

Peter Pett married twice and had 14 children. Many of the sons were shipbuilders and three held the royal appointment of master builder. The eldest, William, whose will has been quoted, had his yard at Limehouse. He died in 1587, two years before his father, leaving a widow and two daughters. His will provided that his yards and building materials should be disposed of to his brothers in preference to other buyers. William's brother Joseph carried on the family eminence, succeeding his father as master shipwright at Deptford. Joseph died on November 15, 1605 and was succeeded by his half-brother, Phineas, Peter Pett's son by his second marriage.

More is known about this Phineas (there were several others of the same name) than any of the other Petts, partly because he appears to have achieved the most but also because he wrote an autobiography. He was born at Deptford on November 1,1570 and educated for three years at the free school in Rochester and for another three years at a private school in Greenwich. He entered Emmanuel College, Cambridge, in 1586, and took an MA degree, but after the death of his father three years later he was left penniless. In 1590 he became apprenticed to a master shipwright, Richard Chapman, at Deptford, and after Chapman's death spent two years at sea as a carpenter's mate on an ill-fated voyage of Edward Glenham. He returned to London as poor as when he had started.

Phineas then worked under Matthew Baker, his father's old colleague, on the *Repulse* which took part in the triumphant raid on Cadiz. Pett and Baker later fell out and their feud is said to have lasted for ten years. The Petts seem to have been a particularly quarrelsome breed. In April 1597 Phineas was taken under the wing of Lord Howard, Earl of Effingham, the Lord Admiral, who employed him first as his servant, then on shipbuilding in East Anglia and in June 1600 appointed him 'keeper of the plankyard, timber and other provisions' at Chatham.

Nine months later he became assistant to the master shipwright at Chatham and in November 1605 succeeded his half-brother, Joseph, as master shipwright at Deptford. His first major achievement came three years later when he laid the keel of the navy's largest ship up to that date, *The Prince Royal*, but soon afterwards his career was threatened when charges were laid against him of

Phineas Pett (1570-1647), with his coat of arms top left; painting attributed to John de Critz (National Portrait Gallery)

incompetence and dishonesty over a ship being built at Woolwich. He claimed that this was jealousy on the part of his brother shipwrights, who wanted to ruin him. The case was tried before the King, James I, at Woolwich and Pett was acquitted on all counts. He went on to become Britain's shipbuilding supremo overseeing all construction at the Chatham, Deptford and Woolwich yards. In 1637 the navy's largest and most ornamented ship (it carried 100 guns) was launched at Woolwich. It was called *Sovereign of the Seas* and in the following year King Charles I and his Queen dined on board. Phineas was in overall charge of the project, though the building was the responsibility of his son, Peter.

Phineas, described by one authority as 'a man of great ability and industry, kind to his friends but short of temper and swayed by quick impulse', died in 1647 and was buried at Chatham. The line of distinguished Petts was continued by his fifth son, Peter, who was appointed master shipwright at Chatham and later commissioner of the navy, an apparent reward for helping to prevent a mutiny. But he was often in trouble, arousing animosity by filling important posts at the yard with close relatives and having to face charges of fraud. He survived until 1667 when he was blamed for the disastrous Dutch attack on Chatham, superseded, sent to the Tower of London and threatened with impeachment. The threat was never carried out but he was not restored to office and he died around 1670.

A cousin of the Peter just mentioned, also called Peter, was a master shipwright at Deptford who produced two notable sons. Sir Peter was advocate-general for Ireland, while Sir Phineas appears to have been the last Pett to have held high office in the navy. Both are mentioned in Samuel Pepys's Diary. Like other members of the family, Sir Phineas had his brushes with authority. In 1660, when assistant master shipwright at Chatham, he was dismissed. But he apparently recovered from this setback, for he later became master shipwright at Woolwich and in 1680 was appointed comptroller of the stores and knighted. He was commissioner at Chatham from 1685 to 1689. If Sir Phineas was the last of the family to build ships, the name of Pett appears frequently in navy lists up to the end of the 18th century.

Miller suggests that the wood was held by the Petts under a long lease, or several leases, from the landowner. This was probably the Wotton family, who owned the manor of Ling Ockmere in St Mary Cray. The wood was certainly in their possession in 1687 when the court roll of the manors of Chislehurst and Scadbury records the death of the last Lord Wotton. He left the wood, with his other estates, to the younger son of his half brother, Charles Stanhope, Lord Chesterfield, who died childless in 1704. The wood then passed to his older brother, the second Earl of Chesterfield. His son was the famous literary earl, author of *Letters to a Son*, and the man who introduced the bill for the adoption of the Gregorian calendar which 'lost' the nation eleven days. It is curious that Petts Wood should be associated both with a change of the calendar and a change of the clock. Chesterfield sold the land to a Thomas Borret, a landowner from Shoreham, who around 1790 disposed of it to Herman Berens, a London merchant of Dutch extraction, who also acquired some 900 acres in St Mary Cray. The wood stayed in the Berens family until the 1920s.

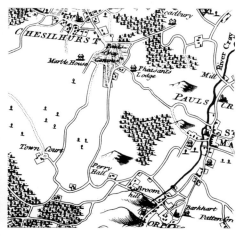

Hasted's map of 1778 shows Town Court but Petts Wood has hardly any trees: had they all been used for the ships?

The gamekeeper's cottage, Petts Wood, taken some time before the Ellis murders of 1880 (Local Studies and Archives Department, Bromley Central Library)

A Victorian Murder

Just over 100 years ago the wood was the scene of a brutal double murder. It came to light in the early hours of Sunday, October 31, 1880, when a 24-year-old labourer, Joseph Waller, was detained at St Mary Cray police station after a complaint from a local farmer who had found the man in his pigsty. Waller was asked why he had blood on his hands and after further questioning told the police: 'If you have eight men and two stretchers, you go to old Ned Ellis's and there you will find two dead bodies.'.

Ellis was the gamekeeper for the Behrens estate and lived with his wife in the cottage just off the Chislehurst-Orpington road. A search in the woods nearby led to the discovery of the bodies first of Mrs Ellis and then of her husband. Both were badly battered around the head. Edward Ellis was 73 and had been working for Behrens for 50 years.

It emerged that Waller was a former policeman who had been discharged from the force two years before for drunkenness and violence. He had worked for Ellis during the winter before the murder. On that fateful morning, Waller had got Ellis out of bed on the pretext that there were poachers about and had taken him into the woods, first shooting him with a revolver and then clubbing him with a staff. Waller then went back for Mrs Ellis and murdered her in a similar way. Waller was committed to Kent Assizes where on January 21, 1881, he was found to be unfit to plead and ordered to be detained during Her Majesty's pleasure. Mr and Mrs Ellis are buried in the churchyard of St Nicholas, Chislehurst.

3. WILLIAM WILLETT AND DAYLIGHT SAVING

After Pett, the most famous Petts Wood name is that of William Willett, who, in the early years of the 20th century, fought a virtually single-handed campaign for daylight saving. It was a campaign that aroused much scorn, and even ridicule, and it was not finally successful until after Willett's death. But his efforts were not forgotten and in 1927 part of Petts Wood was bought by the National Trust as a permanent memorial.

Willett was born in Farnham, Surrey, on August 10, 1856. His father, also William, was a stonemason who later became a builder, and after education at Marylebone Grammar School and commercial training, William junior entered the family business. The firm started building in Belsize Park and established a reputation for quality housing in the more fashionable parts of London - in Mayfair, South Kensington, by Regent's Park and around Sloane Square, where the Willett head office opened in 1897. 'Willett-built' houses also went up in Hove.

A principle which governed the house designs was the young William's love of light and open space. *The Builder* explained his philosophy as follows: 'No matter how many little points in the exterior might be improved by the sacrifice of a little light somewhere inside, yet the sacrifice was never permitted, for he looked on light, and especially sunlight, as all important...' Given this interest, it was hardly surprising that Willett should become the champion of daylight saving.

In 1890 the Willetts bought the Camden Park estate at Chislehurst, which had been the residence of Napoleon III of France and the Empress Eugénie during their exile in England after the Franco-Prussian War. The intention was to develop the whole area but problems arose over access across common land and only two roads, Camden Park Road and Wilderness Road, were laid out. Camden House was preserved and Willett turned the park into a golf course. The club house was opened on July 21,1894 by the future Prime Minister, A. J. Balfour. The first house in Camden Park Road, which he called The Cedars, was reserved by Willett for himself and he lived there from 1894 until his death.

Willett was a keen horseman and each morning, before breakfast, he would ride along St Paul's Cray Common and through Petts Wood. It was during these early morning canters that the idea of daylight saving first came to him. On a beautiful summer day he would notice that the blinds were still down in the large houses and he conceived the notion of saving daylight simply by adjusting the hands of the clock. He set out his case in a pamphlet, *Waste of Daylight*, that ran into 19 editions and was translated into several languages.

Willett proposed that the clock should be moved forward 20 minutes on four occasions in April and put back four times in the autumn. This would give an extra 210 hours of daylight a year and save the nation at least £2½ million on the cost of artificial light. There would be other benefits. As less coal would be burned, there would be less smoke to defile the air. The extra natural light would help eyesight, while longer days spent in the open air would 'make for health and

William Willett (1856-1915), builder and campaigner (Hulton Getty)

strength in body and mind'. Willett asserted: 'Light is one of the greatest gifts for the Creator to man. While daylight surrounds us, cheerfulness reigns, anxieties press less heavily and courage is bred for the struggle of life'. The longer days would also increase the opportunities for rifle practice for which 'the nation may, some day, have cause to be thankful'. Was Willett already anticipating the Great War?

Willett's idea was not original. Benjamin Franklin, a man of many talents who is credited with the invention of the lightning conductor and bifocal spectacles, commended the notion to the inhabitants of Paris in 1784 during his term there as American minister in France. He wrote of people 'living by the smoky, unwholesome and enormously expensive light of candles' when they could have 'as much pure light of the sun for nothing'. But little more was heard on the subject until Willett launched his campaign in the 1900s.

To start with he was a one-man band, firing off scores of letters, year after year, to influential people in parliament, local government, industry, agriculture and the trade unions. He canvassed Chambers of Commerce, clockmakers, astronomers and literary societies. He had moral support from King Edward VII, who had the clocks at Sandringham put forward half an hour, and the South-Western Railway estimated that it could save £92,000 a year through not having to use artificial light. Farmers, on the other hand, argued that it was impossible, by the law of nature, to milk cows an hour earlier; nor could harvesting begin until the dew was off the grass. Theatre managers said their customers would not want to enter playhouses in broad daylight and astronomers claimed that a change of the clock would throw instrument readings into confusion.

But by 1908 Willett had mustered enough support for a daylight saving bill to be introduced in the House of Commons by Robert Pearce, MP for Leek. After a second reading, the bill came before a Select Committee where Willett himself, prepared to argue his case for days if necessary, was the first witness. There was distinguished support from the creator of Sherlock Holmes, Sir Arthur Conan Doyle, and from Lord Avebury, who as Sir John Lubbock had introduced the bill which established the August bank holiday. His grandson, Eric Lubbock, enters the story later. The bill received unexpected endorsement from the manager of Bryant and May. He admitted that extra daylight might cut sales of his matches but thought it more important that working people should get more fresh air and sunlight. The committee's report was generally favourable, though in place of Willett's complicated procedure, it suggested that clocks should be advanced by one hour in a single move.

The Asquith Government effectively killed the bill, however, by refusing to allow parliamentary time for its progress, despite sympathetic noises from the President of the Board of Trade, Winston Churchill. The arguments went on, not least in the correspondence columns of *The Times*, a newspaper which opposed daylight saving as a 'tampering of our standards'. In 1909 a new bill was introduced. Again it was considered by a Select Committee, which heard all the familiar objections as well as some fresh ones, such as that cricket matches would end too late for evening newspapers to carry the close of play scores. This time

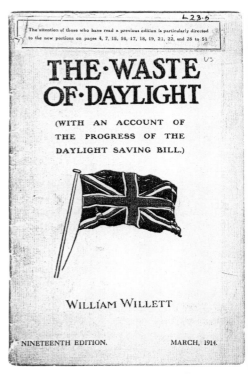

Willett's campaign pamphlet, The Waste of Daylight, *which by 1914 was in its 19th edition (Local Studies and Archives Department, Bromley Central Library)*

The oak-lined bridle path in Petts Wood, looking north; while riding this path William Willett is said to have hit on the idea of Daylight Saving.

the committee sided with the objectors and the bill was lost.

Undeterred by these setbacks, Willett continued his campaign and in 1911 organised a big public meeting at the London Guildhall with Winston Churchill as the main speaker. Now an enthusiastic supporter of daylight saving, Churchill predicted that one day a grateful nation would erect a statue to William Willett and lay sunflowers at his feet on the longest day of the year.

Daylight saving was finally forced onto the statute book by the First World War. Opposition to the measure persisted to the last but it had to bow to the need to save fuel and to ensure that railways and munitions factories were able to operate in daylight as long as possible. Still it was not until May 21, 1916 that daylight saving was introduced. There were protest meetings by farmers but on the whole the nation adjusted smoothly to the change.

Originally a wartime emergency measure only, daylight saving was renewed each year until 1925 when a Summer Time Act made it permanent. In the Second World War it was extended through the winter with 'double' summer time from April to September. In 1968 there began an abortive three-year experiment of the permanent one hour advance, abandoned after concern about schoolchildren having to set off in the dark during the winter months.

William Willett was not able to enjoy the eventual triumph of his campaign. He died at Chislehurst, at the age of 58, on March 4, 1915, and he is buried in St Nicholas' churchyard where a simple marble cross marks his grave. His wife, who lived on until 1957, is buried beside him. Apart from his building business and promotion of daylight saving, Willett took a close interest in medicine and was a benefactor of the London Homoeopathic Hospital and Bromley Cottage Hospital. His daughter, Mrs Gertrude Magrane, in a memoir written for the Petts Wood 21st anniversary celebrations in 1948, recalled other facets: his love for the English classics - Dickens, Thackeray and *Pilgrim's Progress*; a practising Christianity; and a fondness for travel, especially sea voyages.

'Above all', she wrote, 'he loved sunlight, open spaces and fresh air. This, and an untiring fund of energy were his leading characteristics'. Willett Way, the Willett recreation ground and the Daylight Inn perpetuate his name and his work but his official memorial stands, appropriately, in the National Trust woodland.

Willett was married twice. By his first wife, who died in 1905, he had two sons and five daughters; his second marriage, to Florence Strickland in 1910, produced a son and two daughters. But despite this large offspring, family involvement in the company ceased with the early death of his eldest son, Herbert, in 1917. The firm was taken over by a Colonel Mulliner, of the Mulliner coachbuilding business which later became a subsidiary of Rolls-Royce.

During the inter-war period there were Willett developments at Roehampton, Wimbledon, Hampstead and Tunbridge Wells, as well as further building at Hove, and at the request of King George VI the firm carried out extensions and improvements to Royal Lodge, Windsor. In the 1970s, the building side of the Willett business was acquired by Trafalgar House but the company continued to operate as surveyors, auctioneers and estate agents from the Sloane Square building until the late 1980s.

Willett's memory is kept alive by the Daylight Inn; the inn sign was later replaced by an inferior design

4. THE FIGHT FOR THE WOOD

After the First World War there was tremendous pressure for building land around London to accommodate a growing population, swelled still further by a drift to the south from the depressed areas. Areas such as Petts Wood, with fast and frequent electric trains, were prime targets for development and it needed determined local opposition to save land from the builder - particularly as planning legislation was still in its infancy.

The woodland on which the Pett family had held a lease passed in around 1790 to Herman Berens, of Kevington, St Mary Cray, and it was still in the Berens family after the First World War when the owners decided to put it on the market. The decision caused dismay among the people of Chislehurst, who foresaw St Paul's Cray Common being encircled by houses, and a campaign was started by influential residents to buy the wood as a memorial to William Willett. That Willett had himself been a speculative builder was an irony apparently lost on those involved.

In October 1925 the Early Closing Association held a public luncheon in London to celebrate the passing of the Summer Time Act. The association's president, Winston Churchill, now Chancellor of the Exchequer, proposed a toast to the success of the Act and afterwards a meeting was held to discuss the Willett memorial. An appeal committee was formed with Churchill as president and a distinguished list of vice-presidents, including Sir William Joynson-Hicks, the Home Secretary; Sir Kingsley Wood; the chairman of the London County Council; the Lord Lieutenant of Kent; and three Lord Mayors of London. The chairman was a prominent Chislehurst resident, A. Horace Bird, who with friends, had obtained an option to buy the wood north of the Bickley-St Mary Cray railway line. E. T. Campbell, MP for Camberwell North West, was treasurer. It was agreed that if the land could be bought it should be administered by the National Trust, which had been formed in 1895 to preserve 'places of historic interest or natural beauty'.

The appeal, for £12,000, was launched at a dinner at Camden Place on February 17,1926. There was extensive local and national press coverage and on February 23 E. T. Campbell gave a talk entitled 'The Willett Memorial' on the then infant medium of radio. By March 19, £4,500 had been raised and by the middle of April £6,000. In the next 12 months, however, the total advanced by only another £2,000 and although this was enough to purchase nearly 72 of the 87¾ acres, there was a danger that the remaining land, fronting on Orpington Road, would be lost unless the balance of £4,000 could be found quickly. Indeed, a letter to the local paper claimed that the 16 acres in question had already been marked out for roads and pavements and that housing would surely follow. Further publicity was sought through a letter in *The Times* on April 9, 1927: this resulted in another £2,000 being raised and the appeal committee was granted an extension of time.

Meanwhile the committee had agreed that the memorial should take the form of a sundial to be erected in the north-east corner of the wood. The dial, nine feet nine inches high, was designed by G. W. Miller, joint author of the history of Chislehurst, and made by the Westminster firm of Farmer and Brindley out of

Before and after the First World War, Winston Churchill was a leading supporter of Willett and Daylight Saving (caricature by David Low)

grey granite from Shap Fell in Westmoreland. It is set for Summer Time and bears the Latin inscription 'homas non numero nisi aestivas' - 'I will only tell the summer hours'. On the north side of the stone is the legend, 'This wood was purchased by public subscription as a tribute to the memory of William Willett, the untiring advocate of Summer Time. Erected 1927'.

Nearly 1,000 people attended the opening ceremony on May 21, 1927, eleven years to the day since the adoption of daylight saving as a war measure. The sundial was unveiled by the Marquess Camden, Lord Lieutenant of Kent, and he handed the deeds of the wood to Lord Northbourn, a member of the council of the National Trust. William Willett's widow made a moving expression of thanks: 'Nothing would have given my husband greater pleasure than to have known that this wood belongs to the nation and will be forever associated with his name'. It was, *The Observer* newspaper reported, 'a charming little ceremony ... in a clearing in a Kentish wood amidst oak and fir and silver birch'.

The opportunity was taken to make a renewed appeal for the £1,500 still needed to complete the purchase. The money gradually arrived and the remaining 16 acres were officially acquired in February 1928. On March 23 the appeal committee held its final meeting. The accounts showed that a total of £12,834 had been received and the cost of the 87¾ acres was £11,739. The largest donation was £1,500 and the smallest one shilling (5p). The cost of raising the money was £771, or six per cent of the total. The appeal had not been sufficient to acquire a further 47 acres of woodland on the western boundary of Willett Wood but this land was bought in 1927 by Colonel Francis Edlmann and added to the Hawkwood estate which had been in his family since 1852. The whole of the wood was now apparently safe from development.

Responsibility for Willett Wood, meanwhile, had fallen to a Petts Wood management committee of the National Trust under the chairmanship of A. Horace Bird. It was at once faced with the problem of finding money for the upkeep of the wood. The appeal fund had set aside £222 for this purpose but the money would not go very far; and the committee learned, to its dismay, that the National Trust was unable to help. A keeper had been engaged and his wages had to be found; and there were the costs of seats, litter bins, notices and of calling out the fire brigade which, in those days, charged for attendance.

A maintenance fund was therefore launched. In 1934 the West Kent Electricity Company laid a cable along the western edge of the wood for which it agreed to pay a wayleave rent of £20 a year and in the following year the Urban District Councils of Chislehurst-Sidcup and Orpington each agreed to make annual grants of £50. Further income came from individual subscriptions.

The cottage on Orpington Road, which became the property of the Trust when its tenant (the widow of the Berens gamekeeper) left in 1937, posed special problems. It was old and needed urgent repairs and the Trust gave an interest-free loan of £200 to enable these to be carried out. The cottage then became the home of the keeper. In 1948 a member of the management committee, Victor Roques, organised a Petts Wood 21st birthday festival week in aid of the maintenance fund and the money raised allowed the cottage to be connected to the sewer and

Mrs William Willett (centre) and the Marquess Camden (far left) at the unveiling of the Willett Memorial sundial, May 21 1927 (Hulton Getty)

have modern sanitation. A bathroom was installed in 1961.

In 1950 Colonel Edlmann died and his executors decided to put the Hawkwood estate on the market for £22,000. Covering 168 acres, it comprised Hawkwood House, an 18th century mansion with 30 rooms, Hawkwood Farm and Tong's Farm and the 47 acres of woodland. To buy the property was beyond the resources of the National Trust and though the executors were willing to sell the 47 acres separately, the asking price of £2,000 was felt to be excessive. But the management committee said it was prepared to administer the wood if the land could be bought by public subscription.

In 1953 Chislehurst and Sidcup RDC used its powers under the Town and Country Planning Act to zone the estate as agricultural land and refused to permit development for housing. The executors appealed against this decision - a builder had expressed interest and a public inquiry was held in October 1955. Clifford Platt, chairman of the management committee, told the inquiry that there was very strong local feeling that Hawkwood should become a public open space. He went on: 'St Paul's Cray Common, the Willett Memorial Wood and Hawkwood, all adjoining, form an ideal green wedge between the built-up areas and well integrated communities of Orpington and Chislehurst. If Hawkwood were built on, this wedge would be by-passed and the Willett Memorial Wood and St Paul's Cray Common would be entirely surrounded by built-up areas.' The Minister of Housing supported this argument and the appeal was dismissed.

The way was now clear for a private buyer and fortunately one was at hand. Robert Hall, a physiotherapist who worked for a time at Farnborough Hospital, and his wife, Francesca, had come to live in Chislehurst soon after the war. They were keen conservationists and became so impressed by the peace and beauty of the 'bluebell wood' (the 47 acres) that they proposed to buy the Hawkwood estate and present it to the National Trust. After more than two years of negotiations, the official announcement of the gift was made in October 1957.

At a ceremony in the wood on St George's Day, April 23, 1958, the deeds of the estate were handed over to the National Trust and a memorial stone of Cornish granite unveiled which bore the words: 'This woodland was saved in 1927 by Francis Joseph Frederick Edlmann and given to the National Trust in 1957 by Robert and Francesca Hall'. It was decided that the 47 acres would be known as the Edlmann Memorial Wood. There was a tragic sequel: three months later Robert Hall was killed in a car crash at the age of 44 and his wife seriously injured.

With the acquisition of the Edlmann Memorial Wood, the management committee assumed direct responsibility for 134 acres of public land. The remaining 220 acres of the former Hawkwood estate was farmed by tenants of the Trust and public access limited to footpaths. The original Hawkwood House was in such bad condition that it had to be pulled down but a new house was built in the 1960s and for a time became the home of Mrs Hall, happily recovered from her injuries and taking an active part in Trust affairs. In 1964 she succeeded Clifford Platt as chairman of the management committee, continuing in that post until 1981.

The maintenance of the wood is the responsibility of the warden. For 19 years,

Memorial stone in Cornish granite to Colonel Francis Edlmann, unveiled on St George's Day 1958

A 150 year-old oak lying across the bridle path in Petts Wood, one of the casualties of the storm of October 1987; the picture was taken by the keeper, Tony Hall, and shows his eight-year-old son, Barnaby

until his retirement in 1981, the job was held by James Wells. He was succeeded by Tony Hall, a former tree surgeon from Bedfordshire, who was assisted by his wife, Madeleine. The warden's duties included the clearing of undergrowth; the upkeep of paths, bridges and ditches; and the setting out of trees worth encouraging. The trees were mainly silver birch, oak, elder, rowan and sweet chestnut.

Between 1981 and 1984 there was a major renovation of the warden's cottage, with the installation of a new staircase and other amenities. The work, which cost £25,000, was designed to provide essential modernisation while preserving the character of a building that probably goes back to the 18th century. At the same time a new access was provided to Orpington Road, the previous exit having been on a dangerous bend.

In the early hours of Friday October 16, 1987 south-east England was hit by what experts claimed was the most severe wind-storm to affect the area for nearly 300 years. Petts Wood residents had their first inkling of it when they were awoken in darkness by howling winds and found that their electricity had been cut off. When they set off for work, they discovered that roads and railway lines had been blocked by fallen trees. Some trees came down in gardens, others fell on houses and garages.

The National Trust woods were devastated, with many trees flattened and others torn partly out of the ground and left leaning at an angle. In a detailed survey of the damage, Ken Palmer, a member of the management committee, found that out of 18,500 trees in Willett Wood, which was worst affected, 8,800 (47 per cent) had been damaged and 5,800 (31 per cent) had been lost.

The first step was to clear paths and overhanging branches so that people could walk in the woods safely. A storm damage appeal brought in £18,000 and a small area was cleared south of the Willett Memorial. But the cost of clearing the whole wood would have been prohibitive and surviving trees would have been damaged in the process. The management committee decided on a policy of 'natural regeneration', or leaving things more or less alone.

There were positive benefits from this. The soil was poor and would be enriched by the rotting remains of dead trees. The demise of older trees had revealed many young oaks and sweet chestnuts whose growth had been held back. These would now be allowed to develop and it was hoped that in 15 or 20 years, without the planting of any new trees, there would be a beautiful woodland again. The wood lost further trees in the gales of January 25, 1990, including a fine Corsican pine near the Willett Memorial which had survived the storm of 1987. The recent history of the wood is related in Chapter 10.

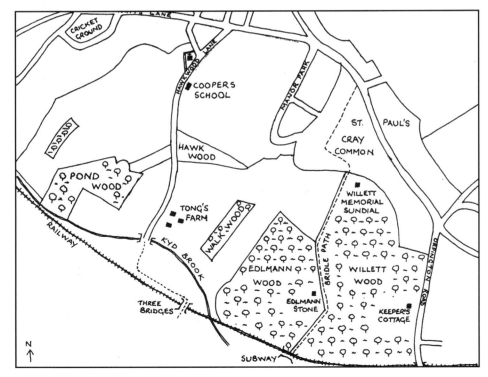

Map of the National Trust Woods, showing the Willett and Edlmann acquisitions

5. BEFORE THE DEVELOPERS CAME

Up to the late 1920s the area now covered by residential Petts Wood was much as it had been for centuries - an unspoilt landscape of woods and fields. The wood once leased by the Petts continued south of the railway and the Ordnance Survey map of 1910 shows portions of it called Great Thrift, Little Thrift, Towncourt Wood, Cornayes Wood and Birch Wood. Smaller stretches of woodland - Birchen Wood, Ashen Wood and Carnwell Wood - lay to the south, with Covet Wood (covering a much larger area than it does today) to the east. To the west of the railway line to Sevenoaks were Oxhawth Wood, Sparrow Wood, Lake's Wood and Roundabout Wood.

Apart from its woods, the area was notable for its many lakes and its streams, of which the largest was (and still is, as Petts Wood flood victims know to their cost) the Kyd Brook. These streams had to be crossed by plank bridges. The land west of Tudor Way was a virtual swamp and the cows which inhabited a meadow where Beaumont Road now meets St John's Road were sometimes up to their bellies in water. Along the lane which became Crossway were watercress beds. In winter, this and the other lanes became so muddy as to be virtually impassable.

As befits the 'garden of England'- the area was still part of Kent - there was much fruit growing. Along what is now Poverest Road, a narrow track without kerbs or pavements, stretched apple orchards and strawberry fields. At Thomas Hudson's Poverest Farm the housekeeper would have a large dish of strawberries ready for William Willett, who called in on his daily ride. Much of the land around Scad's Hill belonged to a jam manufacturer, E. and F. Pink. When enough strawberries had been gathered for the needs of the factory, local people were allowed to pick the surplus.

Town Court and the Walsinghams

The greater part of the land, some 272 acres, comprised the Town Court Estate. It covered all of what is now Petts Wood west and extended east of the railway as far as the Kyd Brook. The name goes back at least to medieval times, for the manor of Town Court, then in the parish of Chislehurst, was in the possession of the Church, through the Abbot and Convent of Lesnes, in 1280. Lesnes Abbey Woods are today an open space in Erith.

The manor was a unit of local government and taxation held by its lord from the king. The lord provided protection to his tenants in return for their services and rents. In its grander form the manor house comprised a high-roofed stone hall, in front of which was a walled courtyard. The house was often protected by a moat against hostile neighbours. It is possible that the rectangular lake which bounded the garden of the later Town Court farm was a remnant of a former moat. The existence of a manor at Town Court in the 13th century appears to be the earliest evidence of human settlement in what became residential Petts Wood.

The Church's interest in Town Court lasted until 1433 when the Abbot of Lesnes exchanged it for Fulham Place in Plumstead and it was acquired by Thomas Walsingham, a vintner and citizen of London. Through his descendants, most of

Tomb of the Walsingham family, which owned much of Petts Wood, in St Nicholas Church at Chislehurst

whom were also called Thomas, Town Court stayed in the Walsingham family for more than 200 years. The Walsinghams held substantial lands elsewhere in Chislehurst, including the manor of Scadbury, while references in wills to Tong's Farm and Hawkwood suggest they may also have owned part of the woods.

Thomas Walsingham IV, who died at Chislehurst in 1630, was the patron of the playwright Christopher Marlowe. In 1956 the Walsingham tomb in the Scadbury chapel of St Nicholas Church, Chislehurst, was opened at the request of an American writer, Calvin Hoffman. Convinced that Marlowe was the author of the works of Shakespeare, Hoffman hoped that the tomb might yield manuscripts of Shakespeare's plays and poems in Marlowe's handwriting. He was disappointed. All it yielded was a large quantity of sand.

A cousin of Thomas Walsingham IV, Francis, was another important local landowner with property in Footscray, North Cray and Bexley. Sir Francis Walsingham, as he became, was nationally famous as the secretary of state to Elizabeth I. He ran an intelligence operation to uncover Catholic plots, employed Marlowe as an agent and put his cousin Thomas in charge of espionage for Kent.

The Walsingham connection with Chislehurst ended with the death of Sir Thomas V in 1669. A few years before he had sold Town Court, with his other lands in the area, to Sir Richard Bettenson. From the Bettensons it probably passed to the Farrington family, who gave their name to Farringtons School. Around 1760 it was bought by Edward Hodsoll of St Mary Cray and he passed it on to his daughter. By now the site of the ancient manor house was occupied by a farm, possibly established in the early 18th century. By the early 19th century the Town Court Estate belonged to Thomas Morgan of St Mary Cray and on his death in 1826 he left part of it in trust to his daughter, Augusta. She married Albert Gossett, who predeceased her, and when she died in 1895 the property passed to her son, Arthur Wellesley Gossett, a retired army captain from Brighton. It was farmed in the early years of the 20th century by the Kemsley family, whose son later started the Dunstonian garage.

One of the biggest landowning families in the area came briefly into the story of Petts Wood when in 1912 Gossett paid £450 for five acres of land to Archibald Cameron Norman. He was a grandson of George Warde Norman who at his death in 1882 held more than half the total acreage (2,446) of the parish of Bromley, as well as substantial land along the edge of what became west Petts Wood in Southborough and Crofton. The most famous Norman was Montagu, another grandson of George Warde, who was Governor of the Bank of England from 1920 to 1944. The five acres Gossett bought from the Normans became the southern tip of Crest View Drive.

The farm house and buildings stood between Kenilworth Road and Queensway. Facing north, the farm house had started as a modest dwelling and been extended to contain seven bedrooms. To the rear was a lawn sloping down to a large lake. To the east of the lawn, adjoining the unmade lane which gave access to the farm, was a kitchen garden. The farm buildings, including cow shed, hay loft, pig sty, granary and cowman's house, stood to the north. Part of the old farm lane can be traced through the gardens on the west side of Queensway, with

Sir Francis Walsingham (c 1532-1590), Elizabethan spy catcher and Kent landowner, whose cousin Thomas held Town Court Manor (National Portrait Gallery)

Town Court Farm in 1895, showing the rear of the house and the lawn running down to the lake; the occupier was a Mr. Allison, a deacon at Spurgeon's Tabernacle

their layers of crushed flints almost impossible to penetrate.

In the winter, when the lake froze, there would be skating parties to which the farmer would invite his neighbours and their families. As darkness fell, coloured lanterns were hung in the trees. In the spring the woods would be covered with bluebells, while in the summer neat green hedgerows framed the golden cornfields. Such attractive countryside on London's doorstep brought people out from suburbs such as New Cross. They would make a day of it, catching the bus to the Crown at Bromley Common and walking the rest. Though the railway to Sevenoaks had been built in the 1860s, there was no station between Chislehurst and Orpington.

Turning off the farm road under the railway and close to the present line of Tudor Way and Crossway was Green Lane, which eventually petered out into a bridle path over the level crossing on the Bickley-St Mary Cray railway line and into the woods. The farmer would use this route when walking to Sunday worship at St Nicholas Church in Chislehurst.

Where Franks Wood Avenue meets Crescent Drive a five-barred gate stood entrance to a field and small boys would sit on top of the gate on Thursday nights watching the fireworks displays at Crystal Palace. It was high ground and there was a clear view for miles. From there a group of youngsters saw the German Zeppelin coming down in flames over Potters Bar during the First World War. There was drama nearer home in 1917 when a French fighter plane made a forced landing in the middle of the cornfield which later became the site of the Embassy Cinema. The farmer and some of his men ran across the field with pitchforks, thinking that the pilot was a German. The farmer's cheeks were red with fury at the sight of his flattened corn but he ended up inviting the pilot to dinner.

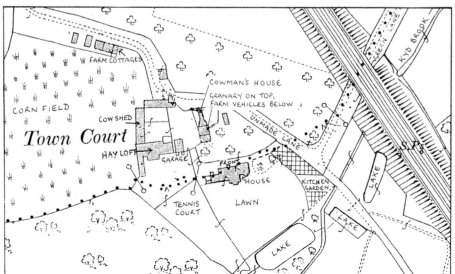

Town Court in 1928, another view from the back of the house; the figures on the lawn are the Langdon family

Map of Town Court Farm as it was in the 1920s, a few years before the land was sold for development; the house stood between Kenilworth Road and Queensway

Ladywood: for a Gentleman of Fortune

Between the Kyd Brook and the Orpington-Chislehurst road was the 120-acre Ladywood Estate. During the 19th century it belonged to the Sydney family, one of the leading Chislehurst landowners. After the death of Earl Sydney and his wife, it passed to a nephew, Robert Marsham, who adopted the family name and became Robert Marsham Townshend. The estate included 47 acres of wood, 26 acres of meadow and nine acres of plantation and its centrepiece was Ladywood House.

Easily the largest building in what became residential Petts Wood, the house stood for less than 60 years, was empty for a long period and went through several changes of occupant. It seems to have been something of a white elephant, an attempt to perpetuate the country mansion at a time when this was no longer viable. Described in a 1879 sales brochure as 'especially deserving the attention of a gentleman of fortune', it was probably too big to be economic.

In August 1871 *The Bromley Record* reported the sale of five acres of woodland with a frontage of 198 feet on the main road from Chislehurst to Orpington. The land was described as 'extremely eligible for building; it is well timbered, beautifully placed and commands fine views.' The house was finished in the following year and stood between The Chenies and the top half of Princes Avenue. The approach was from Chislehurst Road where The Chenies now begins, through large ornamental iron gates and along a carriage drive encircling a lawn and rhododendron beds. At the entrance was a brick-built lodge, big enough to contain four rooms and a scullery.

The house was a square, white building with the hint of a French chateau. It had a portico supported by stone columns and an ornamental gilt gallery over an observatory, offering views in all directions including one to the Thames. There were three storeys and a basement, linked by a stone staircase. The ground floor had an outer and inner hall, dining room, drawing room, billiard room 'lighted from the roof' and library. The upper floors contained nine bedrooms, as well as servants' quarters, while the basement housed the kitchen, scullery, larder and wine cellars.

To the back of the house a lawn gave way to an orchard and a kitchen garden, beyond which was a piggery and cow shed. To the south, at the end of a cart track bordered by lilac trees were a brick farm house, stables for eight horses and a water pump in the yard. A well uncovered in a garden in The Chenies in 1981 probably provided the water for the pump, while a ploughshare, snaffle bit and horseshoes found in another garden suggest that the area was being farmed long before Ladywood House was built.

From 1889 the resident of Ladywood was a provision merchant and brewer, George Burrows; and in 1903 he bought the estate for £6,000. He became well known in the area as a City gent. Dressed in frock coat and silk hat, he would drive down Scad's Hill and along Orpington High Street in a carriage and pair, with a coachman on the box, and at Orpington Station he would be met by the station master, who would ensure that Mr Burrows's compartment stopped exactly opposite the entrance.

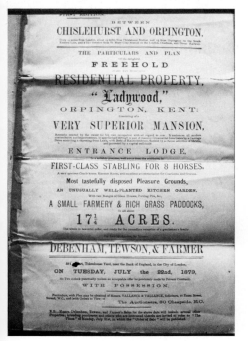

During its short life, Ladywood House changed hands several times; this is a sales brochure from 1879 (Local Studies and Archives Department, Bromley Central Library)

Ladywood House, taken from the front in 1909; it was the largest building in what is now residential Petts Wood (John W. Edwards)

Ladywood House, a view from the rear showing part of the extensive grounds (John W. Edwards)

28

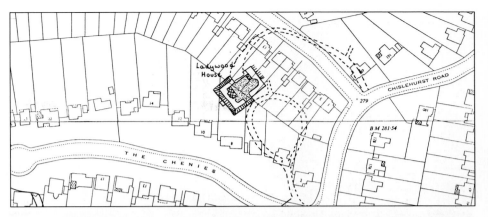

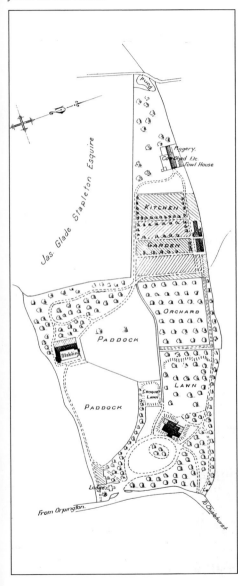

People living in the area also remembered a Miss Burrows, an invalid, being wheeled out in her bed on to the balcony of the house on Friday afternoons. Two camellias, one red and one white, shielded her from the gaze of passers-by. She would stay on the balcony for an hour or so, listening to the music of a barrel-organ brought along by an Italian and his wife in national dress.

In April 1910 George Burrows died at Ladywood, owing all but £520 of his £6,000 mortgage, and the property was taken over by the bank as security. Just before the First World War the estate was bought for farming by Frank Fehr, a resident of Chislehurst and head of a City firm of commodity merchants founded in 1857 by his father, Henry Fehr, who had come to this country from Switzerland. It was a mixed farm, keeping goats, pigs and cows and growing wheat and barley; and it was run by a farm manager with several hands. Ladywood House remained unoccupied, as it had since before the war. In 1923 the estate was bought by a developer, Jack Kent. Its subsequent history is related in the next chapter.

Further down Chislehurst Road towards Orpington, on the same side as Ladywood, was Scad's Hill House, a large red brick building with turrets, balconies and a conservatory at the back. Built around 1890, it stood in six acres of ground and up to the First World War had cesspool drainage. There was a brick-built cottage at the entrance and stabling. The owner was George St Pierre Harris, who held other land in the area and re-enters the story in Chapter 6.

During the First World War Scad's Hill House was used as a convalescent home for wounded soldiers. It later became a maternity home and a training centre for handicapped children. Around 1911 there was a serious accident on Scad's Hill. A wagonette was taking a party of Chislehurst tradesmen on their annual outing when the horse took fright, bolted down the hill and ran into a tree. The wagonette turned over and several of the passengers were thrown out and killed.

Below the Crofton Lane turning off Scad's Hill stood Kingsburgh House, owned

continued on page 33

Gathering the rhubarb; a photograph taken before the First World War near the junction of Crofton Lane and Homesdale Road

Bottom left: Strawberry fields off what became Towncourt Lane; the buildings, since demolished, are a stables (left) and a cottage

Below: Petts Wood just before the roads were laid; this picture of Green Lane, later Tudor Way (looking towards the woods from the junction with Fairway) was taken as late as 1932

The old custom of 'beating the bounds', or going round the parish boundary on Holy Thursday or Ascension Day, was still observed in 1923 when this picture was taken at Crofton Lane railway bridge; the wooden building is the off-licence (Arthur Eldridge Collection, Local Studies and Archives Department, Bromley Central Library)

Scads Hill, Orpington. DB L 3177

Scad's Hill was less busy, but not less dangerous, when this shot was taken in the 1900s (Philip Lane)

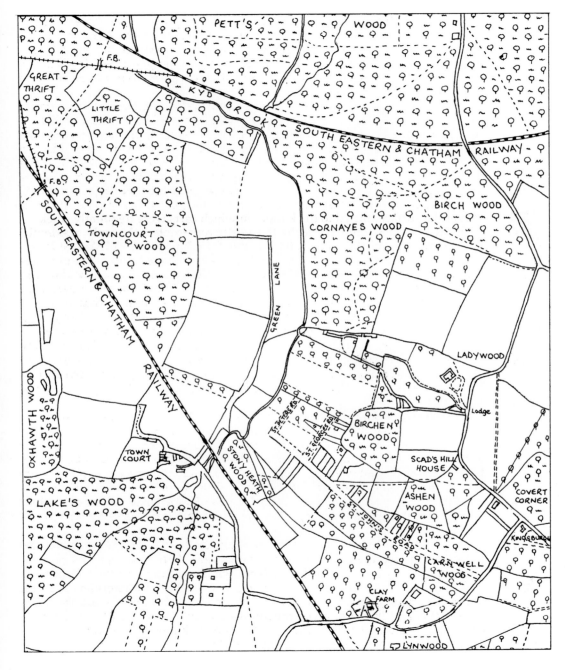

Map of Petts Wood c 1909

PETT'S WOOD

GREAT THRIFT

LITTLE THRIFT

KYD BROOK

SOUTH EASTERN & CHATHAM RAILWAY

BIRCH WOOD

CORNAYES WOOD

TOWNCOURT WOOD

GREEN LANE

SOUTH EASTERN & CHATHAM RAILWAY

LADYWOOD

OXHAWTH WOOD

Lodge

BIRCHEN WOOD

SCAD'S HILL HOUSE

COVERT CORNER

TOWN COURT

STONY HEATH WOOD

ST. PETERS RD.

ST. GEORGES RD.

ASHEN WOOD

KINGSBURY

LAKE'S WOOD

CARN WELL WOOD

CLAY FARM

LYNWOOD

F.B.

Victorian house with sash windows in Priory Avenue; later Petts Wood looked nothing like this

for many years by Captain George Wisely. His other properties included 15 acres of Covet Wood, a six-acre fruit plantation on Chislehurst Road and land in St George's Road, where he built retirement cottages for some of his workers. His cook, Mrs Morris, lived in Hazell Cottage, and the under-gardener, Mr Hodgson, in Blenheim Cottage until his death in 1963. Kingsburgh was later converted into flats and re-named Skehan Court.

Off Crofton Lane to the south was Lynwood, a partly-timbered, partly roughcast house built around 1885, with 10 bedrooms, billiard room and library. In the grounds were stables and an orchard growing apples and plums. The owner was William Jones, a magistrate known locally as Squire Jones. He also had Clay Farm on the other side of the road, the stone granary of which still exists in Elm Cottage between Homesdale and Beaumont Roads. By the railway bridge at the end of Crofton Lane was a wooden building in which Mr Bligh kept an off-licence. The lane was little more than a gravel track until well into the 1920s. In winter the surface turned to thick mud, in which carts were frequently stuck.

The roads off Crofton Lane to the north represented the only residential development in what is now Petts Wood before the First World War. St John's Road ran most of its present length and had several large houses, one of which later became St Dunstan's School. It was demolished after the school closed in 1964 to make way for 'town houses'. St Peter's Road (later Priory Avenue) and St George's Road were only half as long as they are now, ending at a line of poplar trees which formed the southern boundary of the Ladywood Estate. (According to local legend these roads, like St John's, were named after workmen who helped to build them.) By 1914 there were also a few houses in Fairfield Road and the Crofton Lane end of Beaumont. Again, there were no proper surfaces and when, in 1923, a resident of St George's Road died, his coffin had to be carried on foot from the house to Crofton Lane because it was impossible to get a vehicle through.

Before and just after the First World War, several railway workers lived in the area: 'it was almost like a clan', one contemporary remembers. But they had a long and lonely trudge down to Orpington Station, where they kept lamps and gum boots in lockers for the dark winter nights (this was before street lighting). Partly to help the railwaymen, local people, around 1922, got up a petition with 200 signatures calling for a halt where the footbridge crosses the line just south of Tudor Way. The proposal was rejected by the South Eastern Railway, which argued that there was no prospect of the area being developed for the next 50 years!

Before the developers came, the future residential Petts Wood was quiet and attractive countryside and despite the muddy lanes there were many people who were sad to see it go. One was Ernest Neal, who before the First World War lived in a bungalow in St George's Road called Ivy Nook. In an interview with the *Orpington Times* in 1971 Mr Neal lamented the loss of the fields and the lanes, adding 'I hope I have not given the impression that I resent the town that now exists. But I would love the people of Petts Wood to know that where their houses now stand was once a beauty spot of character.'

6. THE MAKING OF A GARDEN SUBURB

Stage One: Chudleigh and Langdon

Residential Petts Wood had its origin in a love affair between the daughter of a chartered accountant working in the City of London and a farmer from Cornwall. The accountant had the splendid name of Adolphus Orchard Chudleigh. A little twinkling man, with a delicious sense of humour, he was affectionately known in the family as Peter Pan. Among his schoolboyish larks was jumping up into the luggage rack during the train journey to town. But he was an astute businessman who was to take a crucial role in the transformation of Petts Wood from an area of unspoiled countryside to a modern, quality estate.

The Chudleigh family used to spend its holidays in Cornwall and here Adolphus's daughter, Irene, met and fell in love with James Langdon, who ran his family's farm at Treviskey, near Portloe, overlooking the sea. They decided to marry but Irene was reluctant to leave her widowed father in London. Chudleigh suggested a solution. He and Langdon would share the cost of buying a farm near the capital. They found the Town Court farm and estate north of Orpington and in 1920, the same year in which Irene and James were married, bought it from Arthur Gossett for £7,474.

Chudleigh, who moved in with the newly weds, always had at the back of his mind the possibility of development. Langdon farmed part of the estate west of the railway, a mixture of dairy and arable. His younger daughter, who was born at Town Court, remembers cows, carthorses and hay stacks. But Chudleigh realised that the bulk of the land was not workable and began to explore the idea of using it to create a new community. He correctly foresaw that an essential prerequisite was a railway station between Chislehurst and Orpington.

Chudleigh saw Town Court as an investment and intended to sell the land to a developer. A possible candidate was Jack Kent, who in March 1923 bought the adjoining Ladywood estate and, later that year, the smaller Cornayes Estate, covering the land later occupied by Birchwood and Hazelmere Roads and the Thrifts. It had been in the hands of the Berens family who owned the woods on the opposite side of the railway. The sale was handled by his brother-in-law, Aubrey Mullock, who started his estate agency in Orpington High Street at the same time and later opened a branch office in Station Square, Petts Wood. A solicitor turned property developer, Kent had been building houses in Grosvenor Road and was seeking to extend his activities, although he intended to preserve Ladywood House as a club house or assembly rooms.

Kent put up two detached houses, for himself and his mother, in Chislehurst Road at the corner of what became Princes Avenue but in February 1925 he died at the age of 34. Chudleigh and Langdon moved in and bought the Ladywood estate for £11,475. They now had 400 acres ripe for development. Mrs Lizzie Kent died in September 1977, aged 89. Had her husband lived, the history of Petts Wood might have been very different.

Adolphus Chudleigh, his daughter Irene Langdon and dogs; their move to Town Court in 1920 led to the development of residential Petts Wood

Stage Two: Basil Scruby

Chudleigh and Langdon were not long in finding the man who would turn the Town Court and Ladywood estates into the new garden suburb. Basil Scruby, from Harlow in Essex, was the key figure in the creation of residential Petts Wood. He was the estate developer who bought the land, laid out the roads, arranged drains, gas, water and electricity and then sold off plots to speculative builders.

Scruby developed several other estates, mainly in Essex, but he regarded Petts Wood as something special. It was the peak of a remarkable career. Scruby's vision was a high class suburb that would be only half an hour's journey from London and yet retain the calm and character of the English countryside.

In several respects the prototype for Petts Wood was Hampstead Garden Suburb, which was established from 1906 onwards by the philanthropist Henrietta Barnett and developed under the supervision of the architects Raymond Unwin and Barry Parker. Mrs Barnett knew Ebenezer Howard and had been influenced by his garden city movement and the success of earlier garden villages at Bedford Park, Port Sunlight and Bournville. Parker and Unwin had designed Letchworth, the first garden city, which was started in 1903.

The garden city and the garden suburb were attempts to create new communities from scratch in which the housing would retain a rural ambience. But while the garden city included carefully segregated industrial areas to provide its citizens with employment, the garden suburb assumed that work would be found elsewhere. Like Petts Wood, Hampstead Garden Suburb was designed as a rural retreat for London commuters. As Alan A. Jackson points out in his masterly study *Semi-Detached London*, 'purchasers of plots were able to employ their own architects but designs had to conform with the general scheme, the objectives of which were to retain an open setting, to maintain as close a harmony with nature as possible and to create a mood of rural peace and security'. The same words could be applied to Basil Scruby's Petts Wood.

Basil Scruby was born in Old Harlow in 1876 into a family of corn merchants and educated at Dunstable Grammar School. But he left school early and had no formal professional training. With private means, he was able to pursue his favourite recreations. He was a keen huntsman and a cricketer good enough to play as an amateur for Essex Second XI. It was not until after the First World War, in which he was a special constable, that he went into business as a developer.

During the 1920s he was responsible for estates in his native Harlow; in other parts of Essex, including Newbury Park, Epping and Theydon Bois; and at Peacehaven in Sussex. In contrast to Petts Wood, these earlier developments were mainly of cheaper, lower quality housing. Why he should have changed direction so abruptly is not clear. But he had the vision of a garden suburb and, possibly because of a contact in the Southern Railway, came south of the Thames for a suitable site. In October 1927 he took an advertisement in the *Evening News* to announce that a 400 acre estate was 'now being opened up for building'.

Scruby was a risk taker. Having secured an option on the 400 acres, he proceeded to buy it in sections, divide these into plots and sell the plots to builders. Much of the money came from trust funds administered by solicitors

Basil Scruby (1876-1946), the developer and creator of the Petts Wood estate

Two of the first railway tickets issued at Petts Wood Station in 1928

from Petty Cury, Cambridge, the brothers Charles and Sydney Ellison. They lent the capital on a mortgage and made further advances as plots were sold. The builders in turn raised enough finance to put up a few houses, hoping to sell them quickly and buy more land with the proceeds. The chain was a precarious one and the story of building in Petts Wood is punctuated with bankruptcies.

Much of the credit for putting Scruby's ideas into practice belongs to his architect, Leonard Culliford (1888-1960), a Fellow of the Royal Institute of British Architects and for many years president of the Beckenham Planning Group. His work included the headquarters buildings of the Amalgamated Union of Building Trade Workers, Union of Post Office Workers and National Union of Seamen, and after the Second World War he designed newspaper offices in Coventry and Walsall. In Petts Wood (one of several estate developments with which he was concerned) he played an important part in the design of the roads, emphasising where possible the natural sweep of the landscape, and he personally supervised builders' plans to ensure that the houses met Scruby's demands for a quality neighbourhood. Culliford also designed houses himself.

The Railway Station

When Scruby first came to the area it had a railway but no station and he realised that there was little point going ahead with a big new housing development if the nearest rail link was more than a mile away at Chislehurst or Orpington. In February 1928 he reached an agreement with the Southern Railway for the building of a station to serve the estate, though the SR drove a hard bargain. Scruby was to provide the land both for the station itself and a goods yard; to contribute £6,000 towards the cost of construction; and take out £1,000 of the railway's 5 per cent preference stock, returnable on successful development of the estate.

The railway had arrived some 70 years before. The line through Bromley South to Swanley opened in 1860; and the route to Chislehurst, Orpington and Sevenoaks in 1868. The companies responsible for the lines amalgamated in 1899 as the South Eastern and Chatham Railway. One result was that flying junctions were built to connect the two routes south of Chislehurst, so that Orpington was linked for the first time to Bromley, Victoria and Holborn Viaduct. During the 1920s the lines, now under the Southern Railway, were electrified, giving faster and more frequent services. When the first plans were laid for the new suburb of Petts Wood, the commuter network was ready.

The station opened on July 9, 1928. It was a modest affair, a single uncovered island platform, 520ft by 30ft, just long enough for the standard eight car train then in use. It was lit by oil lamps and became known as 'paraffin junction'. To the east was the goods yard, soon occupied by A. H. Herbert & Co, the coal merchant. People wanting to take advantage of the new bridge to cross the line had to buy a platform ticket: only later was a partition created along the middle of the bridge to provide separate public access.

With the rapid growth of the estate, the station soon justified itself and by 1932 substantial extensions had been made, notably the addition of a second island

*The well-stocked Petts Wood branch of
M. A. Ray and Sons, ironmongers, in
the 1930s; the shop, in Station Square,
was later acquired by G. E. Read*

platform and the provision on both platforms of waiting rooms, toilets and canopies. In 1934 the station issued 320,597 ordinary tickets, as well as 13,049 seasons; as most of the latter would have been quarterlies, this suggests that already Petts Wood had some 3,000 regular London commuters (by 1982 more than 25,000 seasons were being issued each year). In 1937 there was a further series of improvements, including a new booking office.

Donning dark suits and bowler hats, and carrying rolled umbrellas, the men of the new Petts Wood set out for the daily ritual of the half hour journey to town, catching the same train up and the same train back. Before the roads were made up, the walk to the station was often through mud and puddles and a hut was thoughtfully provided by the station where Wellington boots and galoshes could be left during the day. From May 1929 there was a treat for train spotters when the *Golden Arrow* Pullman began its services from Victoria to the Continent.

With trains available to all the south London termini, Petts Wood was one of the best served stations on the network. City people could travel to Cannon Street, civil servants to Charing Cross or Victoria. The availability of an all night service from Blackfriars (then called St Paul's) explains why so many Fleet Street newspapermen came to live in Petts Wood. In 1928 a quarterly season cost either £4 3s 6d or £5 1s 6d, depending on the destination, while those completing their journey before 8 am could take advantage of the cheap workman's ticket, only 10d return to London Bridge.

As well as making the new suburb possible, the station confirmed its name. The area to the south being known as Crofton, it was suggested that the station should be called Crofton Halt. The Southern Railway rejected this as there was already a Crofton Park and Petts Wood it became.

The Shopping Centre

After the station, the next important prerequisite of the new Petts Wood suburb was a shopping centre and Scruby made plans for this from the start. Originally he designated two areas for shops - around Station Square and in Poverest Road just past the junction with Petts Wood Road and Chislehurst Road. Why the Poverest shops did not go ahead is unclear, but the clue may lie in the estate prospectus of October 1928 which requires purchasers of the lots concerned to undertake not to erect shops or business premises until after September 1931. By that time the Station Square development would be well advanced and potential Poverest shopkeepers may have judged that the competition from the other end of Petts Wood Road would be too great.

The first block of shops to go up in Petts Wood was on the north-east side of Station Square. Echoing the mock-Tudor style of many of the new houses, they had flats above and service areas behind and a generous width of pavement. Building started towards the end of 1928 and within a couple of years most of the block was occupied. On the corner, at the Petts Wood Road end, was the ironmonger and coal merchant, Ray Brothers (later M. A. Ray and Sons), the branch of a Coulsdon firm going back to 1830. Moving along towards the station, were the United Dairies, Nelson's newsagents - which was also the first Petts

Heddle Nash, described as 'the finest English tenor of his generation', pictured in 1933; he was one of the early Petts Wood residents and lived in Towncourt Crescent until his death in 1961

Station Square in the early 1930s, with the first Petts Wood shops and cars outside the estate office waiting to take people to the show houses

The Dunstonian Garage on its original site in Station Square in the 1930s; there is an Austin Seven in front of the discreetly hooded petrol pumps, the sales office is to the right and the workshop behind

Wood post office - Hammett's the butcher and Mrs Yexley's cafe. They were soon joined by Lloyds Bank and Bilham's fishmongers.

On the east of the square the first shops to be built were in the block from Farrants, the chemists, to the Express Dairy at the top of Westway. Work then started at the Petts Wood Road end and the Midland Bank and David Greig (later Key Market) filled the gap in the middle. Starting with the Wine Cellars off-licence, shops spread along the north of Petts Wood Road, among them the Bookman's Library where books could be borrowed for 2d a week or, if new, for 3d for three days.

Up to the Second World War many tradesmen were still prepared to deliver. Playfoot and Bell, the greengrocers, were delivering in Petts Wood before their shop opened; they had two vans and split the area between them. Mr Bilham sent one of his sons out on a bicycle to take orders in the morning and the fish was delivered in time to be cooked for lunch. In the early years, some shops sent out goods by pony and trap.

Bill Twomey started at Ray's as a 14-year-old assistant in September 1930. The opening hours were 8 am to 7 pm (8 pm on Saturdays), with early closing on Wednesday, a 52½ hour week for which the boy was paid 15s (75p). One of his jobs was dressing the window; there were four and they took up to a day each. Customers came in for anthracite for their Ideal or Century boilers - it was sent by lorry from West Wickham - green and cream gloss paint to freshen their houses, and they could get a Qualcast Panther lawnmower for just 50 shillings (£2.50).

The busiest day of the year was Maundy Thursday. The bowler-hatted commuters came off the trains in the evening and made straight for the shop to stock up with their gardening and decorating items for the Easter holiday weekend. Ray's would rarely close before 10 pm and some of the goods had to be delivered the same evening. A notable customer was Heddle Nash, the opera singer, who lived in Towncourt Crescent and had a regular order for half a dozen bottles of spirit cleaner to keep his clothes fresh while travelling to and from engagements.

On the south-eastern corner of Station Square, on Armistice Day, November 11, 1930, 19-year-old Jack Kemsley opened the Dunstonian Garage, naming it after his school, St Dunstan's College at Catford. Before and just after the First World War, his father and uncle had farmed at Town Court but it was pure chance that the family link with the area was revived. Jack Kemsley saw the plot and decided it was just the place for a garage. With money from his mother, and help from a school friend, he went ahead. To conform with the character of the Scruby estate, he agreed to put his petrol pumps under a canopy and to use oak beams on his sales offices and workshop.

He began by selling Riley cars, then took on the Rootes franchise which after the war became Chrysler UK and, eventually, Peugeot. In 1932 a good Hillman Minx cost £165 and a gallon of Shell petrol 1s 1d (6p). The Dunstonian came to play a greater part in the community than purely business. It was the polling station and a popular venue for public meetings, when milk crates were borrowed from the Express Dairy across the road for people to sit on. On New

Jack Kemsley, who started the Dunstonian Garage as a teenager and later took part in the Monte Carlo Rally (caricature by William Wiggins, Petts Wood and District Advertiser, *November 1948)*

Selling the suburb: The Reed and Hoad estate brochure from the early 1930s stresses the convenience of a quick and frequent train service

The 'modern' Davis houses formed a contrast to the mock Tudor style prevalent in Petts Wood east

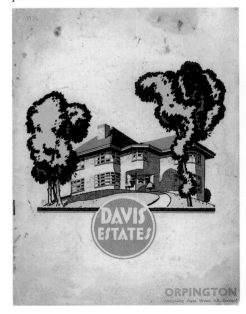

Year's Eve, the Dunstonian held a fancy dress dance for its customers, putting an awning across the square from the garage to the estate office.

The Development of Petts Wood East

Basil Scruby set up his estate office, another building in the mock Tudor style, in the middle of Station Square. Cars were laid on to meet the trains and take prospective buyers to the show houses. Scruby supervised affairs from his office in Cannon Street but left the day-to-day running of the estate to his son, Charles, who lived in Chislehurst Road in a large Culliford-designed house called *Three Chimneys*.

The estate plan of October 1928 shows the roads east of the railway in more or less their present position, though most of the plots were still waiting to be sold. Great and Little Thrift, Silverdale Road and Hazelmere Road were not yet on the map, while Ladywood Avenue was projected south to join Chislehurst Road at what became the entrance to The Chenies, and Willett Way ended in a cul-de-sac instead of going through to Chislehurst Road. Some of the road names were different: Tudor Way was Green Lane, Fairway and Woodland Way were called Station Road and the top half of St George's Road appears as Bower Hill.

West of the railway the proposed roads are only dotted in and bear little resemblance to the original layout. None are named and no plots are being offered for sale. Petts Wood west, in fact, was developed separately and building did not start until 1933.

Local authority building regulations gave Scruby very broad freedom of manoeuvre. Bromley Rural District Council's town planning scheme stipulated a density of no more than eight houses to the acre but otherwise the building byelaws were concerned mainly with relatively technical matters such as drains and damp courses. Much more important in shaping the character of the estate were Scruby's own restrictions, which became legally binding on both builders and residents.

Caravans or 'houses on wheels' were banned and except in one or two places (among them, for some reason, Priory Avenue) no bungalows were to be built. No shops were to go up, except on designated plots. Building lines, minimum cubic capacities and frontages were laid down for each house. Walls were to be of brick, stone or 'rough cast of an approved type', while roofs had to be constructed of 'English tiles made from natural clay or stone laid to a pitch of not less than 45 degrees'.

In his selling of the estate Scruby stressed the rural aspect of a suburb which was only 13 miles and 22 minutes (on the fastest train) from London. An early estate brochure referred to 'orderly roads, tree planted, wide grass verges, low stone walls, hand-made tiles, giving every roof a mellowed appearance, most satisfying to those of artistic taste. Houses that, despite their widely differing styles, merge naturally into the green vistas of woodland that form their background. A sylvan town with birds, trees, flowers - a real country home that, thanks to the boundary of Petts Wood, will always remain country.' The natural

continued on page 47

Four views of Petts Wood taken around 1928 when the roads were being laid and the first houses going up:

Birchwood Road

Towncourt Crescent

Petts Wood Road looking west towards Crossway and the shops

Another shot of Petts Wood Road, this time with some houses

Reed and Hoad's 'baronial halls' were described as 'the house for those wanting mansion comfort with small house expenditure'. Prospective buyers were offered a Tudor hall (left), panelled in real oak, and a spacious lounge (below)

contours of the landscape were exploited, rather than suppressed. As far as possible the old trees were retained and, once the houses were built, new trees were planted. Above all, the houses underlined the idea of 'rus in urbe' by evoking the idealised country cottage.

This explains the popularity of the Tudor or 'Elizabethan' style which flourished in Petts Wood, as it did in other new London suburbs of the inter-war period. Externally it was distinguished by dark oak beams on white walls, the roofs broken up by barge-boarded gables, verges and valleys. The windows had leaded lights, sometimes with coloured glass. There were elaborate porches, with their own red-tiled roofs, and oak front doors with gothic panels, iron hinges and ring knockers. The theme was often continued inside, with oak beams and panels and inglenook fireplaces.

Although Petts Wood east had a common character, it was the product of many individual builders. *The Estates Gazette*, in an article on the Scruby development in November 1930, counted no fewer than 45. One of them was Scruby's own subsidiary, the Petts Wood Building Company, which was responsible for houses in Towncourt Crescent, Chislehurst Road and elsewhere. Another was Reed and Hoad, which was closely connected with Scruby and operated from his estate office.

Walter Reed and George Hoad were friends of Scruby's from Harlow, where Reed was the landlord of a public house called *The White Horse*. Neither man had much experience in the building trade and they saw Petts Wood as a gamble that would either make or break them. They took up residence in the lodge of the Ladywood estate with their workmen and started their first houses, in Petts Wood Road, in the middle of 1928. By the early 1930s they were building in Fairway, Ladywood Avenue, Manor Way, Woodland Way, Kingsway, Priory Avenue and Towncourt Crescent.

Carter-Clout and Tudor House

Other firms active in Petts Wood Road were, at the shops end, H. A. Holland, from West Wickham, and a Cardiff builder, John Davies; and further along Leslie Carter-Clout. Starting in business at the age of 16 in partnership with an employee of his father, Carter-Clout carried out his first substantial development, at his native Thornton Heath in Surrey, between 1920 and 1925. He later built at Forest Hill, Beckenham, Sydenham, Keston and West Wickham and by the time he retired in 1946 he had completed some 10,000 houses.

He had a special fondness for Petts Wood and in 1930 (the date is on the drainpipes) he built Tudor House for his own occupation at the junction of Chislehurst Road and Birchwood Road. Designed by Culliford, it won a 'House of the Year' award from the National House Builders Association. Standing in more than an acre of ground, Tudor House was one of the biggest properties in Petts Wood, an attempt to create a country house in a suburban setting.

Approached through a lych gate and up a drive, the house was an L-shaped design in the Tudor style, with a conservatory at the back and an oak balustraded balcony leading from the main bedroom. Several of the leaded windows had

Crittall's steel framed windows were a feature of many Petts Wood houses; the factory was at the junction of the Orpington and Sidcup by-passes, known as Crittall's Corner

The splendid Tudor House, prize-winning design of the 1930s, successfully saved from demolition in the 1980s

stained glass insets carrying pictures of ships. There were back and front staircases and the butler and his wife, who was the cook, lived in. The spacious grounds contained a kitchen garden and a rose walk, with more than 1,800 blooms. Separate from the house was a garage, large enough to take four cars, and a flat on top designed for a chauffeur but later occupied by the gardener. The Carter-Clout family lived at Tudor House until just after the war; it was then owned by Timpson, of the coach firm, and Sir Thomas Spencer, chairman of Standard Telephones and Cables.

In 1988 the then owner made a planning application to demolish Tudor House and put up four detached houses in its place. After strong protests from residents, the application was refused, as was a second application to build a detached house between Tudor House and the coach house.

Alarmed by the threat to one of Petts Wood's most striking houses, the residents' association approached English Heritage to make it a listed building. This was rejected but Bromley Council decided to include Tudor House in a Conservation Area covering parts of Birchwood and Chislehurst Roads, Wood Ride and Kingsway. This was Petts Wood's second Conservation Area, following a similar designation for The Chenies. An application to convert Tudor House into a residential home was granted in 1990 and the work began, but with a change of ownership the interior was restored and the building continued as a private house. After the property changed hands again the new owner got permission to build a tennis court and swimming pool.

Apart from Tudor House, some of the largest and most expensive properties in Petts Wood were also in Birchwood Road. The builder mainly responsible was W. H. (Freddie) Love, who had put up houses of similar quality in Bickley and Chislehurst. He lived in the road, in one of his houses; it afterwards belonged to the writer, Arthur Mee. Yet another of Petts Wood's builders to settle in the area was John Sutcliffe, who built both on his own and in partnership with Samuel Seel of Wood Ride. Sutcliffe was a stonemason from St Anne's in Lancashire and he brought to his houses a high quality north country brickwork that seldom needed re-pointing. He built in Manor Way, Hazelmere Road, Great Thrift and Woodland Way. His son, Ken, an architect, was captured by the Germans during the Second World War but managed to escape.

Leslie Carter-Clout, builder of Tudor House and 10,000 other houses in south London between 1920 and 1946

Right: The stained glass bathroom window, one of several ship motifs in Tudor House

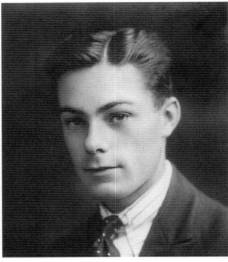

Cecil Pamphilon and his 'Avenue'

During the early 1930s Cecil George Pamphilon arrived in Petts Wood from Bromley. Apart from a house for himself at 54 Birchwood Road, he built in Willett Way and Towncourt Crescent but his most spectacular legacy is the sweep of houses along the west side of Chislehurst Road which became known as 'Pamphilon Avenue'. Pamphilon house fronts were distinguished by a wooden diamond and vertical slit in the gable while inside they had wood panelled hallways and brick inglenook fireplaces with a wooden surround. Prices of up to £1,450 put them at the quality end of the market.

Cecil Pamphilon (the surname is Greek and means 'friend of all') was the son of Walter Pamphilon, an architect whose commissions included the Medhurst (now Allders) store on Bromley High Street. The Pamphilon public house to the north of Allders perpetuates the family name. Cecil was born in Tweedy Road, attended Bromley County School and after a brief spell as a mechanic became a builder, putting up houses in Petts Wood, Chislehurst and Bromley to his father's designs. He employed only a small team, always including a boy to tidy up the site, did much of the work himself and made a point of planting trees in the front gardens. In the late 1950s he left Petts Wood for Seaford, on the Sussex coast, where he also built houses, and lived there until his death in 1990 at the age of 88. His daughter, Sheila, remembers 'a quiet man, who never socialised and always said he liked to build within coffee reach of home'. For that reason, perhaps, he is less well known than he deserves to be.

Top left: Pamphilon houses in Chislehurst Road, 1933.

Above: Cecil Pamphilon and his sign.

Right: The Tudor style at its most flamboyant in The Chenies

Below: Noel Rees and the cigarette holder without which he was rarely seen

Noel Rees and The Chenies

The best known builder in Petts Wood east and the one particularly associated with the Tudorbethan style, was Noel Rees. Fifty years afterwards, his name was still being used as a selling point in estate agents' literature. He was a 'character', a colourful personality with tremendous enthusiasm for everything he did and he lived an extraordinarily varied life to the full.

As Welsh as his name suggested, Walter Noel Rees was born in Merthyr Tydfil and went to Stonyhurst, the Roman Catholic boarding school in Lancashire. He left at 16 and worked for his father's coal mining and shipping company at Merthyr before setting off abroad. He went to Canada and spent more than ten years in Australia, where he was involved in rubber manufacture. By the late 1920s he was in business at Chalk Pit Farm, St Paul's Cray, making breeze blocks - the firm became the largest of its kind in the country - and from this it was a logical step to building and to Petts Wood.

Workmen take a break from putting up Noel Rees houses in Wood Ride:

*back row (left to right): John Collins, Harry Ransley, Tom?, Taffy Jones, Jack Thomson, unknown
front row (left to right): Bill?, Albert Erlock, Mark Logan, Bill?, Mr. Thomas, Harry?
(judging by his suit, Mr Thomas is the gaffer)*

Variations on a Tudor theme: examples of Noel Rees houses in Petts Wood, from 1930s sales brochure

He started in 1931 with a house in Wood Ride called *Westward Ho!* It was both the sales house and, for a time, the Rees family residence. Apart from Petts Wood, Noel Rees, whose office was in Conduit Street in Mayfair, developed other estates around the edge of London, choosing the more select and rural suburbs such as Hadley Wood, Chorley Wood and Walton-on-Thames. During the 1930s, too, he indulged his passion for fast cars by financing a British motor racing team which competed at Brooklands, Donington and the leading Continental circuits. His drivers were Earl Howe and the Hon Brian Lewis, son of Lord Essendon.

By 1939 he had spread his building activities as far as Birmingham and Ireland, but the war left him with many unfinished houses and he was forced to look for other work. He joined Hawker's, the aircraft company, in Yorkshire, and after the war farmed in Scotland and Canada and worked for a company in Bermuda concerned with dissolving the fur in water tanks. Active and enthusiastic to the last, he was talking about introducing the hovercraft to South America when he died, at the age of 76, in 1963.

His estates are his monument and he explained his approach as follows: 'When I began to build houses I had some definite ideas on the subject. I looked about me and saw springing up around London a vast number of houses and I do not think I shall be overstating the case if I say that the majority of them filled me with horror: most of them seemed to me ... to be of a deadly dullness, of an appalling monotony, of a hopeless unattractiveness, and I determined then and there to offer something different.'

As for Petts Wood, 'no sooner had I set foot outside the station, when my heart rose within me. Here was something new. Station approaches are not usually the most beautiful things in the world, but at Petts Wood the view from the station steps is perhaps the key to the district. A pleasant green, surrounded on three sides by well-designed, half-timbered rows of shops, sparkling, clean shops, all live and active.

'Radiating from these are the Drives, Ways and Avenues of Petts Wood, climbing up the hill to the borders of that beautiful land, open and free for all time as a memorial to the man who made our summer evenings longer - William Willett. And away to the back lies Chislehurst Common, a fairyland of birch and gorse, all assuring one that Petts Wood is, and must remain, a *country* home. Birches, hazels, oaks, ash and pine trees have crept away from these common lands and you find them everywhere, little coppices at the corners of the Drives and Avenues; along the paths, in the gardens, everywhere. At the foot of the hill runs a little brook, spanned by charming little white bridges.

'Now walk up Wood Ride, which is the finest example of Petts Wood novelty and charm. Houses of distinctive design, pleasant half-timbering, overhanging bays, sweeping gables, timbered porches, all set well away from the road, bright and sunny in white dress. No fences, but little low crazy stone walls, where irises and rock plants grow, crazy paths, flower-laden beds and bright green lawns, while at the back nod the health-laden pines.'

Rees left his mark on several Petts Wood roads, apart from Wood Ride: Kingsway, Princes Avenue, Willett Way and St George's Road. But his most telling contribution to the area was The Chenies, a distinctive cul-de-sac of 29 contrasting houses with carefully preserved mature trees. The name came from the village of Chenies in Buckinghamshire and was suggested to Rees by a native of that county who was one of the road's first residents.

In October 1982 Bromley Council designated The Chenies as a Conservation Area, being 'archetypal of the best of this sort of inter-war housing' and therefore of architectural and historic importance. This meant that although The Chenies remained a private road, maintained by the residents, no alterations could be made to any house unless the council decided that they conformed to the character of the area. Further, it became an offence to cut down or lop any important tree without the council's permission.

The Tudor style in Willett Way, captured in 1990 by a Petts Wood artist Ron Lawrence

R.A. LAWRENCE

Davis houses in Fieldway, with corner-turning windows and flat roofs which were promoted as suntraps

If Tudor rural-romantic was the most characteristic house style in Petts Wood, it was challenged to some extent by the 'modern' houses of the Davis Estate. 'Modern' had its genesis in the clean functional buildings which began to appear on the Continent before the First World War. The style arrived in Britain during the 1920s and was eventually imitated by speculative builders. In its original form, modern meant flat roofs, smooth white walls and horizontal, steel-framed windows which often turned a corner.

One of the most prolific house builders in the London area in the 1930s, Davis was not part of the Scruby development but came in on its edge - the east side of Tudor Way, including the three Closes, Beaumont Road as far down as Fairfield Road, Eastbury Road and Fieldway. The original modern house was a short-lived phenomenon, for the flat-roof - promoted as a suntrap - was not popular with buyers (or building societies) and it soon gave way to the conventional pitched roof. A few 'suntrap' houses can, however, be seen in Fairfield Road and Fieldway. The latest Davis houses were shown at the Ideal Home Exhibition at Olympia and number one Fieldway was sold from the exhibition in August 1935.

A third popular building style of the inter-war period to reach Petts Wood was the chalet, immediately recognisable through its pantile roof reaching down to the ground floor ceiling, apron-shaped tiled bays and leaded windows. The style was presumably designed to evoke the chalets of Switzerland and Austria, though its precise origins are obscure. Chalet houses were put up at the Orpington end of Willett Way, and in the four closes leading off it, by a Dartford builder, William Brise. This was one of the few pieces of land in Petts Wood not to pass through the hands of Scruby, being sold to Brise by an architect and surveyor, George St Pierre Harris, whose family had owned it at least since the 1840s. As an architect Harris was responsible for the 'arts and crafts' style houses in Aynscombe Angle, Orpington, and also the National Westminster Bank, a 'neo-Georgian' building of 1910 in Orpington High Street; both were later 'listed' by the local authority. Harris sold a nearby plot, off Crofton Lane, to Noel Rees who proceeded to create another mock-Tudor extravaganza, The Covert. In the process Rees, as happened to many a speculative builder of the time, ran out of money, leaving the last house to be finished by his agent, W. A. Kimpton.

The prices of new houses in Petts Wood tended to reflect the sort of area that Basil Scruby was trying to promote. The average price for a house in the London area in the early 1930s was between £650 and £750 but until the Davis Estate went up there was little in Petts Wood east as cheap as that. Reed and Hoad houses started at £795 (semis in Fairway and Tudor Way), rising to £925 (detached houses in Ladywood Avenue) and £1,195 (in Manor Way - the 'baronial halls' - though still only semis). Thomas houses in Greencourt Road ranged from £895 to £1,200 but some of the highest prices were commanded by Noel Rees properties: a detached four bedroom house in Wood Ride, with panelled inglenook fireplace, was offered for £2,200. The higher priced houses included a garage: otherwise it was an optional extra costing £50 to £75. On the Davis Estate it was possible to get a three-bedroomed semi for £695 and the chalet houses could be bought for less than £700.

If the prices were high for the time, there was no lack of buyers. In real terms, houses cost less in the early Thirties than in the 1920s, for thanks to the economic depression building costs fell to their lowest level since 1914. Mortgage funds were plentiful and interest rates fell steadily, from 6½ per cent in 1924 to 5½ per cent in 1932, 5 in 1933 and 4½ in 1935. Also, the deposit required was reduced from 20-25 per cent of the purchase price in the Twenties to 10 per cent and even lower, while repayments became cheaper through being spread over, say 20 years instead of 15, or 23 years instead of 20. In 1932, before the mortgage rate reached its lowest point, a £795 Reed and Hoad semi could be bought for £80 down and £1 a week for 23 years.

The Swiss influence?: chalet house in Oaklands Close

Fact and fantasy in Petts Wood west:

The first houses going up in Lakeswood Road in 1934

How many purchasers of Morrell semis employed a maid to do the hoovering?

Petts Wood West

In the development of residential Petts Wood, the railway line was the great divide and building west of the line had, on the whole, a different character from that on the east. In Petts Wood west the property was generally cheaper, the houses smaller and closer together and the Tudorbethan extravagances largely shunned. The separate development of the two parts of Petts Wood was unfortunate in creating social snobberies that took a long time to break down.

The division was apparent as early as 1936 when much of Petts Wood west was still being built. In his speech at the opening of the Embassy Cinema in October, Sir Waldron Smithers, the local Member of Parliament, said: 'I hear there are two parts of Petts Wood. They are the people who live on this side of the railway line and the people who live on the other and I am told they don't get on well. What utter nonsense that all is! You are all Britishers, you all stood up just now for the National Anthem, you all live in the Chislehurst Division and you all have me for your Member of Parliament, whether you like it or not. Surely that is enough common ground to do away with all this petty nonsense.

'Such rivalries are family relations to the trouble in Spain (a reference to the Civil War) and although I do not suggest it will ever get as bad as that in Petts Wood, I do ask you to live in neighbourliness and love with one another. Just as if it matters what side of the dear old Southern Railway you live!

'I suggest that you do something about it. People who live in number 23 in a road this side should invite a family from some number 23 on the other side to tea on Sunday afternoon. There is nothing like rubbing shoulders, in religion, politics or anything else, to do away with ridiculous and petty differences and bring tolerance and good fellowship instead. I hate these silly squabbles anywhere in the Division I love so much'.

Although Petts Wood west was originally included in the Scruby empire, he exercised far less control over its development and that helps to explain the narrower roads and the higher density housing. By 1933 Scruby was heavily overlent and while Petts Wood east, in the early years at least, had been a financial success, he did not have the resources to continue across the railway. There was great pressure on him, as interest charges piled up, to dispose of the land and this he did, to the builder largely responsible for Petts Wood west, Morrell. He also passed over the bulk of his interest in the estate company to his son, Charles, and son-in-law, Christopher Hutley.

Basil Scruby therefore leaves the story of Petts Wood at this point but he continued to busy himself with a variety of projects up to his death in 1946 at the age of 70. One of them was a factory in Berlin making spirit lotion (or after-shave) which stood opposite Hitler's headquarters. Scruby became very concerned at the rise of the Nazi movement and invited young Germans to stay with him at Harlow when he would try to persuade them against the fascist doctrine.

During the Second World War Scruby tried to do his bit by backing inventions that might help the cause, including a radar system devised by a Captain Roberts. He died insolvent, leaving a young family by his second wife. Petts Wood was the supreme achievement of his career and he is remembered also as a popular

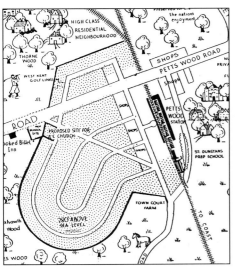

Map of the Morrell estate; note the assumption that a bridge would link Franks Wood Avenue and Petts Wood Road

and outgoing man, kind and generous to a fault, who would rise at four in the morning bursting with ideas which he did not always have the financial acumen to carry through.

In Petts Wood west, as on the other side of the line, the shops were planned at an early stage. Building started along Queensway in 1933 and the first shop to open there was Black's, the newsagent and tobacconist, in March 1934. Arthur Black came from Thornton Heath, where the family had been running a similar business, and the money was put up by his brother. It was seen as something of a gamble since at that time the only houses around were in Queensway itself and Crest View Drive.

For Arthur Black and his family it was a long day's work. Newspapers had to be collected off the train at 4 am and the shop stayed open until 10 at night, six days a week. Then there was bookwork to do. Tables and rustic seats were set up outside so that house hunters could refresh themselves with lemonade and ice creams as they pondered their choice. Sometimes they asked to borrow a ruler from the shop, to measure their windows for curtains. Arthur Black was a great believer in Armistice Day and every November 11 he would stop serving his customers just before 11 am and ask them to observe the two minutes' silence.

While Petts Wood east had 45 builders, Petts Wood west had only two. Both were large and active in many other parts of London and each specialised in standard ranges of low to medium priced houses. Morrell, which created the core of Petts Wood west - the rough oval described by Crescent Drive and Crest View Drive - was headed by two brothers, Cyril and Stanley. They also put up large estates in Bromley, Hayes, West Wickham, Orpington and Chelsfield and had built a few houses in Petts Wood east, along Petts Wood Road and Crossway.

They called their Petts Wood development 'Morrell's Garden Estate', in an attempt, presumably, to echo what was happening on the other side of the line. Their advertising copy was almost as gushing as Noel Rees's: 'In order to do justice to Petts Wood a complete book would be needed and the pen of a poet; all that can be done in these few lines is to give a bare impression of this great Kentish garden … green woodlands, golden in autumn, with deep glades shining with bluebells or the pale stars of the primrose; acres upon acres of the scented fire of the gorse; open parklands where daffodils herald the spring; all these contribute to the abiding charm of Petts Wood …'

The estate, potential purchasers were told, had been planned on garden suburb lines to preserve the amenities of the beautiful open situation. 'The houses, semi-detached and half-timbered, have a charming appearance individually. The general effect of the curved roads and the layout as a whole … makes the Morrell Garden Estate at Petts Wood a veritable paradise'.

Among the facilities of the area mentioned in the Morrell brochure was 'the famous Orpington Lagoon swimming pool, the finest in the South of England'. It was said to be 'in easy walking distance of the Estate', though in fact it was two miles away on the other side of the Orpington by-pass! Amusements 'close at hand' included the Commodore Cinema, also in Orpington (the Petts Wood Embassy had not yet been built). Another touch of fantasy was the picture of a

The Morrell type B semi became a popular house in Petts Wood west

maid in uniform hoovering the carpet of a small two-bedroomed semi.

Morrell houses in Petts Wood started at £595 and thanks to an arrangement between the company and building societies, 95 per cent mortgages were available. The £595 house could be bought for £30 down and repayments of 14s 8d (73p) a week. Morrell's prices included road charges, legal costs, stamp duties and survey fees and furniture removal was free within a 25-mile radius. For £595 you got two reception rooms and two bedrooms and there was 'space' for a garage.

Either side of the Morrell estate, Petts Wood west was developed by one of the most prolific London builders of the 1930s, New Ideal Homesteads. Founded in 1929 by Leo P. Meyer, a former assistant surveyor to Erith Urban District Council, NIH went for the cheaper end of the market, producing a range of semis, chalets and bungalows from as little as £395. Like Morrell, the firm offered 95 per cent mortgages. NIH built around 25 estates in the London area, usually including the word 'park' in their title. They began building in Petts Wood in 1937 and were responsible for the Southborough Park Estate, stretching south from Oxhawth Crescent, and Oakcroft Park Estate, which filled the gap between Crescent Drive and Towncourt Lane/Queensway.

The completion of Petts Wood west meant the end of Town Court farm. Chudleigh died in 1930 and the Langdons were shocked when instead of extending the ambience of Petts Wood east to the other side of the line, Scruby sold to Morrell. The Morrell estate was built right up to the edge of the farm and the Langdons decided to leave. In 1936 they moved to Bickley and after the war lived in Bournemouth, where James Langdon died in 1950 at the age of 83. They named both their Bickley and Bournemouth houses Town Court. Adolphus Chudleigh is commemorated by the stained glass window in the baptistry of St Francis Church, given by his daughter.

A note on road names. The history and character of an area is often reflected in the names of its roads and so it is with Petts Wood. Several were named after former farms and estates: Town Court, Ladywood, Poverest. Others followed the names of the woodland areas: Birch Wood, Great and Little Thrift, Lake's Wood, Oxhawth Wood. In a more general way the rural/woodland nature of the area is evoked in Silverdale Road, Woodland Way and Wood Ride. Tudor Way was, presumably, a reference to the Tudor-style housing (though there are few examples of it in the road). Crest View Drive is a reminder of the fine view once enjoyed to Crystal Palace and beyond. The 'mere' in Transmere and Hazelmere recalls the many lakes and ponds in the area before the houses were built. Franks Wood Avenue was named not after a wood but to commemorate a third Morrell brother, Frank, killed in a car crash at Clock House while the road was being built in 1934. It was originally called Petts Wood Road, in anticipation of the bridge that would link it to the Petts Wood Road on the other side of the line.

A selection of Morrell house prices, with deposits and repayments; in 2000 they hardly seem credible

Petts Wood Estate, Kent.

Type.	Page.	Price.	Deposit.	Repayments.
R1.	43	£595	£60	13s. 11d. per week
			£30	14s. 8d. " "
J2.	47	£625	£65	14s. 6d. " "
			£30	15s. 5d. " "
K1.	51	£675	£70	15s. 9d. " "
			£35	16s. 8d. " "
C2.	— 56	£725	£75	16s. 11d. " "
			£35	17s. 11d. " "
C4 Elev. No. 2.	56a	£725	£75	16s. 11d. " "
			£35	17s. 11d. " "
C4 Elev. No. 1.	55	£735	£75	17s. 2d. " "
			£35	18s. 2d. " "
L3.	56	£750	£75	17s. 6d. " "
			£40	18s. 5d. " "
B.	59	£775	£80	18s. 0d. " "
			£40	19s. 1d. " "
BG.	61	£790	£80	18s. 5d. " "
			£40	19s. 6d. " "
B1.	59	£825	£80	19s. 4d. per week
			£40	20s. 5d. " "
B2.	67	£875	£90	20s. 5d. " "
			£45	21s. 7d. " "
DC2.	71	£895	£90	20s. 11d. " "
			£45	22s. 1d. " "
DC2 with kitchenette extension.		£920	£70	22s. 1d. " "
B3.	69	£925	£70	22s. 3d. " "
A.	73	£995	£75	23s. 10d. " "
A1. S.	77	£1,175	£118	27s. 10d. " "
A1.	75	£1,225	£123	29s. 0d. " "

A constant beef of the early residents was about unmade roads: Manor Way was not as bad as some

The Residents' Voice

Petts Wood was still in the very early stages of development when, on November 20 1929, Petts Wood Residents' Association was formed. The objects, as set out in the rules approved on December 12, were 'to promote a sound economy in the parochial expenditure and the establishment of a just and equal assessment and for the general interest, betterment and improvement of those residing at Petts Wood'. The association was to be non-political in the party sense while 'adopting every legitimate measure for securing the nomination and election of fit and proper representatives to the local councils'. The subscription was initially set at half a crown (12½p) and it stayed at this level until February 1971. During the 1930s the association had at least one, and up to three, representatives on Orpington Rural District Council. By 1937 membership had reached 700.

For much of its early life the association's main preoccupation was to get the roads made up. The builders of Petts Wood east, as was usual at the time, left the roads more or less as they had found them with only a layer of hard core covering the bare earth. In dry weather the surface turned to dust; in winter it became a morass of mud and water. In January 1937 the *Daily Mirror* ran a picture feature under the headline, 'Puddle and Mud(dle) at Petts Wood'. The road under the railway bridge at Tudor Way is virtually a sheet of water and in another part of Tudor Way a bowler-hatted gentleman stares forlornly at his reflection in a huge puddle.

PUDDLE
AT PETTS

A bowler-hatted gent looks at himself in one of Petts Wood's famous puddles (from the Daily Mirror, January 1937)

To get the roads made up meant lobbying the local authority (Orpington UDC), which in turn had to apply for loan sanction to the Ministry of Health in order to carry out the work. It was a long and tedious process. And since 'frontagers' had to pay up to £1 a foot - a lot of money in those days - for having their road adopted, there was opposition from among the residents themselves. By the outbreak of the Second World War in September 1939 many of the roads of Petts Wood east had proper surfaces, but there were still exceptions.

The association was instrumental in getting trees planted along the verges of the newly made up roads, though householders were canvassed first and not all were in favour. That is why some roads have no trees along the footway, while others do. It also campaigned for better street lighting, for more lamps to be installed and for those at important road junctions to remain lit all night. Postal services came under the association's scrutiny, with demands for better deliveries, more pillar boxes and that Petts Wood should have a main Post Office. The Southern Railway was another target for residents, the bones of contention including overcrowded commuter trains, rising fares, the chaos caused to the system by fog and ice and the lack of awnings at Petts Wood Station. Thirty and forty years later exactly the same complaints were being made to the Southern's successor, the Southern Region of British Rail.

Petts Wood Residents' Association was mainly concerned with the area east of the railway but in 1934 the Garden Estates Association was formed to represent residents on 'the other side', taking its name from the Morrell development. In three years it acquired 800 members. The GEA, too, became concerned about the state of the roads. Though Morrell did provide concrete surfacing there was no maintenance and, since the builder went bankrupt, little hope of getting any. Victor Roques, chairman of the GEA, complained early in 1939: 'Some of the roads have been laid for over five years and have not been swept. Rubbish and weeds are everywhere, pavements are dilapidated and dangerous.' Adoption by the local authority did not take place until after the war, in some cases as late as the 1950s. In 1935 a fund was opened for a Petts Wood Community Centre, for which Morrell had given a one-acre site at the junction of Franks Wood Avenue, Lakeswood Road and Crescent Drive. The project was not to be realised until 1949, and on another site in Woodhurst Avenue, by which time the original cost had doubled to £2,500.

The Daylight Inn: its Tudor style helped to overcome the doubters (Local Studies and Archives Department, Bromley Central Library)

A cookery demonstration in the ballroom of the Daylight Inn (the photograph was taken for The Times *and used in a feature on modern public houses on October 10 1936)*

Public House, Parish Church and Cinema

The demon drink came to Petts Wood in rather a curious way. Under an agreement made with Basil Scruby in 1928, Wine Cellars Ltd. was to have a monopoly of the sale of alcohol in the area and to build a public house/hotel. Early house deeds contain a clause requiring the purchaser's undertaking not to oppose this arrangement! The Wine Cellars off-licence was opened at the top of Petts Wood Road but the hotel option was not taken up and Scruby entered into negotiations about a public house with Charrington's, the brewers. The agreement struck was that a building would be put up on the open space behind Scruby's estate office in Station Square, on condition that no alcohol would be sold for consumption off the premises. The Wine Cellars thereby kept its off-licence monopoly.

The prospect of having a pub in their midst was not universally welcomed by the people of Petts Wood and when, in February 1933, an application was made to Bromley Licensing Branch, a petition was handed in opposing the project. But a promise that the building would be in the Tudor style to blend with the surroundings helped to assuage the objectors and the Daylight Inn, taking its name from Willett's campaign, opened in December 1935. Apart from its bar facilities, the Daylight offered a large banqueting hall-cum-ballroom, which also had a stage and dressing rooms. It became a popular venue for dinners, amateur dramatics and public meetings. In its early years the Inn was a residential hotel with 13 bedrooms. The architect, Sydney Clarke of Leigh-on-Sea, designed more than a dozen public houses during the 1930s, many, though not all, in the Tudor style.

Much of the new Petts Wood community came within the parish of St Nicholas, Chislehurst, and as the first homes began to appear the Rector, Canon James Dawson, sent one of his staff to visit the new residents. The next step was the setting up of a committee to oversee the building of a church in Petts Wood. The committee had its first meeting at the rectory in December 1929 and early in the following year Basil Scruby donated a site at the bottom of Greencourt Road.

The first service was held in the hall of Ladywood School on October 26, 1930 and was conducted by the curate of St Nicholas, the Rev James Hampson. Meanwhile Dr Oscar Hardman, who had become rector on the death of Canon Dawson, started a fund to provide a temporary wooden church. It was dedicated by the Bishop of Rochester on March 28, 1931 and served the district for four years until the permanent building was ready. In March 1933 the Bishop dedicated a cross to mark the site of the future altar and the foundation stone was laid in April. In January 1935 the Bishop consecrated the new church and was the first celebrant.

Designed by Geoffrey Mullins, an architect who lived in Chislehurst and had a practice near the British Museum, the church provided a contrast to the more flamboyant styles of the Petts Wood houses. It was built mainly of wood and hand-made Sussex brick and followed the plan of a medieval tithe barn, with a long straight hammerbeam roof. With its woodland setting, the church appropriately took the name of the medieval saint, Francis of Assisi, a man who loved nature,

The temporary wooden church in Greencourt Road which served until the permanent building was ready in 1935

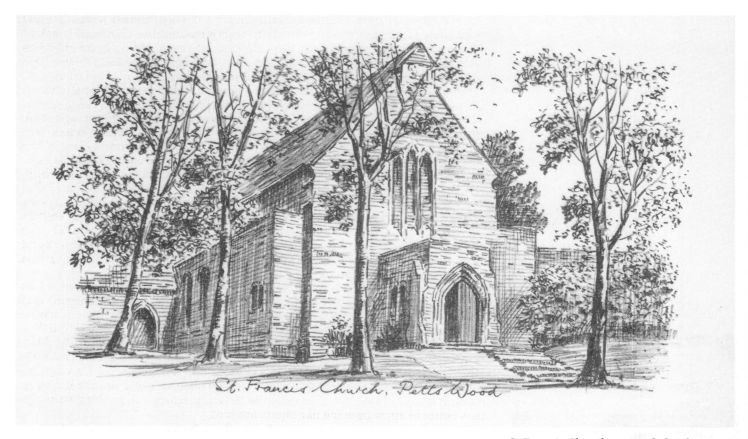

St. Francis Church, Petts Wood

St Francis Church, a simple brick building celebrated in Pevsner (pen and ink drawing by Priscilla Copley)

and the grounds have been kept in their natural state. The church and furnishings cost £12,000, most of which came from the people of Chislehurst.

In July 1935 Petts Wood was raised to the status of parish and the living offered to Father Hampson, who served as the first vicar until his retirement in 1961. Father Hampson brought to St Francis the strong Anglo-Catholicism of the parent church, St Nicholas, and his successors have maintained that tradition.

Before the vicarage, another design by Mullins, was built in Willett Way in 1938, the vicar lived in rooms at the top of Towncourt Crescent with one of the early Petts Wood general practitioners, Dr Guy Milner. A local character, the doctor called his house 'Bedside Manor' and to obtain manure for his garden carried a shovel in the boot of his car to pick up droppings left by the horse pulling the United Dairies milk cart. With the opening of the present church, the temporary wooden building became the parish hall until it was destroyed by fire in 1948. A new hall opened in 1952.

St Francis is the only Petts Wood entry in Sir Nikolaus Pevsner's monumental work, *The Buildings of England*, where reference is made to the 'fashionably jagged treatment of the windows' and the stained glass east window is described as 'above average for its day'. The stained glass, which was installed in 1946, was designed by James Hogan, who also did windows for Liverpool Cathedral.

Among the many gifts to the church were two from famous names. Stuart Hibberd, the BBC's chief announcer, lived in Chislehurst and came to St Francis for the 9.30 service on Sunday mornings, displaying a fine tenor voice. He presented the church with a sanctuary lamp. The other celebrated donor was Field-Marshal Lord Montgomery, who visited Petts Wood in September 1947 for the christening at St Francis of the two-month-old son of an army colleague and personal friend, Major R. C. Macdonald of Great Thrift. Concerned to see the holy water being carried in a milk jug, Monty gave a metal ewer for the font.

Father Hampson was succeeded by the Rev Hector Horobin, a Glaswegian who had come to the priesthood after working in the youth and social fields. In 1977 the church had to spend £15,000 to make good a leaking roof, re-point the brickwork and install new drainage. A similar sum had to be found to rebuild and restore the organ, which went back to the 19th century. Music and singing had been a feature of St Francis from the early days.

In January 1985 the 50th anniversary of the consecration of the church was celebrated by a parish dinner. The chief guest, the Bishop of Rochester, was prevented from attending by snow drifts but made it the next day for parish eucharist. Father Horobin retired in October 1988, two months before his 79th birthday, and early in the following year Father Ross Thompson, a New Zealander, was instituted as only the parish's third vicar. Among his early initiatives was setting up an altar in the nave, to bring the priest closer to the congregation and to complement the move from the Book of Common Prayer to modern liturgy. New lighting made the church brighter and enabled worshippers better to appreciate the hammerbeam roof.

The ordination of women priests in the Church of England proved a contentious matter at St Francis as elsewhere and, unable to accept the change, Father Thompson left to join the Roman Catholic Church. The new vicar, in May 1994, was Father Jeffery Gunn from Larkfield. He served for just over five years before being appointed Dean of Ballarat Cathedral in Australia and in the spring of 2000 Father Owen Higgs, who had trained as an accountant before turning to the priesthood, arrived with his young family from a curacy in Dockland.

The 1930s was the great age of cinema building in Britain and it was inevitable that Petts Wood should soon have its own picture house. The Embassy was one of a chain of cinemas on the fringes of London put up by Shipman and King. It was designed by a Farnborough architect, David Nye, in a restrained version of what became known as 'art deco' and with Bovis as general contractor it took only 4½ months to build. Sir Waldron Smithers, MP, performed the official opening on October 12, 1936 and the first presentation was Ronald Colman in *A Tale of Two Cities*. In view of the separate development of east and west Petts

The Rev James Hampson, first vicar of Petts Wood

The Embassy Cinema in 1938, two years after it opened; the week's attraction is Errol Flynn in The Adventures of Robin Hood *(Alan A. Jackson)*

Wood, the title had a certain irony.

The souvenir programme claimed an unimpeded view from every one of the 1,350 seats and 'perfect projection and audibility in comfortable and luxurious surroundings'. In fact, 'every device that modern science has evolved to increase the comfort and to safeguard the health of the cinema-goer has been adopted.' The auditorium, with its rose and gold decor, was air-conditioned and some seats provided with earphones for the hard of hearing. There was a cafe/lounge on the first floor, with tubular chrome chairs, and a large free car park. The management promised a 'clearly defined policy for the presentation of only the very best films'.

Prices were 1s 3d, 1s 9d and 6d for the stalls and 2s and 1s 6d for the balcony. An application by David Nye for a second cinema at the junction of Petts Wood Road and Woodland Way was turned down by Orpington UDC in March 1939.

For 20 years and more the Embassy was a popular and valued place of entertainment, not least for the children of Petts Wood. Up to 1,000 of them flocked to the Saturday morning shows to watch Laurel and Hardy, Charlie Chaplin and the cliff-hanging serial under the genial eye of 'Uncle Albert'. He was Albert Hazeldene, who had started his cinema career in the silent days and became manager of the Embassy a few months after it opened.

Asked in 1949 about the threat of television, Mr Hazeldene said he was unconcerned as people would always go out for their entertainment. He was soon to be proved sadly wrong. At the Embassy, as elsewhere, cinema audiences fell dramatically from the mid-1950s and while a few films continued to attract long queues, the habit of going to the pictures once or twice a week was broken for good. The end came in April 1973 when the Embassy's last presentation was a children's film, *Snoopy Come Home*. The cinema lay empty for more than four years before being pulled down to make way for a supermarket and office block.

Left: Albert Hazeldene, genial manager of the Embassy before and after the Second World War (caricature by Wiggins, 1948)

Below: Residents celebrate the opening of the cinema in the cafe/ lounge; the tubular chairs were a feature of the period

Schools

In the early years of Petts Wood parents wanting to make use of state education had to send their children out of the area with Chislehurst Road, on the edge of Orpington, being the nearest primary school. Early in 1936 Crofton Lane (later Crofton) School opened in a block of wooden buildings on the left hand side of the road coming from Petts Wood. It was surrounded by farmland, with no hint then of the big housing development in the area that would put such a strain on the enlarged school after the war. But even in 1937 Kent Education Committee was having to authorise the erection of extra classrooms and during the war classes of 60 or more were not uncommon.

For those willing to pay for education, however, Petts Wood did offer a choice of private schools. The earliest, Ladywood, was founded in 1929. Miss M. F. Pigrome had just retired as a primary school headmistress for the London County Council and had come to live at the top of Scad's Hill. Almost at once she was in demand for coaching and what started as half a dozen children in her living room became a respected preparatory school, offering tuition from five to 11. It was very much a family affair: Miss Pigrome was helped by an older sister, known to the children as 'Auntie Annie', while her brother, 'Uncle Charlie', did the gardening and odd jobs. Miss Pigrome, a small woman of tremendous energy and drive, was still teaching until she was nearly 90, finally handing over to her niece, Miss Winifred Cowling. Ladywood was the last private school in Petts Wood when it closed in 1968 on Miss Cowling's retirement.

Another preparatory school was started in Ladywood Avenue in a house built for the purpose with a flat above. Petts Wood School, run by Mrs Sidwell and later by Miss Worthington and Miss Porter, continued until the 1950s when the property was sold and became the Friends' Meeting House. In 1935 St Dunstan's School opened in a large, pre-1914 house in St John's Road. Initially a prep school, by the 1950s it was offering the full range from nursery at three to university entrance at 18. St Dunstan's closed after the summer term in 1964 and the house was demolished.

Sport and Recreation

A recreation ground in the triangle formed by Towncourt Crescent, Kingsway and Crossway was provided for in the original estate plan. By 1930 a Petts Wood Tennis Club was playing on two courts and in 1932 it was decided to develop the rest of the site - 6½ acres of rough ground - and to form a general sports club. A club house was opened in 1934 and a sports field fund started. By 1937 the Petts Wood Club had 600 members and ran tennis, cricket, bowls, hockey, table-tennis and badminton sections. The original sports club disbanded at the outbreak of war, when the ground was given over to allotments and Home Guard training. After the war it was acquired by Orpington UDC and became a public open space, being re-named the Willett Recreation Ground in February 1948. In 1974 and 1975, Petts Wood Cricket Club played matches against the full Kent County side for Mike Denness and Derek Underwood benefits.

Advertisement for Petts Wood School from the Orpington and District Guide of 1935; it was one of several private preparatory schools in Petts Wood

ONE OF THE CLASSROOMS

PETTS WOOD SCHOOL
for GIRLS

Corner of GREENCOURT ROAD, PETTS WOOD

KINDERGARTEN *and* PREPARATORY *for* BOYS

Principal : Miss H. E. STYLES.   Assisted by a fully Qualified Staff

The school is conducted on public school lines and pupils are prepared for public examinations, including London Matriculation, Oxford Locals, etc.

Instruction is individual and a high tone of work is maintained throughout the school.

Physical Culture is under the direction of a competent games mistress.

Games : Tennis, Netball, etc., played according to the Season.

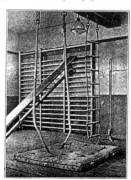

A CORNER OF THE GYMNASIUM

OPENING OF THE TENNIS COURTS AT PETTS WOOD.

A group taken at the opening of the Tennis Courts at Petts Wood on Saturday last. Mr. Basil Scruby is seated at the table on which is displayed the Petts Wood Sports Association trophies. On his right are Miss Chuter, Miss Smith, and Miss Williams. On his left are Miss M. Palmer (lady captain) and Mrs. Clarke. Standing, from left to right, are A. T. Scopes, L. Fuller, L. E. Hopwood (club captain), Miss Collins, Mrs. Farrow, L. V. Gingell, H. H. Pearson (chairman of the association). Mrs. Rogerson, G. Carter-Clout, P. Chaplin, Charles Scruby, Mrs. C. Scruby, A. E. Carter, Mrs. Hutley, J. J. Webster, Miss Scruby, and Mr. E. T. Hemsley (Lloyds Bank), treasurer.

Basil Scruby (with the big moustache) and other local notables gather for the launch of Petts Wood Tennis Club in 1930

In August 1985 the Willett sports pavilion was badly damaged by fire. Out of the ashes arose a new building, with better showers and changing facilities, and two self-contained areas, each with its kitchen and cloakrooms. The new pavilion was greatly appreciated by its principal users, the cricket club, the bowls club and the children's playgroup, and was ready just in time for the 1987 cricket season.

On the other side of the line, between the railway and Blackbrook Lane, was the West Kent Golf Club, founded in 1916 by the developers of the Bickley Park Estate. Between the wars it was recognised as one of the leading clubs in the district and many famous golfers played there, including the great American, Bobby Jones (whose picture hung in the club house). West Kent also entertained the visiting Australian cricket teams and among those who enjoyed their golf were Bradman, McCabe, Oldfield, Woodfull and Hassett. The club was strictly for the well-off, asking a subscription of eight guineas a year. In the early part of the Second World War an anti-aircraft battery was built on the course and in September 1940 a parachute mine wrecked the clubhouse. West Kent moved first to Bromley Common and after the war to Downe.

The early years of Petts Wood saw the formation of many clubs and societies. One of the first was the Dramatic and Operatic Society, which was so successful that it split in two, one for plays and the other for opera. In November 1936 the Operatic Society's production was interrupted so that the audience could listen to Edward VIII's Abdication broadcast: before resuming the show, cast and audience joined in singing the National Anthem. The Horticultural Society held its first show at Petts Wood School in Ladywood Avenue in October 1933 and attracted 242 entries.

What became a Petts Wood institution started in 1935 when Rita Emmerson's School of Dancing held its first class in Ladywood School. In the early 1930s Miss Emmerson was busy pursuing a professional stage career, which took her abroad for long periods, but her home was in Petts Wood and friends suggested that she should run a dancing class. The school proved so popular that it soon outgrew its original premises and moved to the ballroom of the Daylight Inn, where Miss Emmerson also put on tea dances on Saturday afternoons. After the war the school held several charity dances to support the appeal for the Memorial Hall. It moved to the hall in the 1950s and was still going strong, with classes on six days a week, into the 21st century.

A Petts Wood institution: Vanessa Corbett (left) and Susan Cambridge, pupils of the Rita Emmerson School of Dancing, c. 1972

Celebrating the Coronation

An early example of Petts Wood community enterprise was a Gala Day on May 12, 1937, to celebrate the Coronation of George VI. A committee drawn from local organisations arranged a programme of special events, from 'kiddies races' in the afternoon to a fireworks display in the evening and dancing into the small hours, the festivities pausing at 8 pm to hear the King's speech on the wireless. But the most unusual event was a 'flitch trial'. The flitch was a side of bacon offered to married couples prepared to prove before a 'jury' of spinsters and bachelors that they had lived in matrimonial harmony for a year and a day previous to the trial. The winners were Mr and Mrs S. A. Thompson, of Queensway.

The attractively produced souvenir programme discussed two possible ideas for marking the Coronation in a permanent way by improving the amenities of the district. One was to create a 'Coronation Avenue' leading from Hazelmere Road to the then level crossing over the railway to the National Trust woods. The other was to acquire the waste ground in the angle of Tudor Way and Willett Way, familiarly known as 'the dump', and lay it out as a public garden. Already, in 1937, it was felt desirable to retain as much open space as possible in 'what is rapidly becoming a built-up area'. Neither scheme came to fruition. The level crossing was eventually replaced by an underpass and the 'dump' became the site of the Congregational (later United Reformed) Church.

As Television Saw It

The creation and early development of the Petts Wood suburb was the subject of a BBC television documentary broadcast in June 1983 as one of a series on Britain in the Thirties. The title, *22 Minutes From London*, echoed one of the main selling points of the new estate and the film was built around the memories of people who had lived in Petts Wood during the period. As well as arousing much local interest, the programme was widely reviewed in the national press.

In it, people spoke of the excitement of being part of a new community, of taking pride in a well-kept house and garden and enjoying the life of a modern 'village'. The programme also brought out the respectability of a middle-class society, in which the men went off to work in black coats and pinstripe trousers and their wives wore gloves to go shopping. A trip to the shops was a more leisurely affair than the later rush round the supermarket with a trolley. Mrs Rose Fletcher remembered Cullens grocers, with its aroma of ground coffee and chairs by the counter where shoppers could sit and give their orders, knowing that anything they could not carry would be delivered.

There were sharp memories of the division between east and west. Like many residents of Petts Wood east, Mrs Margaret Jenkins was distressed by the sudden appearance on the other side of the line of vehicles and builders, by the felling of trees and the construction of large bonfires to dispose of them. She recalled: 'I actually cried and so did a lot of people'.

The social divisions were reflected in membership of the sports club, which was unofficially but deliberately reserved for people in Petts Wood east. Morrell, the main builder in Petts Wood west, tried to break down this exclusivity by offering trophies. Mrs Joan Edwards, who lived in Petts Wood west, said: 'You got chatting to someone on the train and when they found you lived on the other side they didn't seem to want to continue the friendship.' Much of this was to change with the war, to which we now turn.

Radio Times *billing for* 22 Minutes From London, *broadcast on the day of the 1983 General Election*

GENERAL ELECTION DAY 9 JUNE 1983

THURSDAY tv

BBC 2

9.30 pm
Britain in the Thirties
22 Minutes from London

A garden city to rival Letchworth and Welwyn was created in the woodland south of Chislehurst between the years 1929 and 1939. Almost unchanged to this day, Petts Wood reveals an astonishing array of British suburban designs for living in the 1930s. When the first residents moved in, their only link with the metropolis of London, where most of them worked, was a tiny railway halt. By 1939 a thriving community had grown up, but not without teething problems.
Narrator ANDREW FAULDS

Film editor PETER SYMES
Director VICTORIA WEGG PROSSER

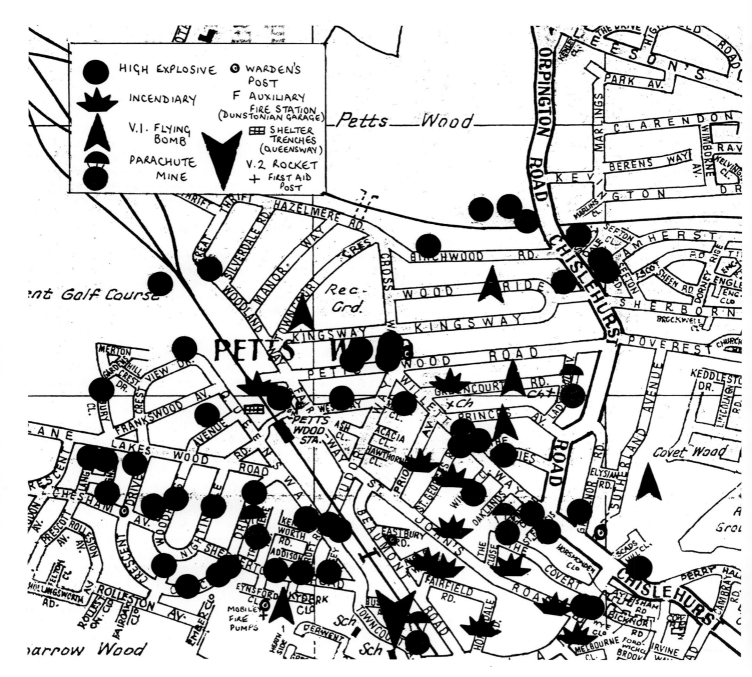

7. PETTS WOOD AT WAR

The Second World War disrupted the Petts Wood community in many ways – men went off to the forces, women and children were evacuated to safer places, private houses were taken over by the army and many properties were damaged or destroyed by bombs. At the same time, the common danger brought people closer together, creating a sense of comradeship and in particular helping to break down the unfortunate social barrier between east and west.

Preparations for war started in 1938 when the first ARP (Air Raid Precautions) volunteers were recruited in Petts Wood. From June instruction courses were held in St Francis Church Hall on first aid, the use of the gas mask and dealing with fires caused by bombs, There were 50 volunteers originally and by the Munich crisis that autumn the number had trebled. In April 1939, when war seemed almost inevitable, the residents' association organised a recruiting rally for 'national service' which was addressed by the author, L. A. G. Strong, and filled the Daylight Inn to overflowing.

War broke out in September 1939. A line of concrete pyramids and other anti-tank defences were built along the southern edge of the National Trust woods, overlooking the railway line, and three nests of anti-aircraft guns erected on the West Kent Golf Course. By the start of the war the ARP volunteers were trained and ready, though it was almost another year before the air raids began. Houses and roads were allocated to sectors and four to five sectors were grouped around a post, a bomb-resistant shelter, either above or below ground and manned day and night. Men would come home from a day's work, have a hurried meal and then report for duty. One of the ARP posts, on the corner of Petts Wood Road and Crossway, was known as 'the hole'. Wardens gained access via a manhole cover, then descended some 25 feet on the metal rungs to a small, fusty room which had two beds, a lamp and a desk with a telephone. Wardens' duties included giving out gas masks, enforcing the blackout and advising householders on preparations against attack. When the bombs started to fall, wardens did their best to help victims while fire, ambulance and other rescue services were summoned. Those bombed out of their houses were taken to rest centres and looked after by the Women's Voluntary Service.

While Petts Wood itself was not a prime target for German bombers, it did have an important railway junction, there was Biggin Hill airfield only a few miles away and the industrial and dock area of London directly to the north. The worst periods were during the Battle of Britain (August to October 1940); the Blitz which followed and lasted well into 1941; and during the flying bomb and rocket attacks in the second half of 1944. During the war, according to figures compiled by the ARP, the four square miles of residential Petts Wood suffered 99 high explosive bombs, five land mines, five flying bombs and one rocket.

The first V1 flying bomb to hit Petts Wood landed in Towncourt Crescent in June 1944. Others fell in Princes Avenue, Wood Ride and Greencourt Road. The V2 long range rocket followed in November, falling at the junction of Bushey Avenue and Towncourt Lane and killing two people. In the worst V2 incident in

Petts Wood under fire: where the bombs fell, compiled from ARP records by Fred Walford

Dad's army at the ready:

Above: Petts Wood Home Guard pose with an anti-aircraft gun

Left: 'Who do you think you are kidding, Mr Hitler?'

the area, also in November 1944, there were 35 fatalities at the Crooked Billet in Southborough Lane. Petts Wood just missed the last rocket to arrive in Britain. It fell in Court Road, Orpington.

One of the early victims of the war was George Reed, of Reed and Hoad, the builders, killed with one of his daughters and a neighbour when a land mine demolished his house in Ladywood Avenue in September 1940. In St George's Road, a few weeks later, C. E. Wallace would probably have lost his life if he had not decided to write a letter. On the evening of October 15 Mr Wallace was sitting alone in the small sandbagged shelter at the back of his house, Thrift Cottage, when he was visited by two neighbours, Mr Brown and Mr Bachelor. They often called round and the three men would have a hot drink together. But on this occasion Mr Bachelor suggested they should all go to his house for something to eat. Since this was the first time Mr Wallace had had such an invitation, he jokingly asked Mr Bachelor what he had to offer to justify a hazardous 300-yard walk across the road! Anyway, Mr Wallace said he would come, later, after first writing the weekly letter to his wife who was staying with relatives in Cumberland. He had no idea what made him do this, since he had a regular day for writing and he was breaking a routine. But a couple of minutes after the two neighbours left a bomb dropped, killing Mr Bachelor and sending Mr Brown to hospital with a shrapnel wound on his forehead.

The Dunstonian Garage in Station Square became a fire station and Jack Kemsley joined the fire service as a column officer responsible for some 2,500 vehicles over an area stretching from Lambeth to Biggin Hill. At Crofton School the staff operated a fire watching rota, sleeping in the school overnight; and during the V bomb attacks in 1944, the children had their lessons - and lunches - in a huge underground shelter. On the 61 bus route blue Leeds City Corporation buses were brought in to replace London Transport stock damaged by bombs.

On May 16, 1940 the Minister of War, Anthony Eden, made an appeal on the wireless for civilian volunteers to defend the country against invasion which at that time seemed imminent. Quarter of a million men enrolled for the Local Defence Volunteers (later known as the Home Guard) in the first 24 hours. Orpington was the base of the 53rd Kent Battalion, whose B Company was recruited in Petts Wood. With Major Horace Crouch as commanding officer, the Petts Wood Home Guard set up its headquarters in Lynwood House, Crofton Lane. The duties included day and night patrols - keeping a special watch for German parachutists - guarding the anti-aircraft battery on the Golf Course and target practice at Botany Bay, Chislehurst.

Like the *Dad's Army* of television fame, the Petts Wood Company had its lighter moments: on more than one occasion a platoon got lost during exercises in the woods and found itself going round in circles. But the Petts Wood Home Guard, like the ARP, was a tremendous morale-booster and there was sadness among the men when the stand-down order came at the end of 1944. One of the by-products of the Home Guard, and its women's nursing section, was the amateur dramatic group, the Lynwood Players. It was formed at Lynwood House, gave its first performance in 1945 and continued to flourish long after the war.

The call to duty: Home Guard recruiting leaflet issued in Petts Wood

JOIN THE HOME GUARD!!

YOUR LOCAL COMPANY
"B" COMPANY
WANT MEN !
(17 to 65 years).

Vacancies for
Riflemen, Machine Gunners, Bombers, Signallers, Despatch-Riders (M/Cycle & Cyclist), Runners, Lewis Gunners, etc.

On formation over a year ago applications for membership had to be refused, but now organization is advanced and arms, equipment and qualified instructors are available.
MORE MEN ARE WANTED.

The more spare time men have the faster they can be trained, but as a minimum "B" Company men train one evening per week and every Sunday morning with a night guard roughly every ten days. Specialists attend on additional evenings.

Men of seventeen and upwards who are liable to be called up are specially welcome as instruction they receive will be invaluable to them later on. Older men up to 65 years of age are particularly wanted to increase strength of "B" Company.

Remember Mr. Winston Churchill said "Be ready by September 1st."

JOIN NOW
JOIN "B" COMPANY & DEFEND YOUR OWN LOCALITY

For particulars apply at "B" Company Orderly Room, or ask any member of "B" Company in Petts Wood and Orpington District. Nearest Officer is :—

The Social side is encouraged and enjoyed by all ranks.
Herbert, Printer, 10a, High Street.

ORPINGTON URBAN DISTRICT COUNCIL

FUEL AND LIGHTING ORDER, 1939.

Article 3 (2) and (3).

Application for Registration of Controlled Premises with a Licensed Coal Merchant.

FORM FLO/6 should also be used if registration is required with Companies, etc., producing coke.

Before completing this Form, the notes overleaf should be carefully read.

To *(Name and address of Coal Merchant, dealer, etc.)*

Messrs. F Warren & Co:
Orpington.

I Général De Gaulle, the occupier of the premises known as 41 Birchwood Road Petts Wood Kent declare that I wish to obtain from you supplies of coal (and coke) for consumption on those premises, and I hereby request you to register those premises in accordance with the provisions of the above Order.

I propose to register these premises also with .... in respect of the supply of coke.

(See note 6 overleaf.)

During the year ended 30th June, 1939, I did not acquire, save as shown below, any coal and/or coke for consumption on those premises except from you.

Quantities of Coal or Coke obtained from other Suppliers.

Amounts obtained in each Quarter of the year ended 30th June, 1939.		Name and Address of Other Supplier.
Quarter ending.	Basic Quantity.	
	Tons. Cwts.	
30th September, 1938 ...	1 - 0	N.R. Yreation by
31st December, 1938 ...	2 . 0	SRI. application
31st March, 1939 ...	2 - 0	See Y. I. O. l. Au 2493
30th June, 1939 ...	1 - 0	

Signature of Applicant ....

Date 23/8/40

Fuel for the General: General de Gaulle's application, signed by him, for his coal ration while living in Petts Wood in August 1940 (Bromley Museum, London Borough of Bromley)

General and Madame de Gaulle in England early in the Second World War (Imperial War Museum)

Houses left empty by evacuation were requisitioned by the military. Stanley Nickelson, whose work had taken him temporarily away from Petts Wood, first heard from a neighbour's letter that his house had been occupied by the Scots Guards and was being used as a sick bay. Later the Royal Corps of Signals moved in to prepare for D-Day, storing their boots in the main living room and filling the garden with telegraph poles and cables. Tudor House opposite was an officers' mess. The Scots Guards became a familiar part of the Petts Wood scene, parading up and down the roads and providing partners for the local girls at Saturday night dances.

The most famous soldier to stay in Petts Wood during the war, indeed the most distinguished resident Petts Wood has had, came from France. At 49 Charles de Gaulle was the youngest general in the French army and had briefly been under-secretary for defence. When in June 1940 the government of Paul Reynaud fell and an armistice with Hitler was inevitable, de Gaulle decided to carry on the struggle from exile.

On the morning of June 17 he flew from Bordeaux to London. He had only the 100,000 francs (less than £600) which Reynaud had given him from a secret fund, no troops and little following. He spoke hardly any English. On June 18 he made a famous broadcast to his fellow countrymen in which he declared: 'The flame of French resistance must not and will not be extinguished.' From a two-roomed office opposite the House of Commons and later in more spacious premises in Carlton Gardens, he put himself at the head of Free France.

His first home in England was a flat in the West End of London but when the rest of the family joined him on June 19, something bigger had to be found. The de Gaulles moved into the Rubens Hotel in Buckingham Palace Road while Madame de Gaulle looked for a suitable house. Within days, through the estate agent A. F. Mullock in Station Square, Petts Wood, she found one. Mr and Mrs Leonard Pummell, owners of the mock-Tudor house at 41 Birchwood Road, had put the property on the market, intending to sell. But in the special circumstances they agreed to let it while they stayed with friends.

The de Gaulles were to pay a rent of £14 1s 8d a month in advance, to give one month's notice and to keep the garden in good order. Since they had arrived in England with only their personal possessions, the house was let fully furnished. There was a radiogram, with a stock of Gilbert and Sullivan records, and a television set although programmes had been suspended at the outbreak of war. Madame de Gaulle used the sewing machine to make clothes. The only air raid shelter was the cloakroom under the stairs.

The de Gaulles had three children - Philippe, who had left school and was about to join the navy, Elisabeth, in her early teens, and 12-year-old Anne, mentally handicapped and looked after by a nurse. Anne died a few years later. Mrs Pummell introduced Madame de Gaulle to the local tradesmen: her Express Dairy milkman, Playfoot and Bell the greengrocers, Griggs the butcher, Bilhams the fishmonger and the Marlborough Bakers. During the first week women in the road clubbed together to buy a basket of fruit and flowers, tied with the red, white

Volunteers running a 24-hour canteen for ARP workers in the showroom of the Dunstonian Garage, September 1939. The photograph was taken by Eric Greenwood, chief photographer of The Times, *who lived in Princes Avenue, Petts Wood*

and blue ribbon of France.

Madame de Gaulle made a point of calling on each of the donors or leaving a note of thanks. She took Elisabeth to tea with the Clarks at *Lone Pool* and was amused by the tea cosy. The general was a more shadowy figure. He could be seen walking in the garden on Sundays and sometimes striding up to the station to catch a train to Victoria. More often he was collected in a large car.

August saw the start of the Battle of Britain and intensive German bombing. Whether the Germans knew de Gaulle was in Petts Wood is impossible to say. Certainly the local residents became convinced of it and there was some relief when, in September (while the general was in Africa), Madame de Gaulle wrote to Mrs Pummell that they had decided to leave: 'The nights are too noisely and my little Anne is frightened'. Elisabeth was now at school in Shrewsbury and the family moved north to be near her. The de Gaulles remained in Britain until May 1943 but did not return to Petts Wood. Their stay at 41 Birchwood Road is marked by a small plaque fixed to the panelling in the hall.

Among other foreign visitors to Petts Wood were refugees from Belgium, who were put up in empty houses in Silverdale Road and Hazelmere Road. With space in short supply, several families had to live together in the same house. There were also some guests from the enemy side. In December 1940 bombs had destroyed four houses in Crescent Drive. When in 1942 the owner of number 144, G. M. Dyce-Keele, returned home from service overseas (he was a press attaché at the British Embassy in Baghdad) he found that the Ministry of Works had put up huts on his and the adjoining land and that the occupants were 70 Italian prisoners of war.

Although Mr Dyce-Keele was found a requisitioned house in Poverest Road, he received no compensation for the use of his land and continued to pay a mortgage on a house that no longer existed. Furthermore, the POWs were still there several months after the war ended and the matter was finally raised with the Government. The Minister of Health, Aneurin Bevan, replied that the Italians were engaged on urgent Government work and that there was no other suitable accommodation for them. The site, which was known as 'Camp 49', was not cleared until the middle of 1946.

War Weapons Week at the warden's post in Beaumont Road (Philip Lane)

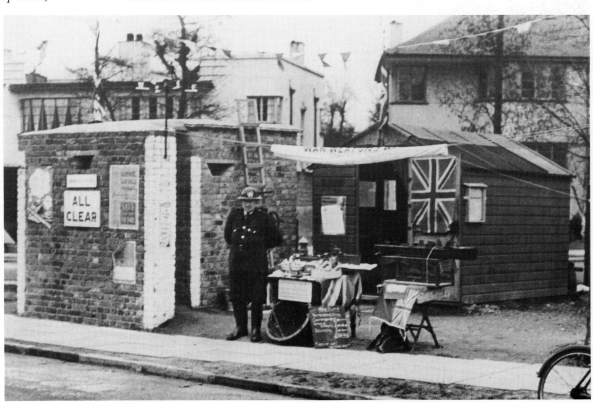

A popular feature of the Petts Wood social scene during the 1980s was the fair held annually in Station Square on May Bank Holiday, when stalls, sideshows and entertainers drew large crowds from Petts Wood and beyond

8. THE POST WAR YEARS

The Memorial Hall

A memorial to the fallen citizens of Petts Wood was first discussed at a public meeting in the Daylight Inn on March 2, 1945. Several suggestions were put forward including houses let free to the disabled, a youth centre and a community hall. Mr and Mrs Joseph Cast then entered the picture. They had lived in Woodland Way since 1936 and had bought a piece of land opposite their home which they had never used: they decided to donate it for the hall and a garden of remembrance. A scheme was formally launched in August 1945.

Bands of volunteers went out in their spare evenings and weekends to clear the site and at the same time a series of fund raising events was started - house to house collections, whist drives and, from 1946, an annual fête. When Mr and Mrs Cast celebrated their golden wedding in 1948 friends were asked not to bring gifts but to make donations to the war memorial fund: £93 was collected.

On May 7, 1950 the Garden of Remembrance was dedicated and it became the focal point of the local British Legion's Armistice Day observance. Although limited by the then building regulations to an outlay of £4,000, the Memorial Hall was completed, with a temporary stage, in 1954 and officially opened by Mr Cast in January 1955. His ambition to see the hall erected in his lifetime had been fulfilled. Cloakrooms were added later and in 1964 an £18,000 appeal was launched to provide major improvements - a permanent stage with a box unit extension and an addition at the back with two committee rooms, kitchen, toilets, store, office and caretaker's flat. The sponsors of the appeal included such well-

Right: An ambition fulfilled: cartoon by Wiggins in 1949 anticipates the opening of the Memorial Hall six years later

Baby Keith Atkins and his mother receive the challenge cup for best baby in the show from the radio personality, Anona Winn, at the Garden Estates Association fête at Eynsford Close in August 1948. The cup, which was competed for annually, was donated by Mrs Sarah Hardiman (centre) of Franks Wood Avenue

known residents of the time as the cricketer, Colin Cowdrey; the broadcaster, Peter West; and the opera singer, John Heddle Nash (whose father Heddle Nash, one of the finest English tenors of his generation, had also lived in Petts Wood). Orpington Urban District Council granted a mortgage loan of £9,000 secured on the premises and there was a generous donation from General de Gaulle, now President of France. It was made on condition that the fact was not revealed during his lifetime, but the secret leaked out.

Run on a non-profit basis, with fees well below those of similar halls in the area, the Memorial Hall became the focus for a wide range of community activity. It was used for a nursery school, a dancing class, whist drives, amateur dramatics, exhibitions, jumble sales and meetings. Bookings averaged nearly 90 per cent of capacity and the more popular spots had to be secured up to two years in advance. But in 1989 bookings fell after the decision to stop Saturday evening wedding receptions and birthday parties because of noise and drunken behaviour.

The War Memorial Trust, a registered charity, was administered by a 15-strong committee of management, of whom three were trustees, six elected at the annual general meeting and six appointed to represent the hirers. The only paid staff were the caretaker, and his deputy, and a part-time gardener. A ways and means committee was formed as a fund raising body to supplement the income from lettings and raised some £3,000 a year.

The debts on the building were quickly paid off, which meant that any surplus money could be spent on improvements. These included lighting, curtains and decorations (1978) and a public address system (1983). But in 1985 an appeal had to be launched for £12,000 for substantial repairs to the floor, which had to be lifted and re-laid because of subsidence.

There was more subsidence in the early 1990s. To deal with it some oak trees were pollarded to reduce their intake of water from the soil and the drainage system was renewed. At the end of the decade a generous bequest from a former resident enabled the hall to be redecorated and have new chairs, tables and curtains while leaving enough in hand for the trust to consider a further extension at the back. The 50th anniversary of the trust was celebrated in July 2000.

Residents' Voice Revived

Both the Petts Wood Residents' Association and the Garden Estates Association suspended their activities during the war but the GEA was soon revived after hostilities and in October 1949 realised a long-held ambition by opening a Youth Centre and Community Hall in Woodhurst Avenue. The hall has proved a popular addition to the facilities of Petts Wood west. GEA membership then stood at a record 900 but it has become less active in recent years and administration of the hall is now the association's main function.

The residents' association was still dormant some years after the war when a fatal accident at the level crossing leading from Hazelmere Road to the National Trust woods brought it back to life. Concern about the danger of the crossing had been expressed back in the 1930s and for some time the railway company had provided a watchman: but he was eventually dispensed with on economy grounds. One factor making the crossing more hazardous was that noisy steam engines were gradually giving way to quieter electrics. Another was the increase in traffic: in 1950 it was estimated that 50,000 people were using the crossing every year and about the same number of trains were passing the spot.

Charles Pratt, first post-war chairman of Petts Wood Residents' Association and later Mayor of Bromley

As local feeling ran high, there were protest meetings and calls for either a bridge or a tunnel. Out of this a new residents' body was formed, holding its first committee meeting on June 26, 1950. The files and funds of the original residents' association were acquired and a new association formally constituted. Until 1962 the chairman was an Orpington Councillor (later Mayor of the London Borough of Bromley), Charles Pratt.

The argument about the level crossing went on. Much of it hinged on whether or not the crossing was a public road: the authorities claimed that it was a bridle path and that therefore the Minister of Transport had no power to order safety measures. British Rail did, however, offer to meet half the cost of a bridge or tunnel (about £3,000). The issue was eventually settled in 1958 when the track was widened and the railway constructed a subway under the line.

The association had meanwhile set itself two main objects: to preserve and develop the amenities of the district and to promote an active interest in local government. In 1962 Charles Pratt was succeeded as chairman by Stanley Nickelson, who had been secretary of the original association in the 1930s. He held the office until 1967, and again from 1976 to 1978, continued to be a member of the committee and finally retired in his 93rd year. To mark his services to the association over 59 years he was presented with a silver rose bowl. Membership of the association grew steadily, from just over 1,000 in 1962, and finally broke the 3,000 barrier in March 1999.

From 1946 a useful source of local news and views was the *The Petts Wood and District Advertiser*. A monthly magazine published from 172 Petts Wood Road, it expanded as the post-war paper shortage eased and ran to 36 large pages. Regular features included forthcoming attractions at the Embassy Cinema, profiles of local personalities, news of church and social clubs and an extensive letters column.

The *Advertiser* ceased publication in 1951 but the gap was later filled when the residents' association started its magazine, *The Gazette*. Although more modest in size and scope, from its first issue in August 1953 it not only performed the valuable function of keeping residents informed about local issues but provided an invaluable record of local news and opinion.

On the Buses

Another concern of the revived residents' association was the lack of local bus routes. The first bus to serve the area had been the East Surrey Traction Company's 422 from Eltham to Orpington, which from October 1934 became the London Transport number 61. Using Chislehurst Road and Scad's Hill, it ran along the edge of the Petts Wood estate and was of limited use to most residents.

The development of the suburb on both sides of the railway increased the demand for additional services and in May 1953 the route 161a was inaugurated, to Petts Wood Station along Petts Wood Road. Getting a service from the Bromley direction proved more difficult. It was approved in principle soon after the war and in May 1952 London Transport announced that the 94 bus would be extended from the Crooked Billet in Southborough Lane to Petts Wood Station by July. The condition was that West Approach be widened so that buses could turn round.

The real obstacle, though, was that the most favourable route, Franks Wood Avenue, was still a private unmade road, unsuitable for heavy vehicles. London Transport's proposed use of Lakeswood Road as an alternative was vetoed by Orpington Council. As an interim measure, London Transport suggested an extension as far as Oxhawth Crescent. But bus crews said they would refuse to work it, as there would be no toilet, washing or refreshment facilities.

In October 1952 Harold Macmillan, the Minister for Housing and Local Government, gave Orpington Council the go-ahead to make up Franks Wood Avenue and the impasse was broken. West Approach was enlarged and at 6.20am on May 19, 1954 a 94 bus reached Petts Wood Station for the first time. Not surprisingly at that hour there was only one passenger.

By the end of the 1980s the three bus services in Petts Wood had become five.

The first bus service to serve Petts Wood was the East Surrey route 422 from Eltham to Orpington via Chislehurst; it became the 610 and then the 61 (picture taken c 1931) (John W. Edwards)

Stanley Nickelson, one of the earliest Petts Wood residents and a pillar of the residents' association for 59 years

The 161 and 61 continued, the 61 being operated as a result of deregulation by a private company, Metrobus. The 94 was replaced by the 208, which ran from Orpington through Petts Wood west to Bromley and Lewisham. In May 1984 the 284 single-decker was introduced for a six-month experimental period from Petts Wood Station via Poverest Road and Cray Avenue to Orpington Station. Two years later the 284 became the R3, using smaller vehicles and operated by Roundabout. The R3 was soon joined by the R7, which linked the Coppice and Cockmanning estates and became the first bus route along St John's Road.

In 1994 the 161a was replaced by the 162, which ran between Petts Wood Station and the Gordon Arms at Chislehurst, and from Chislehurst to Bromley and Beckenham Junction. The R3 was extended to Chelsfield and Green Street Green, serving Orpington Hospital, and the R7 to St Mary Cray, while a new R2 service ran from Petts Wood Station Square to Poverest Road, Orpington, Green Street Green, Downe and Biggin Hill. All this meant that Petts Wood was better served by buses at the beginning of the 21st century than ever before, though the 208 was notoriously bad on punctuality and there was no service from the centre of Petts Wood to Farnborough Hospital. The planned upgrading of the hospital was likely to increase the pressure to fill this gap.

Two Celebrations

The post-war years of rationing and shortage were relieved by two notable celebrations in Petts Wood, one local and the other national. In May 1948 a Festival Week was arranged to mark the 21st anniversary of the purchase of the wood as a memorial to William Willett. The week started with a community service and pilgrimage to the wood to see the bluebells and continued with a Whit Monday fête at Eynsford Close Recreation Ground attended, so *The Kentish Times* reported, by more than 3,000 people.

There was also a two-day 'entertainment of plays, music and dancing' at the Daylight Inn. One of the plays was written and produced by Pat Keysell, later to be presenter of the award-winning children's television programme, *Vision On*. Her father, Peter Keysell, was secretary of the Festival Week committee. The Keysell family ran an amateur drama group, the Proscenium Club, whose members included a young resident of Beckenham, Robert (now better known as Bob) Monkhouse. In the souvenir programme published for the festival, residents were invited to choose six improvements to Petts Wood most urgently needed by the community. The list included a permanent library, modern primary school, community centre, rebuilt railway station, bus service to Bromley and open-air swimming pool.

The 1953 Coronation celebrations, in which Petts Wood joined forces with Crofton North, were not at first enthusiastically welcomed: six weeks beforehand a leaflet distributed by the celebrations committee complained of 'very little co-operation and support from the community'. All the same, a full week's programme was arranged, including dances, a carnival procession and a sports gymkhana. As on VJ Day there were street parties and over-60s were invited to watch the Coronation free on television in the Daylight Inn.

The Methodist Church in Queensway, with its sharply angled roof, opened in 1961

New Churches

St Francis was the only permanent church to be built in Petts Wood before the war, though other denominations started holding regular services in the late 1930s - in some unlikely places - and eventually acquired their own buildings.

Petts Wood Methodists held their first meeting in 1944 at the home of Miss Grace Cooke in Nightingale Road and met occasionally thereafter in the restaurant of the Embassy Cinema. In September 1945 they moved to what was then the end shop in Chatsworth Parade, later to become the betting shop. But during the war a site had been bought at the corner of Queensway and

Lakeswood Road and a new brick building, seating 100 people, was opened in April 1949. Site, buildings and furnishings cost £5,700. Now the Lakeswood Hall, the building doubled as church and hall until the present church, designed by Victor J. Syborn and with a distinctively angled roof, opened in February 1961. By selling off part of the site for shops it was possible to build the church for the modest sum of £27,000.

Originally there was no provision for an organ and the intention had been to use a grand piano. But church members, supported by the minister, the Rev John Chamberlayne, decided that an organ was preferable and hit upon an unusual solution. Since funds were limited a Compton cinema organ was bought for £100 as scrap from the Capitol, Upminster, and rebuilt in the chapel by enthusiastic members of the congregation. It gave good service for 18 years before being replaced in 1979 by a six-rank two-manual and pedal instrument by a local organ builder, Ralph Arnold.

In the Methodist tradition of an itinerant ministry there was a succession of ministers in Petts Wood. But new ground was broken in 1985 with the appointment of a woman, the Rev Sheila Purdy, who served for five years before moving on. The church celebrated its 50th anniversary in 1994 and nine former ministers either attended or sent greetings.

While the church continued its spiritual mission, the prominent position of the building meant that it had also become a centre of social and community activities for Petts Wood, embracing drama, exercise, educational and sports activities for all ages. Shoppers and passers-by were invited to pop in for a coffee and a chat. Through its various connected organisations, the church provided activity and nurture for more than 300 children and young people, a strong riposte to the frequent complaint that there was 'nothing for youngsters to do'.

In the early days of Petts Wood the small number of Roman Catholics had to make their way on Sundays to churches in Bromley, Chislehurst, Orpington and St Mary Cray. Before the age of mass car ownership, most of them did so on foot. As Petts Wood and its Roman Catholic population grew, new arrangements were made and in 1937 the ballroom of the Daylight Inn was hired for Sunday morning mass. The *Daily Mirror* thought this newsworthy enough to run a story and a picture. But the congregation continued to grow and it became necessary to find other premises. In 1939 a modest building was erected and opened for worship on a site in Lakeswood Road. Curates from Orpington and Chislehurst were given the care of the Petts Wood community and an energetic young priest, Father Hubert Simes, carried the burden of the war years.

In 1946 Petts Wood had its first resident priest with the appointment of Father Cyril Scarborough, a former army chaplain who had been a prisoner of the Germans in Colditz Castle. He was transferred to Caterham in 1955 and after two ministries Father John Wright became rector and served until his death 22 years later. Meanwhile the church building had become increasingly inadequate and in 1964 the present church of St James the Great was opened next to it.

In April 1970, almost 30 years since it was first mooted by Father Simes, St

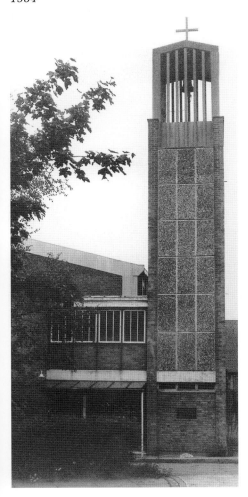

The bell tower of St James the Great Roman Catholic Church, completed in 1964

James Roman Catholic Primary School was opened in a single storey brick building in Maybury Close. It started with 121 pupils, a head teacher, Miss Philomena Lennon, and five teaching staff. Within two years it had reached its capacity of around 230 children, with an intake mainly from the parishes of St James, Petts Wood, and St Swithins, Bromley Common. Miss Lennon guided the school through its first 25 years, retiring in 1995.

Father Wright was succeeded in 1978 by Monsignor John Elliott, whose ministry saw the church into the 21st century. During his tenure considerable work was carried out. The sanctuary was enlarged and the altar and tabernacle reconstructed in line with changes in the liturgy, and extra rooms were added to the hall enabling it to become a social centre. In an age of declining church attendances, Sunday mass at St James regularly had between 850 and 900 worshippers. The crowning event in the life of Petts Wood Catholics was the consecration of the church by Archbishop Michael Bowen on July 17, 1988, 25 years after the laying of the foundation stone by Archbishop Cyril Cowderoy.

A large extension was added to the front of the church in 1995 and the inside was refurbished in 1997, when the walls were tiled and the pillars and ceiling covered in oak. The 3rd Petts Wood Scout and Guide group started by Father Scarborough later expanded to include Beaver Scouts, Venture Scouts and Rainbows and celebrated its 50th anniversary in 1999.

The Quaker community in Petts Wood goes back to 1934 when half a dozen Friends met in the home of George and Edith Cons in The Chenies. Numbers grew and in the following year the Society of Friends rented the schoolroom in Ladywood Avenue for Sunday meetings. After the war there were abortive attempts to find and buy a site for a permanent Meeting House but when, in 1958, the Misses Porter and Worthington retired and Petts Wood School closed they suggested that the Friends might buy and convert the building. There was some local opposition to the change of use and a restrictive covenant was drawn up which forbade letting. In 1962 Petts Wood Amnesty Group started in the Meeting House, later gaining support from other local churches.

The Quaker journal, The Friend, *features the opening of Petts Wood Meeting House in 1958*

The Friend, September 26, 1958. Volume 116, No. 39

THE FRIEND
The Quaker Weekly Journal
" In essentials unity, in non-essentials liberty, in all things charity "
SEPTEMBER 26, 1958   NINEPENCE

Petts Wood Meeting House (see Page 1221)

Since the 1960s the Meeting House has undergone a succession of repairs and improvements, mainly to combat damp. Substantial renovation of the children's rooms was an early priority and the flat roof was replaced by a sloping one. Pianos, too, fell victim to the cold and damp, prompting the decision in 1991 to use an electric keyboard instead. In the garden the tennis court was replaced by lawn and shrubs, and additional trees have been planted over the years. Although membership has fluctuated, Petts Wood Meeting has had a wide catchment area and played a prominent part both in the work of the Society of Friends and in the wider community.

Christ Church (United Reformed) was planned by a small group under the leadership of S. Rawlings-Smith, S. J. Kingsbury and W. T. Betterton which met in Kay's Pantry, a teashop in Petts Wood Road. In March 1939 consent was given for erecting a church at the junction of Tudor Way and Willett Way and in the

Christ Church, at the junction of Willett Way and Tudor Way, which opened in 1954 (Roger Hiscocks)

following month the first services were held at St Dunstan's School. Petts Wood Free Church was officially constituted in November. From June 1943 services were conducted in a prefabricated hut on the site of the later Kingsway Hall and in April 1946 the Rev Robert Duce, who had been newly ordained in the temporary church, became the first minister, serving for 15 years.

A foundation stone for the permanent church was laid in October 1953 and it opened 12 months later, now known as Petts Wood Congregational Church. The church itself, the halls and the manse in Tudor Way cost £74,000. No less than £40,000 was raised by members and the balance came mainly from the sale of churches in Bermondsey and the New Kent Road. The Rev Duce was succeeded by the Rev R. W. Hugh Jones, minister from 1961 to 1969, and the Rev Douglas Bale (1970-76). During Douglas Bale's ministry the Congregational Church of England and Wales united with the Presbyterian Church of England to form the United Reformed Church.

After a three-year interregnum, the Rev Kenneth Chippindale was inducted in the autumn of 1979. On his initiative Community Care was started in 1983 as an ecumenical venture to help the elderly of the neighbourhood 365 days a year with

continued on page 94

Petts Wood in the age of steam, captured by a rail enthusiast, B. C. Bending, from Bromley

Victoria to Ramsgate train, hauled by a BR Class 5 locomotive, passes the level crossing to the National Trust Woods, March 2, 1958, as the crossing was being replaced by a tunnel under the line (see page 85)

The Golden Arrow from Victoria to Dover Marine, hauled by locomotive 34085, 501 Squadron, at the junction north of Petts Wood Station on August 30, 1958, during the formation of the new down loop

Charing Cross to Ramsgate train, hauled by West Country class locomotive Exeter, *passes through Petts Wood Station on September 12, 1959*

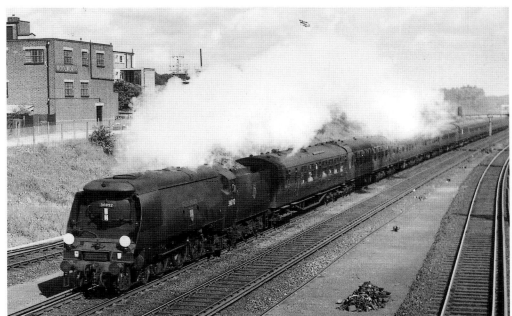

Victoria to Folkestone Harbour boat train, hauled by West Country class locomotive City of Wells, *passes the back of Petts Wood Woolworths on June 6, 1961, the last weekend of steam working*

transport, shopping, visiting and jobs in the home. To extend its work in the community the church launched a £190,000 appeal fund and new premises dedicated in 1991 included a purpose-built room for the Petts Wood playgroup for children with special needs which Christ Church sponsored. Reaching further afield, Christ Church established links with churches in Germany, leading to regular exchanges.

The 50th anniversary was celebrated in April 1989 with the Rev Bale and the Rev Hugh Jones sharing the service. The Rev Chippindale left Petts Wood in 1992 and was succeeded, after a two-year vacancy, by the Rev Julian Thomas. When the Petts Wood councillor, Peter Woods, became Mayor of Bromley in 1996, Christ Church hosted the borough's civic service and Julian Thomas served for a year as Mayor's Chaplain.

During the late 1990s the church celebrated a succession of landmarks: the 25th anniversary of the United Reformed Church, 50 years of its Anvil youth group and 60 years of the fellowship in Petts Wood. During 1999 new links were established across the Atlantic when the Rev Thomas exchanged with Rev Lincoln Dring, a Presbyterian minister from Washington DC, who served in Petts Wood for the summer. In the same year Christ Church was the first Petts Wood church to launch a website on the internet.

In 1971 an ecumenical initiative was launched which became known as Petts Wood Churches Together and involved the ministers and representatives of all the local churches in regular meetings, acts of witness, services and discussion groups. From 1997, in co-operation with Petts Wood Residents' Association, the churches held an annual open-air service in the Memorial Gardens.

A Purpose-Built Library
The branch library which had opened in a shop opposite the Embassy Cinema in 1938 became increasingly inadequate to serve a population which by the 1950s had grown to 15,000 and in 1958 Orpington UDC agreed to provide new, purpose-built premises. A single-storey building in Franks Wood Avenue, with space for 10,000 books, the library opened in May 1961. It was set out on an open plan and the main colour was cleverly provided by the books themselves. The development, which had a final cost of £14,000, also included a four-storey 'higher income group' block of maisonettes. At that time there was no footbridge over the railway at Bluston Parade and library users from Petts Wood east faced a long walk round. The library helped the case for getting the bridge built.

In response to growing demand, the library was extended in 1968. A record section was added in 1976 and the stock was further expanded to include music and spoken word cassettes, compact discs and videos. The video section included many titles for junior borrowers. In the spring of 1990 the junior library was decorated with a jungle mural by a local artist, Ian Ramage.

The installation in September 1983 of a computer system meant that borrowers had a single ticket for all items and a more efficient reservation service. In July 1989 the library changed to a new computer holding details of cataloguing,

The changing face of Station Square. The JDM estate office, above, filled an unsightly gap in the square and proved that a 1990s structure need not be out of sympathy with traditional Petts Wood building (see page 115)

The Village Sign, right, was put up in 1989 to mark the 60th anniversary of Petts Wood Residents' Association (see page 113)

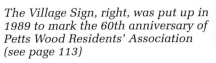

Petts Wood Library was modernised in the 1990s, with a new display window and more prominent sign

acquisitions and the circulation of items. Terminals allowed the public to call up information on any item in stock throughout the borough and to receive the latest news about the library service. The computer system was upgraded at the end of 1999 and as this book went to press (summer 2000) two further initiatives were imminent: the provision of internet access in the library for educational purposes and the facility for those with personal computers to call up the library catalogue at home and order books, videos and other items.

The 1990s saw a radical modernisation of the library building. Floor space was extended by building out at the back, and the frontage was brought forward to create a display window. A new, bolder sign made the library more eye-catching for passers-by. The shelves were reorganised to give a more spacious feel and to make the stock easier to find, with books being labelled by categories, such as romances and thrillers in the fiction area and gardening and holidays in non-fiction. A security system was installed, through which borrowers had to pass when items were issued.

Work started in late 1993 and it was planned to close the library for six weeks from January 1995 so that asbestos could be removed from the ceiling and boiler cupboard. While this was being done, however, it was discovered that the underground heating system had flooded. There was nothing for it but to install a new system, though this meant the library having to shut not for six weeks but nearly five months, while a mobile van did its best to fill the gap.

Show Stoppers

The founding of Petts Wood Operatic Society was noted on page 72. Although one of the most successful local societies, it has, because of a lack of a suitable venue, only once performed in Petts Wood itself. This was at the Daylight Inn in 1938 when other halls were unavailable. With facilities limited, the society opted for a musical revue rather than a specific show. The first production, *The Street Singer*, was presented at the Village Hall, Chislehurst, in May 1936 and cost £52. The society put on a show a year until interrupted by the war and resumed in 1948 with *The Geisha* at the Civic Hall, Orpington. It was given on a concrete stage, with the scenery hung on sky hooks, and the auditorium was also concrete.

In 1950 hall and stage were re-laid in wood. Later an orchestra pit was installed and an enlarged apron increased the useable stage area and, at the society's expense, raised seating was put in for the back rows. There were few types of show the society was unable to attempt and from 1972, with *Salad Days* and *Kiss Me Kate*, one production a year became two. Thanks to inflation and more ambitious staging, costs rose steadily and in 1978 the bill for the 13 performances of *Lady Be Good* and *Showboat* was £5,300.

Always looking to improve its presentation, the society considered the Churchill Theatre in Bromley as a venue and even explored the possibility of building its own theatre. In 1988, with the Civic Hall closed for refurbishment, the society staged its first production at the Stag Theatre in Sevenoaks and alternated thereafter between Sevenoaks and Orpington, where the new Crofton Halls had superseded the Civic Hall. In 1994 the Stag became the regular venue but despite its distance from Petts Wood the productions continued to be produced, performed and supported largely by Petts Wood people.

Politics, Local and National

In its early years Petts Wood came partly under Chislehurst Urban District Council and partly under Bromley Rural District Council, with Kent County Council at Maidstone the first-tier authority. In 1934 Orpington Urban District Council was created and it took over responsibility for the whole of Petts Wood, which elected three councillors out of a total of 33. By the mid-1950s Orpington was one of the largest UDCs in the country, ninth out of 569 in England and Wales on population, which was 61,000, and eighth on rateable value. Petts Wood had the highest rateable value of any single ward.

In the 1960s local government in London was reorganised into larger and, it was hoped, more efficient units. The London County Council was replaced by the Greater London Council covering a much larger area and 32 new boroughs were created by amalgamating more than 80 existing boroughs and urban districts. Petts Wood became part of Borough 19, the London Borough of Bromley. In area the largest of the new second-tier authorities, and with a population of just over 300,000 (bigger than cities such as Nottingham or Bradford), it comprised the boroughs of Bromley and Beckenham, the urban districts of Orpington and Penge and part of the Chislehurst and Sidcup urban district south of the Sidcup by-pass. The first elections for the borough of

Programme for the first production by Petts Wood Operatic Society, at the Village Hall, Chislehurst, in May 1936. By the first year of the new millennium the society had put on more than 90 shows

THE PETTS WOOD
OPERATIC SOCIETY

presents

THE

STREET

SINGER

THE PLAY BY FREDERICK LONSDALE
MUSIC BY HAROLD FRASER-SIMPSON
Additional Numbers by IVY ST. HELIER
LYRICS   BY   PERCY   GREENBANK

Bromley were held in May 1964 and it came into operation a year later.

Whether the change was beneficial for a community such as Petts Wood was a matter of argument. With three councillors out of 60, Petts Wood had less weight on the new Bromley Council than it had on Orpington UDC. On the other hand, services such as education, which were formerly controlled from Maidstone, were run from Bromley and in that sense became more 'local'.

From the start of the new borough, Petts Wood Ward, later extended to take in Knoll, returned three Conservative councillors and that remained the case until two remarkable by-elections in 1980. Feeling that the interests of the area might be better served by getting away from party labels, Petts Wood Residents' Association, in conjunction with Knoll residents, put up its own candidates. Peter Woods and Maureen Huntley were voted in by large margins and on taking his seat in June 1980 Peter Woods became the first independent councillor in the borough's history. Maureen Huntley joined him in October.

Both councillors served until the full Bromley Council election in May 1982 but with only Peter Woods standing, and beaten into fourth place, Petts Wood reverted to three Conservative councillors. One of them, Joan Hatcher, was elected Mayor of Bromley in 1983 and served on the council for 27 years before retiring in 1998. Meanwhile Peter Woods, now standing as a Conservative, was re-elected and served as Mayor of Bromley in 1996-97. In 1998, after securing the highest vote for any candidate in the borough, he became the council's provisional deputy leader. But the election produced a hung council and the Liberal Democrats, joined in a coalition by Labour, took control.

There was a further radical restructuring of local government when the Thatcher administration carried out its pledge to abolish the Greater London Council. The measure was enthusiastically supported by Bromley, which claimed that doing away with the GLC would mean lower rates, greater efficiency and less delay. As the GLC ceased to exist on March 31, 1986 many of its services passed to Bromley. These included planning, housing, main roads and traffic management. Rates were cut by 10p in the pound, an annual average saving of £30 for a householder and £80 for a shopkeeper.

Next to go were the rates themselves, replaced by the Community Charge or Poll Tax in April 1990. By setting the charge at £283, only £5 above the government's guideline, Bromley managed to avoid the heated protests which erupted in many other parts of the country. When the Poll Tax was replaced by the Council Tax, however, Petts Wood residents found themselves facing much bigger bills. London government returned in May 2000 with elections for the Mayor and Assembly. With Bromley and Bexley forming one constituency, and a complicated voting system for the assembly, the voters of Petts Wood may not have felt involved enough to turn out in large numbers, though such apathy was capital-wide.

Until 1945, when the Orpington constituency was created, Petts Wood belonged to the Parliamentary division of Chislehurst. The MP for Chislehurst and then Orpington, from 1924 to his death in December 1954, aged 74, was Sir

Four Tories and a Liberal. The MPs who have represented the Petts Wood area since the 1920s are, opposite page from the top, Sir Waldron Smithers, Donald Sumner (in his judge's wig) and Eric Lubbock (on the day of his 1962 triumph); and, on this page, Ivor Stanbrook, top, and John Horam.

Waldron Smithers, a Conservative of staunchly traditional views and a devoted churchman. His death created a by-election and on the shortlist of Conservative candidates was 29-year-old Mrs Margaret Thatcher, who had twice stood unsuccessfully in Dartford. She was up against Donald Sumner, a barrister, Orpington councillor and chairman of the local party. He told the selection committee: 'You want someone in Parliament who knows the state of the roads in Locksbottom'.

Impressed by this argument, the committee chose Sumner though four years later, ironically, Mrs Thatcher went to live in Locksbottom. The family bought a house in Farnborough Park and Carol Thatcher attended Farringtons School in Chislehurst. Had she been elected for Orpington, Mrs Thatcher would have been one of three Conservative Prime Ministers with adjoining constituencies, for Harold Macmillan was MP for Bromley and Edward Heath represented Bexleyheath, later Bexley and Sidcup. In addition, Orpington would not have staged one of the most famous by-elections of the 20th century.

This came about in March 1962, when Sumner, who had become Orpington's MP in January 1955, and held the seat in 1959, resigned on being appointed a County Court judge. The Liberal Party had always been strong in the rural hinterland of Orpington but had polled poorly in Parliamentary elections. Its candidate was Eric Lubbock, who had gained an engineering degree and boxing blue at Oxford and served in the Welsh Guards. He came from a well-known local family, being the grandson of Sir John Lubbock, and was a member of Orpington UDC.

Although the Macmillan government was going through an unpopular phase, the result went far beyond the wildest Liberal dreams as Lubbock turned a Conservative majority of 14,760 into a Liberal victory by 7,855. Macmillan was deeply shocked. He saw the result as a revolt of the middle class, hit by the credit squeeze and resenting the growing prosperity of the working class. The press invented a new species, Orpington Man, to describe disaffected suburban Tory voters. Later that year, in the wake of Orpington and other setbacks, Macmillan sacked one-third of his Cabinet.

Indefatigable in his pursuit of local concerns, Lubbock held Orpington at the 1964 and 1966 general elections but in 1970 was narrowly defeated by a Conservative barrister, Ivor Stanbrook. Soon afterwards Lubbock succeeded his cousin to the family peerage and became the fourth Baron Avebury. Orpington gradually reverted to its traditional status as one of the safest Conservative seats and Stanbrook, a hard-working and independent-minded MP, notable for his opposition to Sunday trading and working mothers, served for 22 years.

His successor, John Horam, elected for Orpington in 1992, had an unusual political background. He had first entered Parliament as a Labour MP, becoming a junior minister in the Callaghan Government, and joined the new Social Democrat Party in the early 1980s before moving over to the Conservatives, again reaching junior minister rank. He was re-elected in May 1997, with a greatly reduced majority, after a campaign in which his Eurosceptic views on the single currency put him at odds with party policy.

9. CHANGE FOR THE BETTER?

Most of residential Petts Wood was completed before the Second World War and post-war house building was mainly to close the few remaining gaps and to replace properties destroyed or damaged by bombs. By the early 1960s a rising south-east population was putting renewed pressure on building land and there came to areas such as Petts Wood a different, and arguably less welcome, form of development for which a special word was coined: 'infilling'.

This meant squeezing as many new houses as possible on any piece of land that could be found. There were several examples of the larger, older houses in the area, particularly the former St Dunstan's School in St John's Road and around Crofton Lane, being demolished to make way for several smaller houses. Given the housing shortage, and as long as these buildings complied with the by-laws, the local authority was reluctant to withhold planning permission. Equally, in a free society, householders with long gardens could not be prevented from selling off chunks of their land to developers. But there was a feeling that such high density building must, by cutting down trees and reducing open space, damage the amenity of the area. Nor did the new architectural styles - by the 1960s mock Tudor was being replaced by mock Georgian - necessarily blend with existing ones.

The first commercial building to go up in Petts Wood after the war was Farley House at the north end of Queensway. Completed in 1958 it was the headquarters of the Peachey company, later to become the country's largest owner of residential property. Peachey grew out of the Petts Wood estate company and its chairman and joint managing director was Christopher Hutley, son-in-law of Basil Scruby.

Hutley and his co-managing director, George Farrow, had worked with Scruby before the war. In 1940 they formed a property company, Anthony Hutley and Partners, which operated from the estate office in Station Square. In 1947 they acquired A. Peachey and Company , a building and contracting business which had started in Chingford, Essex, in the 1930s. In the same year Farrow came to live in a Sutcliffe house in Hazelmere Road. The Farrows were opera lovers and had music piped to several rooms in the house, as well as illuminating the garden at night. The group expanded rapidly and its properties in Petts Wood included houses in Crescent Drive, Woodhurst Avenue and Towncourt Crescent, as well as shops and flats. With the acquisition early in 1958 of Bell London and Provincial Properties, the company was renamed Peachey Property Corporation.

After the death of Hutley in January 1961, Farrow became chairman and sole managing director. Peachey moved from Farley House (Farley was a contraction of Farrow and Hutley) to a new headquarters at Park West, Marble Arch, in 1965. Farrow resigned through ill-health three years later. Peachey continued to own property in Petts Wood, including shops, flats, the estate office in Station Square, the Dunstonian Garage site and its old headquarters, but most had been sold by the end of the 1980s. By this time the company had been taken over by a Dutch firm, Wereldhave.

George Farrow, by Wiggins, late 1940s: Peachey boss, opera lover (and looking rather older than 32)

Farley House in Queensway under construction in 1958; it was the first big office development in Petts Wood

Farley House was successively occupied by Vidor Batteries and the Keston-based Seismograph company. A plan in 1988 to extend the building and provide more office space was rejected by Bromley Council but after a face-lift and internal changes it was re-named Mega House and became the headquarters of the *News Shopper* free newspaper group.

A Shopping Revolution

Infilling took place also at the shopping centre. Chatsworth Parade was extended northwards along Queensway, the new Bluston Parade (named after its landlord) went up opposite the Memorial Hall and there was Rice Parade in Fairway, the creation of a builder called Rice from New Eltham. Although these blocks, which appeared in 1960 and 1961, lacked the character of the original shopping development they attracted little criticism.

More controversial was the substantial redevelopment of the 1970s. On the south side of Station Square, three-storey shop and office blocks went up on the former Dunstonian Garage site and on land released by the closure of the railway goods yard. The newsagents, in the middle, remained as a sole and incongruous reminder of the Petts Wood that was. The Lipton's supermarket building aroused much hostile comment. At the planning appeal the residents' association and a Petts Wood Councillor, Mrs Joan Hatcher, spoke forcefully against the proposed development as being out of scale and character with the rest of the shopping area.

The Safeway supermarket, built on the site of the former Embassy Cinema, had a dramatic impact on Petts Wood shopping when it opened in 1982

But the building went ahead and when it was finished in 1975 one resident described it as 'a modern monstrosity' and Mrs Hatcher promised 'to use my best endeavours to see that this disease does not creep all around the square'.

Apart from considerations of size and aesthetics, the Station Square development raised fundamental questions about the sort of Petts Wood people wanted. Some welcomed the influx of office blocks and big new shops. Others felt they were destroying the 'village' character of Petts Wood. The time taken finding tenants for these sites suggested that the area was already becoming saturated. The arguments were heard all over again when International Stores applied to put up an office and supermarket complex on the site of the Embassy Cinema and car park.

The plan was for a supermarket on the ground floor, with a car park for shoppers underneath. There would be two floors of offices and space for a small cinema. International Stores intended to run the supermarket but changed its mind and leased the premises to the American food group, Safeway. Walls and Birdseye took over the offices, thereby doubling the office population of Petts Wood to more than 200, and with nobody claiming the cinema shell it went to a snooker club.

The Safeway supermarket opened in March 1982 and its impact was felt almost at once. It was between four and five times larger than any existing store, with a floor area of 33,800 square feet and 18 checkouts. Several shops were rolled into one: grocer, greengrocer, butcher, fishmonger, baker, delicatessen, off-licence and even florist. With such a wide range, Safeway could offer 'one-stop' shopping.

This was one challenge to existing Petts Wood shops. The other was Safeway's generous opening hours, eight in the morning to eight at night (nine on Fridays), with no half day closing. In some cases the competition proved too great and within months of the new store opening, five other food shops had closed - the two Express Dairies, the Co-Operative Society, Lipton's and Hammett's. That left Key Market in Station Square as the only other grocer in Petts Wood. With Sainsbury's freezer centre closing soon afterwards and the Lipton's site still lying empty after nearly four years, Safeway had a virtual monopoly.

Residents of Petts Wood east now had to cross the railway for their groceries, which meant either negotiating the hazardous steps to the station footbridge or making a detour to the other footbridge by Bluston Parade. Late in 1986 the Lipton's site was reopened by Bejam as a freezer centre but the former Gateway shop became a liquor store, Bottoms Up. Bejam failed to prosper and it was taken over by another frozen food group, Iceland. Refitted and promising to carry a wider stock, the store reopened under the Iceland name.

There was concern at the disappearance of Petts Wood's retail shops but not all of this could be attributed to Safeway. In 1985 Mrs Joan Cuell, for 19 years in business with Queensway Fisheries, wrote: 'The blame has to be laid fairly and squarely at the door of the landlords, whose demands at each lease renewal or rent review (the latter usually every three years) have become so crucifyingly high that small shopkeepers are eventually forced out of business'. She added that only estate agents and building societies could afford the rents, and what they agreed to pay became the norm. 'I fear that until landlords become more realistic in their demands, sadly more and more retail shops will disappear'.

There were social factors as well. When one of Petts Wood's long established butchers closed, deciding that he could no longer make a decent living, he blamed not only competition from the supermarket but more women going out to work and people having less time, or inclination, to cook and relying on instant meals. He also cited the trend towards vegetarianism.

Working women, certainly, appreciated the longer hours that supermarkets were open and this helped to increase the pressure for Sunday opening. It was first introduced by Safeway during the pre-Christmas period but by 1992 had become a permanent feature. Some, including the local MP, Ivor Stanbrook, regretted what they saw as a further erosion of the traditional British Sunday. But for others the extension of weekend shopping was a boon.

The decline in the number of food shops continued relentlessly, from 37 in 1975 to 18 in 1983, 12 in 1990 and nine in 2000. Widely regretted was the loss of Petts Wood's last wet fish shop when Queensway Fisheries closed at the end of 1998. Other long-standing businesses disappeared during the 1990s including Southerns, the china and glass shop, after 40 years in Queensway, while the closure of The Book Cellar in Petts Wood Road meant that there was no bookshop in that part of the shopping centre for the first time since the 1930s.

Woolcrafts in Queensway was one of the few original shops to survive into the 21st century, still with its art deco front. The shop was started in 1936 by a mother and daughter, Mrs and Miss Boyce, after Mrs Boyce was widowed and had to earn a living. In the early years it was lit by gas. During the Second World War when knitting wool was in short supply, people would queue outside on Monday mornings for the delivery from Paton and Baldwin and the week's stock could be sold in a few hours. In 1976 Woolcrafts was acquired by Marian and Colin Barwick, who were still there 24 years later by which time the stock had expanded to include needlework, haberdashery and dance wear

The start of the new millennium saw the end of yet another shopping landmark, G. E. Read Ltd in Station Square. George Read had arrived in Petts Wood from Plumstead in 1946, setting up a hardware store in the former ARP post in Queensway. Six years later he bought a second shop in Queensway, which became a grocer, and the ironmonger, originally also a coal and timber yard, in Station Square. The Queensway stores were later sold but G. E. Read Ltd carried on. Robin Read eventually took over from his father and when he retired in August 2000 he had been in the business for 45 years. Read's was the best type of traditional shop, carrying some 11,000 lines and able to meet most needs, particularly for small items. But like all hardware stores it faced increasingly strong competition from the big DIY chains.

If there were fewer outlets for fresh food, the opportunities to eat out or buy ready-cooked meals increased dramatically. In 1983 there were six restaurants and/or take-aways and in 2000 16. While welcomed by some, take-aways were criticised for generating smells, noise, particularly late at night, and litter. There was also a boom in hairdressers and beauty salons. In 2000 there were 12, as well as businesses specialising in fake suntan, manicure and face and body treatments. During the 1990s the Daylight Inn finally ceased to be the sole Petts Wood pub when Wetherspoons opened The Sovereign of the Seas, named after Peter Pett's ship, in Queensway. Bromley Council had objected to the application but been overruled by the Department of the Environment.

Petts Wood had developed as a predominantly local shopping centre and that was the pattern up to the 1960s. In a council survey in 1967, 90 per cent of people interviewed said they were shopping for everyday purchases and nearly half had come to the shops on foot. But there was increasing evidence of a widening catchment area, helped by greater car ownership and provision of new bus routes. In a Saturday morning survey by the residents' association, half the shoppers questioned were from outside Petts Wood.

Saving the Green Belt

Not the least of the attractions of residential Petts Wood, and unusual for a built-up area so near to London, was that it was surrounded on almost every side by open space. But while the National Trust woodland was secure, one by one the other pieces of open land - Sparrow Wood and Crofton Heath, the former West Kent golf course and Covet Wood - were threatened with development during the 1970s.

An application to develop 139 acres of land at Sparrow Wood, Roundabout Wood and Crofton Heath was made public in March 1973 and envisaged the building of some 1,100 new houses. At the public inquiry 13 months later Stanley Nickelson handed in a petition opposing the development signed by more than 2,200 members of Petts Wood Residents' Association and Bromley Borough Residents' Federation. The application was also opposed by Bromley Council and by amenity groups who argued that Crofton Heath had become a sanctuary for wildlife. In refusing the application, the Department of the Environment

End of an era: G. E. Read, the ironmonger in Station Square, closed in August 2000 after 48 years as a family business. It had been a hardware shop since the 1930s.

inspector remarked: 'I have little doubt that the scale of public interest aroused by the proposals is a reflection of the concern which is felt that this land should retain the protection offered to green belt land.'

The open space bounded by the railway to the east, Blackbrook Lane to the west and Southborough Lane to the south became an important wedge between Petts Wood and Bickley. Between the wars it was used by the West Kent Golf Club. During the Second World War it was taken over by the Ministry of Defence for an anti-aircraft battery and became popularly known as 'the gun site'. After the war the land was acquired by the Bank of Scotland, which leased out portions to a pony club and Catford Football Club. Most of it was grazed by horses from the stables in Southborough Lane. In 1967 Bromley Council announced its intention to buy the land by compulsory purchase for 'a variety of open space uses'. The following year, when an application was made to build around 500 houses on the site, Bromley repeated its determination to preserve the land as green belt. The application was refused.

In April 1974 a public inquiry was held into two further applications for residential development, on 113 acres and 54 acres respectively of the former golf course, and Petts Wood Residents' Association once more voiced its opposition. In both cases the Environment Secretary upheld Bromley Council's refusal to allow the applications. His inspector had concluded that 'in spite of the shortage of housing land in the Greater London region, there are no exceptional circumstances which would justify ... this incursion into green belt land'.

Bromley Council finally made the area safe from development by announcing late in 1977 that it was acquiring 82 acres for use as a public open space. Four years later 49 acres, in time extended to 70, were made available for recreation as Jubilee Country Park. The name was chosen because the site was bought in the year of the Queen's Silver Jubilee. The policy was to keep the land in its natural state, part meadow and part woodland. The park contained ancient London clay meadows supporting many plants, butterflies and animals. Unusual plants found within the damp meadowland were the corky fruited dropwort, the only example within a 20-mile radius of London, and dyer's greenweed.

The council planted more than 500 traditional English trees, including oak, ash, sweet chestnut, poplar, hazel and field maple, and it was hoped that careful management would preserve and promote wildlife. Picnic areas were created, an orienteering course laid out and, using the old service road for guns, a cycle track linked Crest View Drive car park with Thornet Wood Road. The former allotment site by the railway signal box, cleared in the early 1970s for a school which was not built, was left to grow naturally, with Orpington Field Club, helped by children from St James Primary School, monitoring progress.

In 1996 with the approval of English Nature, the advisory body on conservation, Bromley Council declared the park a nature reserve to give it more protection and allow better management of the plant and wildlife. Not all the council's initiatives were welcomed. The construction of a gravel path for walkers, while appreciated by those who found the going muddy in winter,

Leaflet from the 1974 campaign to save Sparrow Wood, Roundabout Wood and Crofton Heath from development

ORPINGTON & DISTRICT AMENITY SOCIETY

SAVE OUR GREEN BELT

Sparrow Wood, Roundabout Wood & Crofton Heath

Developers want to build 1,000 houses on the 139 acres of this Green Belt—open country, woods and heath land—between Petts Wood, Crofton, Southborough and Bromley Common. Yet this is a valuable area for recreation and is a sanctuary for wild life. Join Bromley Council, residents' associations and this society in opposing the developers.

Evidence will be heard at a public inquiry at Bromley Town Hall at 10.30 am on Tuesday, 2nd April, 1974, YOU CAN HELP:

● Sign petitions being organised in your locality,
● Object in writing, addressing your letter to the Inspector, c/o Town Clerk, Town Hall, Bromley, marking the envelope 'Local Planning Inquiry.'
● Attend the inquiry to object in person.

REMEMBER — individual protest letters really count, so please write.

For further information please telephone: Mrs Joyce Pitt (Orpington 20133), Mrs Iris Jones (Orpington 27806), Mrs Anne Hammond (Orpington 30662) or your local residents association or ward councillor.

brought criticism that the park was being 'urbanised'. The balance between conserving the meadow and woodland and encouraging public access and recreation was a tricky one but Bromley Council insisted that there was no intention of turning a wild area into a formal type of park.

References to Covet Wood can be traced at least as far back as the 17th century but it was not until the 1970s that the area came under threat from developers. The first indication was an application in 1973 by the private owners of the land to develop field and woodlands adjacent to the Poverest Recreation Ground. This was followed three years later by an application to build blocks of 60 flats on part of the wood, a plan vigorously opposed by Petts Wood Residents' Association and local councillors on the grounds of the wood's high amenity and natural history value. The plan was later withdrawn. A further application, for 50 detached houses, was made by the then owners of the land, Rush and Tompkins, in 1983. This was turned down by Bromley Council after local opposition which included a petition signed by 1,300 Petts Wood people.

There was a new public inquiry in 1986, at which the residents' association pressed Bromley Council to buy the land. The inspector's decision was that the site should be valued as 'private open space or private open-air recreational facilities'. This was a victory for the conservationists and in 1991, after Rush and Tompkins went into receivership, the wood was finally bought by Bromley Council. There was much satisfaction that the long campaign to save the wood from development had finally succeeded. The wood was left in its natural state and whatever Bromley Council had done in Jubilee Park it could not be accused of 'urbanisation' here.

Map and information sign for Jubilee Country Park, which opened in 1981

The Kyd Brook

One consequence of the building of the Petts Wood estate was to hide the local stream, the Kyd Brook, though its progress could be traced through the stone balustrades marking the points where it ran under the roads. The brook rises, in two small tributaries, in Locksbottom near Farnborough Hospital. It enters Petts Wood at the open space around the recreation ground at Eynsford Close and then goes mainly under ground, crossing Willett Way and Petts Wood Road before running parallel to, and behind, the houses on the east side of Crossway. After crossing Hazelmere Road it enters the National Trust woodland on its way to Chislehurst. At Lewisham it runs into the Quaggy River, which joins the River Ravensbourne, which in turn flows into the Thames at Deptford.

During the 1960s and 1970s, as many Petts Wood residents discovered to their cost, the brook became unable to cope with heavy summer and autumn rains and regularly overflowed its banks. For those with homes nearby the risk of being flooded became a constant anxiety. One householder said it was like living in a state of emergency. In the areas worst affected, the first hint of heavy rain saw residents putting sandbags round their houses in an attempt to keep the water out. A cloudburst on the August Bank Holiday Saturday in 1977 led to some of the most serious flooding and renewed calls for remedial action.

Thanks to relief work, including the widening of the stream, improved maintenance and lower rainfalls, the threat of flooding receded. But a shortage of rain brought its own problems. Wildlife along the banks and in the brook itself decreased dramatically and the fish, ducks and swans virtually disappeared. The lack of flow-through allowed the build-up of silt and other debris on the bed of the stream and a proliferation of weeds on the bank sides. Residents unaware that the roadside drainage gulleys were connected to the brook unwittingly fouled the stream by pouring oil, petrol or detergents into roadside drains. The dumping of rubbish in the stream itself was less excusable and in any case illegal.

Coping with the Car

The rapid growth of car ownership from the late 1950s left Petts Wood, largely built before the age of mass motoring, with a dilemma. If the extra traffic was to flow smoothly, there would have to be road improvements. But better roads would attract even more vehicles. The traffic problem was increased by the railway cutting Petts Wood in half and forming a barrier which could be breached at only one point. This was along Tudor Way which by the early 1960s had become a busy and dangerous junction.

To relieve Tudor Way the idea was revived for a bridge over the railway linking Franks Wood Avenue with Petts Wood Road and creating a through route from Bromley to the Orpington by-pass. From the beginning of residential Petts Wood it was assumed such a bridge would be built and it is sketched in on one of the earliest estate plans in 1928. At a public inquiry in 1937 into the making up of roads, the inspector said the bridge was likely to come within two years.

The war put paid to the idea but in 1962 Petts Wood Residents' Association was convinced of the need for a bridge and started campaigning for it, arguing that it would relieve the heavy traffic using Tudor Way, provide proper access to the library, shops and banks for people on both sides of the line and unify the artificial division of Petts Wood. It was also claimed that the bridge would relieve the shopping area of through traffic.

But the residents' association may have misread local opinion. Its arguments were fiercely denounced by, among others, Eric Watkins, who lived in Petts Wood Road and feared the worst. He wrote: 'We have always known that a road bridge, with its attendant traffic problems, might be thrust upon us. But we never dreamed that a group of our fellow residents would *ask* for it.' If the bridge were built, he went on, motorcycle cowboys would murder sleep for children and parents alike, monstrous articulated vehicles would make day and night hideous with noise, vibration and smell, children and old people would no longer be able to cross the roads safely and property values would slump.

With opinion divided, and since a bridge was unlikely to be built for some years, the residents' association decided to explore the possibility of a footbridge instead. For this it found overwhelming support, not least because British Rail was threatening to close the station footbridge as a through route. The footbridge was erected at the end of Bluston Parade in 1966 and with no steps to negotiate proved specially popular with old people and mothers with prams.

A bridge over the Kyd Brook as it passes through a Petts Wood garden. The waters were not always as tranquil

Two possible solutions emerged for the Tudor Way junction, a mini-roundabout or traffic lights. The Greater London Council argued that traffic lights would increase accidents and cause more delays on surrounding roads. A scheme for a mini-roundabout was approved in 1972 but abandoned because it would take land from residents on the corners of the junction. A new scheme, which involved no loss of private land, came into operation in November 1983.

The initial reaction was favourable, particularly from motorists who found that long traffic queues in Tudor Way were a thing of the past. But there was concern that the roundabout had made the junction more dangerous and accident figures seemed to bear this out. The main problem seemed to be drivers approaching the junction too fast from Towncourt Lane and not yielding right of way. To dissuade them, the blob at the centre of the junction was increased to a hump. During 1993 temporary traffic lights were introduced to reduce accidents but the experiment proved unsuccessful and was soon abandoned.

To ease congestion along Franks Wood Avenue, Queensway and Lakeswood Road a one-way system was approved by the Greater London Council and came into effect in September 1983. Traffic approaching Petts Wood from Southborough Lane could no longer turn right into Lakeswood Road, which became one-way from Crescent Drive to the junction with Franks Wood Avenue. The idea was to make Franks Wood Avenue and Queensway the main route for traffic entering Petts Wood from the west. To further help traffic flow in Franks Wood Avenue, parking was banned on the side opposite the library and later on both sides of the road. From June 1987 one-side parking was introduced in West Way and Fairway.

In the centre of Petts Wood parking became a growing problem from the early 1960s. Solutions were sought in the provision of off-street car parks, plus restrictions on street parking to discourage commuters from outside the area leaving their cars in Petts Wood all day. Public car parks opened behind the Memorial Hall in 1962, at the end of Queensway in 1966 and alongside the Embassy Cinema and off Crest View Drive in 1969. Two years later a fifth car park opened next to the station on the site of the former coal sidings. The first yellow lines appeared in 1971 and they were gradually extended to residential roads.

Still the streets were clogged with cars and lorries. The introduction by Bromley Council of a 'pay-and-display' system for car parks, cheap though it was, seemed to dissuade motorists from using them, putting even more traffic on the streets. The shortage of traffic wardens meant that enforcement of yellow line restrictions was spasmodic and the police and GLC refused to extend them for this reason. The opening of the Safeway supermarket, despite the provision of 125 parking spaces underneath, intensified the problem and there was a noticeable increase in the number of cars parked on nearby residential roads.

The indiscriminate and thoughtless parking in Station Square, which often obstructed buses, prompted a radical new scheme which was introduced in May 1989. It provided for one-way traffic, in a clockwise direction, and pay-and-display parking, nose to kerb, for 43 cars on the outer sides of the square opposite

Aerial shot of Petts Wood centre in 1983, with Station Square in the foreground, the railway and station behind and Petts Wood west stretching out beyond. But dominating everything is the Safeway supermarket block (Kentish Times)

A happy group of Crofton Junior School teachers in June 1958, outside the since demolished 'annexe':

Back row: Fred Liles, Derek Heritage, David Lindsay   Next to back: Monica Court, Mavis Reese, Joyce Davies, Mrs Dempster
Back middle: Louis Court, Mrs Tolhurst, George Reeve, Mr Urquhart, Len Marsh
Front middle: Mrs Usher, Mrs Andrew, Elizabeth Wardle, Mrs Challis, Vivien Abbott
Front row: Mrs Stribley, J. Ramsden, C. Grevatt, Pam Reynolds, Barbara Baxter

the shops. The maximum stay was two hours. Other parking in the square was banned. In 1993 parking meters were introduced in Queensway after shop-keepers complained that the extension of the morning parking ban from 9.30 to 10 to deter commuters was losing them business.

During the 1990s there was growing concern about safety at the interchange of Woodland Way, Petts Wood Road and Bluston Parade. A proposal for a mini-roundabout to regulate what many felt to be a confusing junction was turned down by Bromley Council, but Petts Wood Residents' Association continued to press the case, as well as arguing for traffic calming measures in Petts Wood Road. Road humps had already made their appearance in Grosvenor Road, which had become a notorious short cut for traffic to Orpington, and a combination of humps and traffic tables (raised sections) at junctions had been introduced in Crofton Lane. While reducing traffic speeds, they were disliked by the fire and ambulance services.

By 1996, according to a Bromley Council survey, 45 per cent of households in the Petts Wood and Knoll Ward had two or more cars. One consequence of this was the growing practice of concreting over front gardens to give extra parking space. There was nothing in the planning regulations or anywhere else to prevent 'hardstanding', but some regretted the disappearance of those green front gardens which had been one of the most attractive features of Petts Wood.

The Next Generation
Education problems in the 1970s focused largely on one school, Crofton. It was not the only school used by Petts Wood children up to the age of 11 but it was the main one, and it was bursting at the seams. After the war the original wooden buildings were supplemented by the new Infants' School (1950) and Junior School (completed in 1967). But the enormous influx of young families into the area - particularly with the building of the Crofton Place Estate from the early 1960s - meant that what had seemed to be generous provision would hardly be enough. By 1970 Crofton had become one of the biggest schools of its kind in the country, with some 600 infants and 900 juniors. More than 300 of the juniors were still in the wooden huts, now called the 'annexe', which had been officially declared 'totally unsuitable' back in 1961.

The solution could only be another school and in 1971 one was announced for Crofton Heath, at the back of St Thomas Drive. It was to have 320 junior and 240 infant places and was intended to relieve what was admitted to be 'gross overcrowding' at Crofton. In 1972 Bromley Education Committee proposed that a third primary school should be built north of Petts Wood, on the signal box site adjoining the railway.

But two years later the Crofton Heath school was postponed because of government spending cuts and the other project cancelled. The Education Department hoped that the pressure on Crofton would be eased towards the end of the 1970s by the falling birth rate, but with a constant turnover of young families this did not happen and in 1979 some children were having to wait until well past their fifth birthday before being admitted.

In February 1986 Crofton School celebrated its 50th anniversary. On its first morning, in 1936, just 128 children arrived for lessons. Now there were more than 1,200. The annexe was finally abandoned at the beginning of 1989 when children returning from the Christmas holidays went to a new eight-classroom block. The junior school was at last on one site.

The new block was officially opened in May when a plaque was unveiled by a former pupil, Emma Johnson, of Crossway, Petts Wood. In 1984, at the age of 17, she had gained national celebrity as a clarinettist by winning the BBC Young Musician of the Year competition. She had first played in public while at Crofton and went on to pursue a successful career as a concert and recording artist. Appointed OBE in 1996, she was the latest in a distinguished line of musical talent from Petts Wood, following Heddle Nash and his son, John, and yet another opera singer Sir Geraint Evans, whose residency in Birchwood Road was marked by Petts Wood's first blue plaque.

Crofton infants also gained new classrooms while on the annexe site the wooden huts were pulled down to make way for a housing development. In 1992 Crofton Junior School obtained grant maintained status and was no longer the responsibility of the local education authority. Although numbers had dropped, with 736 pupils Crofton was the largest junior school in the country and could claim to be one of the best, having been named as 'excellent' in a report by Ofsted, the standards authority.

Crime and Policing

In the formative years, policing of Petts Wood was down to a bobby on the beat and that, for a generally law-abiding community, seemed enough. There was no clamour for Petts Wood to have its own police station, though residents found it confusing that Petts Wood was split among three police areas, served by stations at Chislehurst, St Mary Cray and Farnborough.

During the 1970s, however, the police presence (or lack of it) in Petts Wood became an increasingly contentious issue. One reason was that the area had become a prime target for burglars. Housebreaking reached almost epidemic proportions and the police seemed powerless to stop it. They appealed to residents to be more security conscious and many households went to the expense of installing electronic alarm systems. Still the thieves broke in, often in broad daylight, no doubt encouraged by the fact that they stood a less than one in ten chance of being caught.

An equally serious problem was vandalism, mostly perpetrated by mindless youths, some of whom lived in the very area they set out to desecrate. Residents were abused and threatened as they tried to stop their gardens being trampled and their walls knocked down. The cost of damage to the Garden of Remembrance and Memorial Hall was running at £900 a year. In August 1983 the Kingsbury Hall of the United Reformed Church was gutted by fire.

The opening of the new police station in the Walnuts, Orpington, at the end of 1983 meant that all of Petts Wood was served from one place. In the following years Petts Wood's first Neighbourhood Watch Scheme was launched, covering

Emma Johnson of Petts Wood with the BBC Young Musician of the Year trophy, April 1984; she went on to make a successful career as a clarinettist

Priory Avenue, St George's Road, St John's Road, Berger Close, The Close and The Covert. By October there were 15 schemes in Petts Wood. The combination of more vigilant and safety conscious householders and an increased police presence seemed to have its effect. Burglaries in the Orpington police division went down by nearly 30 per cent in 1985, compared with 1984, though this encouraging trend did not continue.

In August 1984 many hearts were touched by the courage of Yerba, a six-year-old Alsatian police dog fatally wounded in Station Square as he gave chase to two gunmen who had tried to rob a security van collecting money from Lloyds Bank. Yerba was shot three times but may have saved the life of his handler, PC Martin Coxon. A collection organised by Mrs Joan Gardner of Green Street Green raised £300 and in October a brass plaque was unveiled on the wall of the Daylight Inn opposite the spot where Yerba died. Yerba was buried at the Metropolitan Police dog training school at Keston. The gunmen got away but Yerba's killer later shot himself dead with the same gun during a police siege. His accomplice was arrested at Gatwick Airport while on his way to Tenerife and sentenced to 12 years in prison.

During the 1990s graffiti began to disfigure Petts Wood on a serious scale. Petts Wood Station, no longer manned in the evenings, and the bridge across the railway from Bluston Parade, became favourite targets but were by no means the only ones. Although graffiti was classed as criminal damage, nobody ever seemed to be caught doing it. The police said that they did not have the resources to mount round-the-clock watches. The more traditional crimes continued. In 1993 there was an arson attack on the Garden Estates Association Hall, a popular venue for toddlers' play groups, dancing classes and whist drives and the main polling station for Petts Wood west. In the same year PC Bob Gay received serious stab wounds while making an arrest after an armed robbery in Queensway. During the summer of 2000 Petts Wood experienced one of its most dreadful criminal acts yet when five cars, some on private driveways, were set on fire during the same night.

One answer to crime, at least in the centre of Petts Wood, was closed-circuit television. Railtrack installed it in and around the station in 2000 and prompted by Councillor Peter Woods, Bromley Council looked set to follow suit. Although the necessary four cameras would cost £20,000 each, annual running costs of £2,000 seemed a modest price to pay.

A Village Sign

In 1989 Petts Wood acquired its own village sign. A joint venture between the residents' association and Bromley Council, it stood 12 feet high and had a design by Ian Ramage with four motifs: the white horse of Kent, the Pett family crest, an oak galleon representing the Petts as shipbuilders and a symbol of William Willett's daylight saving campaign. The sign was unveiled by the bus stop in Station Square on November 29, 1989 to mark the 60th anniversary of the residents' association. A second sign, together with seats and flower beds, was erected in Queensway.

Sir Geraint Evans, the opera singer, lived in Birchwood Road, Petts Wood, from 1961 to 1981. A blue plaque marks the house

10. INTO THE NEW MILLENNIUM

What sort of place was Petts Wood at the beginning of the 1990s? Some of the answers were revealed by the 1991 Census and although the figures related to the local government ward which also included the Knoll area, this did not affect the general picture. The population of the ward was 15,224, a fall of nearly 5 per cent on 1981. This was partly because more people were living alone. Some 21 per cent of the 5,815 households were occupied by one person. The majority were pensioners, who made up 18 per cent of the total population.

Nearly 42 per cent of households had a dual income, compared with a borough average of 36.8 per cent, and 92 per cent of houses were owner occupied. Just over half the population lived in semi-detached houses, nearly 30 per cent in detached properties and 10.7 per cent in purpose-built flats. Perhaps surprisingly, 17.6 per cent of households had no car, while 47.8 per cent had one car and 34.5 per cent two cars or more. The rapid increase in car ownership soon made these figures out of date and by 1996 the 'two-or-more' category had jumped to 45 per cent.

On the Right Tracks?

Petts Wood had been established by Basil Scruby as a commuter suburb, with the railway at its heart. Although travellers had cause to grumble from time to time, London could still be reached in the 22 minutes promised by the early estate brochures and Petts Wood was one of the few stations offering services to all the south London termini. The introduction of Thameslink in 1986 enabled people to travel from Petts Wood through to another terminus, King's Cross, and on to St Albans, Bedford and Luton. The service was withdrawn after only a few years, though an expansion of Thameslink planned early in the 21st century raised hopes that it would return.

In 1989 the station booking hall was enlarged and modernised, with a newsagents kiosk underneath and wider steps to the footbridge. During the summer of 2000 a coffee bar opened on the main platform.

On suburban services modern Networker carriages finally replaced the Southern Railway 'slam-door' design which went back to before the Second World War. The Networkers were smoother and quieter, with better acceleration, though they seemed to have been designed for maximum carrying capacity rather than comfort. There was more standing space but passengers who did get seats found them short on legroom. Plans for 12-carriage trains, for which platforms at Petts Wood and elsewhere were lengthened, were put on hold, initially because of a shortage of rolling stock and then to await improvements to the signalling system. Commuters had usually to make do with eight cars, sometimes ten and sometimes only four.

During the 1990s the privatisation of the railway network meant that British Rail's Network South-East was replaced for Petts Wood travellers by two bodies. Railtrack was responsible for the station, signalling and track, while the French-owned Connex South-Eastern sold the tickets and ran the trains. The change

The new booking hall at Petts Wood Station, with newsagents kiosk underneath, opened in 1989. The station had changed in other ways. In the 1940s it employed two foremen, three porters and two ticket collectors. These had now all gone.

proved politically controversial, though the Orpington District Travellers Association, which had been monitoring local public transport since the 1960s, concluded that, possibly in face of the general perception, services were becoming more punctual and had fewer cancellations.

Of great concern in the late 1980s was the effect of the Channel Tunnel, particularly if, as at one time seemed likely, the new high speed link from the tunnel to London used the route between Bickley and St Mary Cray. The prospect of more, faster and noisier trains was not one which appealed to residents living near the line, not to mention the possibility of depressed house prices. But after a huge environmental protest throughout Kent and south-east London, the Government announced that the high speed link would run through a relatively under-populated area of north Kent and enter London via Stratford.

There was, however, no prospect of the link being completed before the opening of the tunnel, which after many delays took place on May 6, 1994. The Eurostar trains had to be carried on existing tracks, including those running through Petts Wood Station. Passenger services to Paris and Brussels started in November but although the diesel engines had their own distinctive noise nobody found this unduly intrusive and children had a new train to wave at.

Petts Wood Station continued to be heavily used. A survey by Connex in 1996 found that with 6,400 travellers each weekday it was the third busiest of the 26 stations in Bromley Borough, after Bromley South and Orpington, with St Mary Cray fourth. Not all of those using the station came from Petts Wood, however, and all-day parking on residential roads by commuters from outside the area was not always appreciated, particularly when it began with ear-splitting music in the early morning.

From the mid-1990s the Eurostar became a familiar sight as it passed through Petts Wood to and from the Continent

Station Square and Beyond

In 1991, after a recommendation from English Heritage, Petts Wood Residents' Association launched a campaign to make Station Square a Conservation Area. The association argued that it met the criteria of having 'special architectural and historic interest, the character and appearance of which it is desirable to preserve and enhance'. The proposal was supported by the 20th Century Society, Petts Wood councillors and the local MP, John Horam. Bromley Council was less convinced and turned it down twice before finally relenting in the face of considerable local feeling in January 1995. Station Square, including the 1930s shops at the top of Petts Wood Road, became the third Petts Wood Conservation Area after Birchwood Road/Chislehurst Road and The Chenies.

Any future development or alterations which required planning permission would have to be specially scrutinised to ensure that they preserved the character of the area. The sub-standard post-war buildings on the south side of the square were deliberately excluded, as not being worthy of preservation, and it was hoped that when they came to the end of their life, sooner for most tastes rather than later, they would be replaced by buildings more in keeping.

The first substantial change in the square after conservation status was granted was the office block adjoining the railway. The site, which belonged to British

Rail and was next to the station steps, had long been an eyesore. Single-storey offices of no visual distinction gave on to an area of garden which despite the efforts of the residents' association, which paid for planting, had never been maintained. Eventually British Rail sold the land to the Alan de Maid company for development.

Rising to three storeys with a car park underneath and mainly occupied by JDM estate agents, the block was completed, after months of building delays, in 1997. Its size guaranteed that it would make a strong visual impact, but by adopting the half-timbered mock-Tudor style on the upper storeys, albeit in brown timber rather than the traditional black with the walls cream instead of white, it was generally felt to improve the appearance of the square.

There was concern that in clearing the site for the new building the lychgate which had stood there for some 40 years might also be lost. But Philip de Maid generously agreed to donate it to the residents' association, which offered it to the Memorial Hall Trust to be erected over the path leading from Woodland Way to the hall and memorial garden. The gate was in its new position in the summer of 1995, as Petts Wood marked the 50th anniversary of the end of the Second World War.

Meanwhile the Daylight Inn had been taken over by Bass Taverns, who announced a substantial programme of renovation while insisting that the original character would be preserved. After building work in the spring of 1996 the inn reopened in May. The restaurant had been turned into a function room and the barrelled ceiling of the ballroom was restored, while externally the building was smartened up, with the white walls repainted pale yellow. The renovation won a Bromley Design Award. A previous award in this borough scheme launched in 1994 had gone to the new front of the dental surgery in Petts Wood Road.

The square's other locally listed building, the former Estate Office, had been empty for some time and both the building and surrounding garden were showing signs of neglect. Then came an application for a change of use from offices to a restaurant. Although Petts Wood was not short of eating places, the prospect of the building being occupied again was generally welcomed, particularly as it involved no change to the exterior and would not be a take-away. In April 1998 the estate office reopened as Trencherman's Brasserie, seating 64 diners with al fresco eating in the summer.

One building from the 1930s which was in desperate need of refurbishment but seemed destined never to get it was the Victoria Works in Fairway, originally the depot for the Express Dairy. Long in disuse, it became the subject of a succession of planning applications during the 1990s. They included office block with car parking spaces at ground level, restaurant, pre-school nursery (this was granted but came to nothing), MOT and car repair centre and, finally, health club-cum-gymnasium. The main sticking point was the high cost of restoring the building, most of which, the landlord insisted, would have to be borne by the new tenant.

For many years Station Square was the setting for a May Fayre, held on the first Bank Holiday Monday of the month and organised by Petts Wood Round Table.

The lychgate, long a feature of Station Square, moved to the Memorial Gardens entrance in 1995

That the weather was often unfriendly did not dampen the enjoyment, as local organisations and good causes set up their stalls around the square, there was much dressing up in period costume and entertainment was laid on for all ages, from bouncy castles to jugglers and fire eaters. At the first Fayre, in 1982, the staff of Bilham's, the fishmongers, sold jellied eels outside the shop and the shot putter, Geoff Capes, entertained the crowds with feats of strength. The event usually had a medieval flavour, though that did not prevent an appearance from Henry VIII. By the early 1990s the Fayre was attracting an estimated 6,000 visitors.

But eventually the Round Table found that the traditional family-based event was no longer viable and decided to introduce a commercial fairground. While some, especially younger people, welcomed this, for others the thunderous noise from the rides and the heavily-amplified music were unacceptable. The 1995 Fayre was the last, though stalls representing local charities continued each May in the Memorial Gardens. Three years later the Round Table was itself wound up because of falling membership. In its 33 years, apart from the May Fayre it had organised an annual fireworks display, taken Father Christmas round the roads of Petts Wood on his sleigh and raised thousands of pounds for charity.

In the Woods

We left the National Trust woods in the wake of the 1987 storm (see page 21) and the hope that a policy of 'natural regeneration' would allow the wood to recover without the planting of new trees. On balance this seemed to work well. Some of the trees thought to be dead proved not to be and visitors to the wood could spot several new oaks growing out of the fallen trunk of an old one. Where trees were destroyed this opened up parts of the wood and encouraged fresh growth though this worked both ways, as bird enthusiasts discovered.

Letting light in, while beneficial in some respects, allowed bramble to proliferate and this greatly reduced the number of winter finches who were no longer able to get at the birch seed they relied on for food. In the March of 1975, the peak year, some 1,000 redpoles and 600 siskins came in one flock to feed off the birch seed. But 25 years later it was rare to see such birds in the wood, and attempts to pull the bramble failed to bring them back. Other species once common in the woods, such as yellowhammers, skylarks and tree sparrows, had gone by the turn of the century, though this was more a national trend than a consequence of storm damage.

Woodpeckers, on the other hand, benefited from the storm, which opened up new holes in which they could nest. At the end of the century woodpeckers were thriving. Parakeets, which also like holes in trees, were on the increase as well. Two rare butterflies on the verge of extinction, the grizzled skipper and the dingy skipper, were spotted in the Brick Field.

From March 1994 the Petts Wood Management Committee ceased to act as the local manager of the woods, having fulfilled the role since 1927. The management of the wood was taken over by the National Trust from its regional headquarters at Scotney Castle, though a new Petts Wood and Hawkwood Committee continued to represent local interests on an advisory basis. After

The great spotted woodpecker could be seen in the National Trust Woods in increasing numbers after the 1987 storm created new nesting sites

serving as warden for 14 years Tony Hall left in 1995 and was succeeded by David Clarke, aged 33, from Cornwall. He was part of the trust's North Kent wardening team and able to draw on additional support when required.

In 1997 the National Trust launched a ten-year improvement plan for the Hawkwood Estate, the work to be carried out by the tenant farmer and trust wardens. It included the restoration of hedgerow, the return of arable fields to fenced grazing land, pollarding of willows and poplars along the Kyd Brook and the improvement of public footpaths and bridleways. The aim was to bring out the historic features of the estate, while conserving its landscape and nature and improving public access.

Marking the New Century

As the new millennium approached, the residents' association asked members for their suggestions for commemorating it. The main proposal to emerge was for a millennium stone, to be placed outside the library. But when residents were asked through *The Gazette* to endorse the project there was such a poor response that the idea was abandoned.

Meanwhile, and quite coincidentally, Ravensbourne Geological Society was thinking along similar lines. With a grant from the Heritage Lottery Fund it planned the permanent siting of 20 large boulders each weighing around four tons in prominent locations in the borough, including Petts Wood. More than 2,000 million years old, the boulders were of Lewisian gneiss rock and came from Lochinver in the North West Highlands of Scotland. The Petts Wood boulder took its place on the lawn to the left of the library entrance.

Past, Present and Future

Petts Wood has been acclaimed as one of the best examples of the inter-war London suburb, deriving its character from Basil Scruby's aim of providing quality housing in an attractive rural setting only a short train journey from London. By the arrival of the 21st century, more than 70 years had passed since the building of the railway station and the first shops and houses marked the start of residential Petts Wood and, inevitably, much had changed.

Mass car ownership and the pressure for office space made their impact, particularly on the centre of Petts Wood, as, sadly, did vandalism and graffiti. People's lives were different. Many women now worked, a factor behind the rise of supermarkets open seven days a week and the closure of the small shops which had helped to give Petts Wood its 'village' ambience. But there was still much that could be preserved and, encouragingly, a will to do so. Initiatives such as Jubilee Country Park and the saving of green belt land at Covet Wood and elsewhere owed much to local pressure, articulated through the residents' association. In Petts Wood itself the designation of three Conservation Areas ensured that important parts of the historic estate would be protected.

Thanks to these efforts Basil Scruby's vision of a garden suburb remained largely intact. The challenge for the future was to continue to strike the right balance between conservation and change.

The new millennium was marked in Bromley Borough by the permanent siting of 20 large boulders of Scottish rock. The Petts Wood boulder took its place on the lawn outside the Library

SOURCES AND ACKNOWLEDGEMENTS

Books consulted on the Petts included *The Autobiography of Phineas Pett* (there is a copy in Petts Wood Library) and *The Dictionary of National Biography* (19th century series, vol 15), which contains several Pett entries. Neither source, unfortunately, mentions the woods. William Willett's campaign is recounted in E. S. Turner, *Roads to Ruin: The Shocking History of Social Reform* (Penguin Books, 1966) and I also drew on *The William Willett Story*, by Anne Bouillot, produced by the Willett company. Clifford L. Platt's booklet, *In Trust for Chislehurst* (privately produced, 1975) tells how the National Trust acquired the woods. *The History of Chislehurst* (1899) by E. A. Webb, G. W. Miller and J. Beckwith was useful for its references to the Town Court Manor and the Walsinghams.

Alan A. Jackson's detailed and absorbing *Semi-Detached London* (Allen and Unwin, 1973) charts the growth of new London suburbs between 1900 and 1939 and includes references to Petts Wood. Charles Devereux's monograph, *Railways to Sevenoaks* (Oakwood Press, 1977) describes local railway building. For details of General de Gaulle's stay in Petts Wood I am indebted to Susan Raven's article in *The Sunday Times Magazine*, May 5 1968. Aspects of the Petts Wood community are covered in J. P. Edwards, *History of the Petts Wood Sports Association* (1976); Robert Haskins, *History of St. Francis Church* (1985); and Fred Walford, *The Story of Petts Wood Memorial Hall* (1985). A tree-by-tree survey of the effect of the October 1987 storm on Willett Memorial Wood is given in Ken Palmer, *Counting the Cost* (1988).

The Petts Wood and District Advertiser (published between 1946 and 1951) is a source for local news and views. Even better coverage of Petts Wood issues is provided by *The Gazette*, the magazine of Petts Wood Residents' Association, which started in 1953. The Bromley Local Studies Library, and the branch libraries at Petts Wood and Orpington, hold valuable material, including local newspapers and street directories. Their staffs were unfailingly helpful. I also made use of the library of the Royal Institute of British Architects.

But much of the material in this book came directly from the residents of Petts Wood, past and present. They lent me house deeds, estate brochures, early estate maps, commemorative booklets and photographs. Several of them also gave me their personal memories of Petts Wood. For information on key figures in the development of Petts Wood, such as Adolphus Chudleigh, James Langdon, Basil Scruby and Noel Rees, I was fortunate to make contact with their families.

I would like to renew my thanks to those who helped with the first edition, namely: Miss E. M. Adams, Mr S. R. Allen, Miss C. Baker, Mr K. Barrett, Mr S. F. Barrett, Mr D. N. Beauchamp, Mr and Mrs H. J. Cannon, Mr I. A. England, Mr and Mrs E. Evans, Mr W. J. Farrelly, Mrs D. Foot, Mr C. Fox, Mr and Mrs D. R. Goad, Mr P. J. Green, Mrs K. A. Greenwood, Mrs E. Grimshaw, Mr P. D. Haskins, Mr R. J. Haskins, Mr and Mrs R. J. Hiscocks, Miss G. Holmes, the Rev. H. S. Horobin, Mrs M. Jenkins, Mr M. J. Judd, Mrs E. D. King, Mr A. M. A. Lowe, Mr I. B. McLeish. Mrs D. Mason, Miss M. Merfield, Mr G. Morley, Mr A. Newing, Mr A. S. Nickelson, Mr J. A. Partridge, Miss B. J. Pattison, Mr E. G. Pearce, Mr N. Peel, Mr H. B. Percival, Mrs D. E. Place, Mr P. D. Reddick, Mr S. A. Ridge, Mr A. G. Stanton, Mrs I. Taylor, Mrs M. A. Taylor, Mrs M. C. Vincent, Mr F. Walford, Mr and Mrs G. Wharton, Mr J. Wheeler and Mrs M. Winterton.

I also wish to thank again those who contributed to the second edition: Miss C. Alabaster, Miss A. Allen, Mrs K. Angell, Mr T. Baistow, Mr L. G. Baldwin, Mr A. Black, Miss C. M. Buckland, Mr C. G. Burton, Dr. R. H. Carpenter, Mr D. G. Carter-Clout, Mr S. W. Clayton, Mr J. W. Edwards, Miss R. Emmerson, Mr B. H. F. Fehr, Mr A. E. Gilbert, Mr J. W. Gowanloch, Mrs P. Hooper, Mr A. A. Jackson, Mr D. Jones, Mr J. H. Kemsley, Mr R. W. Kidner, Mrs L. Margo, Mr A. F. Mullock, Mrs K. M. Murray, Miss E. M. Payne, Mr D. Pilkington, Mrs W. E. Pye, Mr R. Ravenhill, Mrs M. Rees, Mrs D. M. Remington, Mrs M. Roberts, Mr T. Scruby, Mr M. Smith, Mr C. Tippett, Mr A. G. Turner, Mr W. J. L. Twomey and Mr C. E. Wallace.

Many of the above gave further help with the third edition. In addition I would like to thank: Mrs K. Bacon, Mr and Mrs K. G. T. Bishop, Mrs D. R. Bray, Mrs P. M. Francis, Mr G. F. Jones, Mrs H. Long, Mr M. Roffey, Mr H. Saunders, Mr H. F. W. Saunders, Mrs A. Tilley and Dr. A. Tyler. Mr I. C. Gilchrist again gave me the benefit of his proof-reading skills.

For the millennium edition, in addition to further help from several people mentioned above, I would like to thank: Mrs M. Barwick, Mr B. C. Bending, Mr A. J. Brown, Mr A. Burlace, Capt L. H. T. Court, Mr and Mrs R. P. Elms, Mr D. Hardiman, Mr P. Hook, Mrs L. Hooper, Mr W. J. Howard, Mrs R. Huzzard, Mrs E. O'Donnell, Mr K. H. Palmer, Ms S. Pamphilon, Mrs J. Percival, Mrs P. Perry, Mr R. Read, Mr and Mrs V. Spears, Mr R. F. Spivey, the Rev J. P. Thomas and Mrs T. Troy. Special thanks to Mrs J. E. Guntrip for reading the proofs, as her father, Mr I. C. Gilchrist, had done for previous editions.

Last, but not least, renewed thanks to my wife, Janet: for drawing the maps, taking many of the photographs, her encouragement and so much good advice.

INDEX

Printed by: Bishops Print, Orpington, Kent

kawaii Origami

Super Cute
Origami Projects
for Easy
Folding Fun

CHRISSY PUSHKIN

Race Point
PUBLISHING
www.quartoknows.com
New York, NY

Contents

So much fun awaiting!

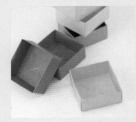

Cat & Dog
Hearts   50

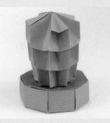

Cactus
57

Round Pot
62

Bento Box
67

Mini Trash Bin
75

Mini Drawer
80

Stationery Boxes
86

Ice Cream
91

Sushi Roll Boxes
99

Nigiri Sushi Boxes
107

Flower Bowl
115

So many cute
projects!

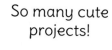

Star Bowl
121

Twinkle Star
123

Introduction

Welcome!

ORIGAMI HAS BEEN A FAVORITE HOBBY OF MINE since I was a child. In fact, I loved all sorts of paper crafts, but origami is the one that has continued to intrigue me to this day. That you can create something very beautiful from just a simple sheet of paper is what makes origami magical to me.

Although I learned a few origami models by heart when I was a child, it wasn't until I was about twenty that I really got interested in it as a serious hobby. I found that, depending on what you want to create, origami can be challenging or relaxing. Folding can be quite meditative in some cases, especially repetitive, modular origami that requires you to make the same forms over and over. But what I really enjoy making is origami that looks "Kawaii."

The word *Kawaii* translates simply as "cute" in Japanese, but it is now used to describe a certain style that is adorable, bright, and friendly. I was really interested in Japan and Japanese culture as a teenager, and when I created my origami blog in 2008, I decided to include this word in my title, *Paper Kawaii*. I started making video tutorials, and Paper Kawaii became a YouTube channel in 2009. Since then it has slowly grown to become a popular how-to origami resource for people around the world, which is something I never expected would happen!

So how do you make your origami look *Kawaii*? The end result of any origami model can be Kawaii if you choose a pretty pattern or color! Each of the origami models included in this book can look Kawaii if you use the paper provided, or you can make them with paper of other colors and patterns to produce any style you like. For instance, using red, blue, and white can give you a nautical style; black, purple, and red will give projects a gothic feel, or if you want something that looks rustic and

natural, use brown, white, and gray papers. Those are just a few examples; there is honestly no limit to what can be created with origami.

Kawaii Origami is the very first full book that I have put together, so I want to cover quite a wide variety of origami models but keep them all in the same kind of style. Practical origami models that serve a purpose, like boxes, have always been my favorite, so I have tried to strike a balance of practical models and models that are just for display. All of the models included can be given as gifts, and in some cases, made into jewelry, so even when they aren't "practical" they can still serve a purpose!

There are several new origami models in this book that have not been seen anywhere else. These include the projects: Kawaii envelopes (page 15), tea bag (page 21), cute purse (page 39), cactus (page 57), bento box (page 67), mini drawer (page 80), stationery boxes (page 86), sushi roll boxes (page 99), and the flower and star bowls (page 115 and page 121).

Models such as the origami cat & dog hearts (page 50), mini trash bin (page 75), and ice cream (page 91) were featured on my blog and YouTube channel and received great receptions, so I am very happy to include them in my first book. These three origami models in particular represent the Kawaii theme and style of origami models that I enjoy designing the most.

You will also find a few traditional origami models that are great for beginners to fold, such as the masu box (page 8), the lucky stars (page 11), which is made from strips of paper; one of the simplest origami models ever (and one of my favorite boxes to make!); and the water balloon (page 19) which is lovely to hang up and super fun to make as well!

I hope you enjoy creating Kawaii origami with me!

Tools & Techniques

Before we start our super fun Kawaii origami projects, there are a couple of basic tools and techniques that you will need to start, and some that come in handy when you want to make variations of the basic origami project.

Paper

All you really need for most origami models is . . . paper! There are quite a few different kinds of paper that you can use. The most popular and easy-to-use paper for origami is known as *kami* paper. Kami paper is thin, crisp, and easy to fold but doesn't rip easily like regular printer paper. You can find kami paper in packs of 50, 100, or 500 in most craft stores and many places online. Depending on your budget, you can get inexpensive packs for under $3 or higher-quality papers that cost a good deal more. Another paper that is commonly used in origami is *chiyogami* paper, which is traditional Japanese paper that is printed in a countless array of beautiful patterns and colors.

But you don't need specialized paper to make origami. There are lots of different types of paper you can fold with, some which you may already have around your house. Wrapping paper, pages from a magazine or newspaper, fancy handmade paper, and even parch-

ment paper used for baking all work!

When you first begin learning origami, it helps to use paper you don't mind throwing away so you can experiment without worrying about wasting special or pricy paper. This could be cheap kami paper or even just printer paper that you cut into a square.

Included in this book are 50 sheets of 6 × 6-inch (15 × 15-cm) origami paper to get you started, which is both the most common size of origami paper and the one needed for most of the projects included in the following pages. In a couple of projects, you will need to cut a sheet of origami paper into one or more smaller pieces or strips.

Other Tools

A few tools can make origami easier to do. I suggest making an origami tool kit that includes:
- A folding tool, or "bone folder," which is used to flatten creases.
- A ruler and a pencil, because some models require that you measure something.
- Scissors, or another cutting tool.
- A paper scoring tool to make precision folds.
- A chopstick to round the edges of the paper.
- Glue to reinforce a box or attach decorations like glitter and ribbons.

Kawaii Art Style

Kawaii is a Japanese concept that started in the 1970s. The word itself translates to "cute" in English. Although the word *Kawaii* in Japanese can be used to describe almost anything that is "cute," ranging from clothing to jewelry, it is commonly used to describe the immensely popular and immediately identifiable art style seen in emojis and characters like Hello Kitty and Pokémon. Like most art styles, there are countless interpretations of what is considered "Kawaii," the common attributes to this pop style are simple black lines, rounded characters with a youthful appearance, and the use of pastel colors. Kawaii art also makes use of simple facial expressions on characters with oversized heads on top of small bodies.

In this book, use your imagination and turn any, or all, of the origami models into fun and whimsical Kawaii characters. Use pens, markers, or crayons to transform your paper art into fully realized animals, characters, and personas!

Basic Origami Folds

Throughout the book, you will see symbols that represent common origami folds in the instructional diagrams. Always be sure to align the fold sides as precisely as possible in each step before moving on to the next. Hold and rotate the origami model according to the instructional diagrams, and use whichever fingers are the most comfortable for you and allow you to make a correct fold. Over time, you will develop a preference. Remember, practice makes perfect, and after a couple of trials and a few errors, you will soon be folding like an origami pro.

FOLDING TIP
When following an origami diagram, it helps to look at the next step in order to see how the model should look after completing the step you are currently on. Using large paper helps when a model is new to you or complex.

FOLD
Fold the paper in the direction of the arrow.

VALLEY FOLD
This is one of the basic origami folds. It indicates you should fold the paper *over* itself to make a crease so the paper bends downward, resembling a V shape or "valley."

MOUNTAIN FOLD
Like the valley fold, this is another basic origami fold. It indicates you should fold the paper *behind* itself to make a crease so the paper bends upward, resembling a "mountain" peak.

DOUBLE FOLD
Fold the paper two times.

FOLD AND UNFOLD
Fold once and then unfold.

TIP
You can find video tutorials online for some of the origami projects in this book!

Visit: paperkawaii.com/kawaiiorigami to view them.

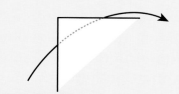

FOLD BEHIND
Fold the paper behind itself.

FLIP OVER
Flip the origami model over from either its front to its back or vice versa as indicated.

ROTATE
Rotate the origami model in the direction indicated.

INFLATE
Blow air into the origami model.

PRESS OR PUSH
Firmly press or push on the fold where indicated.

CUT
Using scissors, cut where indicated.

CLOSE-UP VIEW
Indicates an enlarged view on a particular area of the origami model.

STAR SYSTEM
You will see stars next to each project, with one star being the easiest and five stars representing the most advanced. In addition, the projects are arranged sequentially, starting with easier origami models to build your folding skills as you go.

DIFFICULTY: ⭐ = Easiest ⟶ ⭐⭐⭐⭐⭐ = Hardest

Masu Box

This traditional origami masu box is probably the easiest project in this book. Besides being easy, it is a very good model to start with because it incorporates lots of different folding techniques. Masu boxes were originally used to measure rice, but nowadays serve lots of different uses such as storage for little cute things, a thoughtful gift box, a stand for an adorable figurine—and it is fun to fold.

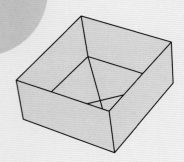

DIFFICULTY:

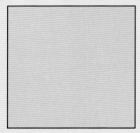

1. Start with your paper color side up.

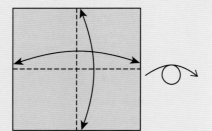

2. Fold the paper in half and unfold, then fold the paper in half in the other direction and unfold.

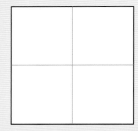

3. Flip the paper over to the other side.

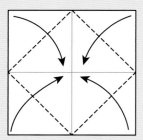

4. Fold each corner to the middle.

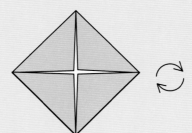

5. Rotate the paper.

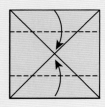

6. Fold the top and bottom edges to the center, making sure the edges are aligned.

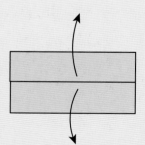

7. Unfold the top and bottom flaps.

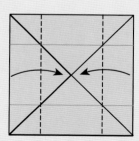

8. Fold the left and right edges to the center.

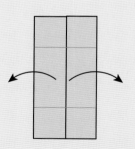

9. Unfold the left and right flaps.

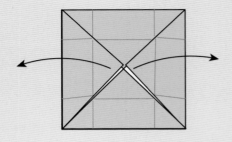

10. Open the left and the right sections.

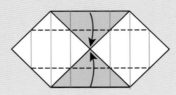

11. Refold the top and bottom edges to the center.

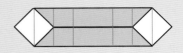

12. This is what it should look like.

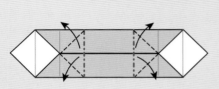

13. Using the existing diagonal creases, open up the middle section.

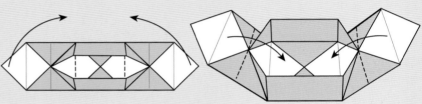

14. Lift up the left and right ends, making the model become three-dimensional.

15. Continue to push the left and the right sides of the model together.

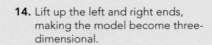

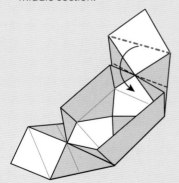

16. Fold the right end over and inside the model, locking it into place.

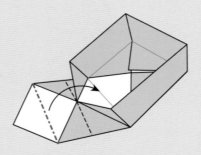

17. Repeat on the left side to complete your masu box.

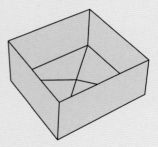

Lucky Stars

A traditional origami lucky star is made using a long strip of paper. You can cut strips from your own paper using scissors; they do not need to be exact. These cute, little stars make for perfect ornaments or little tokens of good luck for family and friends!

PAPER SIZE: 8 × .5 inches (20 × 1.5 cm)

DIFFICULTY:

1. With your strip color side up, bring the right end of the strip down and to the back.

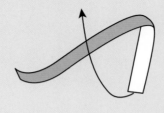

2. Bring that same end up and over the left end.

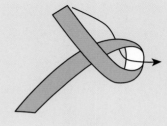

3. Bring the same end under and through the loop.

4. Pull the end through, tightening the loop.

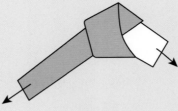

5. Continue to tighten the loop by pulling both ends of the strip, until you have a pentagon-shaped knot. Do not flatten the knot too tightly. You should only have a little overhang on the right side and a good amount of paper on the left.

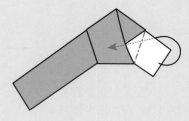

6. Fold the right end of the paper backwards behind the pentagon.

FOLDING TIP

If your lucky star does not take shape when you push in the sides, you may have wrapped the star too tightly or too loosely. Just unwrap and try again. You'll get the hang of it in no time!

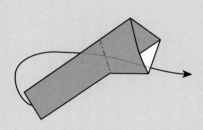

7. Next fold the left end of the strip behind to the right.

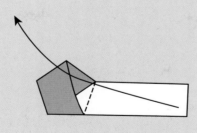

8. Fold the strip diagonally up to the left.

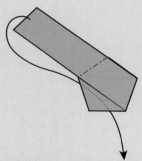

9. Fold the strip diagonally down behind.

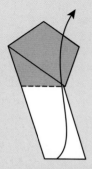

10. Fold the strip up and to the right.

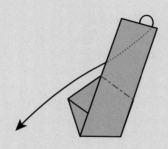

11. Continue wrapping the star in the same manner until only a small tail remains.

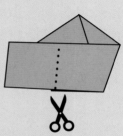

12. If needed trim off some excess paper.

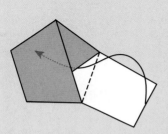

13. Lastly tuck the end of the strip inside the pocket.

14. Use your fingers to push the sides of the model in firmly but gently, causing the lucky star to puff up into shape.

Kawaii Envelopes

These little envelopes are as easy to make as they are cute! They are great for party invitations, as their rounded corners allow for lots of ways to decorate the envelopes depending on the occasion. The envelopes can also be decorated like mochi, which is a round Japanese dessert—or you can draw a cute emoji face, donut, or cake on them!

DIFFICULTY:

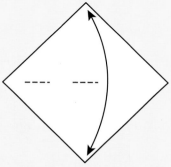

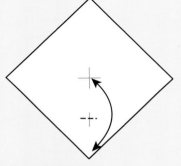

1. Create small horizontal creases by bringing the bottom point up to the top point and pressing your nail lightly across the paper where indicated.

2. Rotate the paper so that the creases you made in the previous step are on the lower section, and create another small horizontal crease in the center.

3. Bring the bottom point up to the middle, creating a small horizontal crease in the lower section. You should now have two plus-shaped creases.

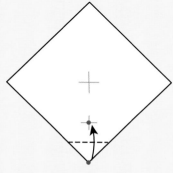

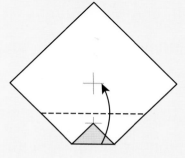

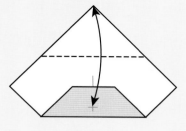

4. Fold the bottom point up to the middle of the lower plus-shaped crease.

5. Fold the bottom edge up to the middle crease.

6. Fold the top point down to the lower plus-shaped crease and unfold.

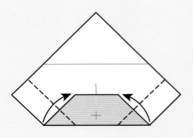

7. Fold the bottom left and right edges up diagonally.

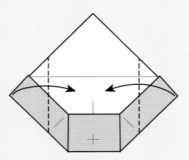

8. Fold the left and right edges inward, using the layer underneath as a guide.

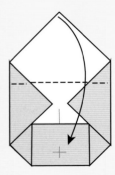

9. Fold the top point down. It should reach the lower plus-shaped crease.

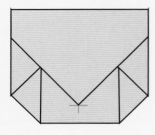

10. Now you've got a super-cute Kawaii envelope!

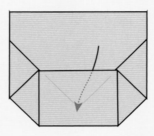

11. You can insert the point inside the envelope to secure it.

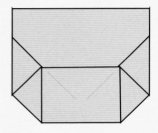

12. Here is what a closed Kawaii envelope looks like.

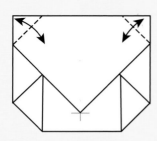

13. To make a rounded envelope, fold the top left and right corners diagonally inward and unfold.

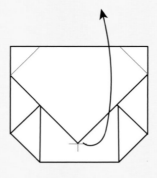

14. Unfold the top flap.

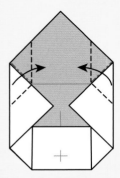

15. Fold the left and right points inward, creating new vertical creases where indicated.

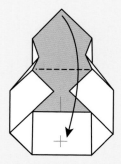

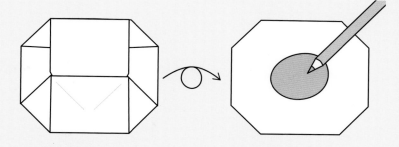

16. Refold the top flap down.

17. You can secure the envelope by inserting the point back into the pocket.

18. Flip the envelope over to the other side, and draw whatever you like here!

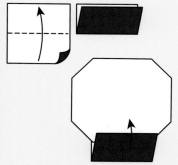

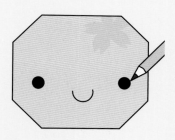

19. You can even make an onigiri rice ball by just folding a small sheet of black paper in half . . .

20. . . . and gluing the black paper to the envelope!

21. Make a Japanese mochi by using pastel paper and drawing a cute face!

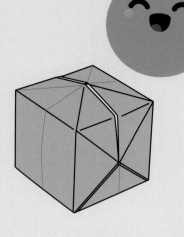

Water Balloon

This traditional origami water balloon is easy to make, and you can use it as a hanging decoration, a round object such as an apple, or even a little cube of wasabi, as on page 73. What makes this origami model extra fun is that you have to blow into it to make it take shape!

WASABI VARIATION PAPER SIZE: 3 × 3 inches (7.5 × 7.5 cm)

DIFFICULTY:

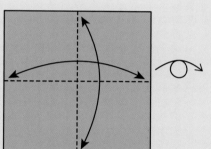

1. Starting colored side up, fold the paper in half from top to bottom and unfold, then fold the paper in half from left to right and unfold.

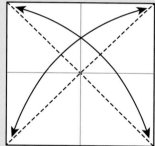

2. Flip the paper over to the other side. Fold the paper diagonally in half in one direction and unfold, then repeat in the other direction.

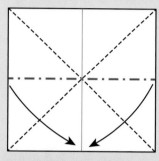

3. Bring the left and right folds diagonally down and inward while folding the top section down as well.

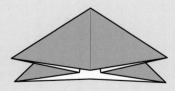

4. This is an origami water bomb base. Flatten the paper.

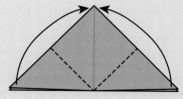

5. Fold the left and right lower points diagonally up to the top point.

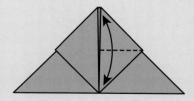

6. Next make a horizontal crease on the right flap by folding the top point down to the bottom and then unfolding it.

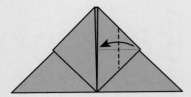

7. Fold the right point to meet the left end of the crease you made in the previous step.

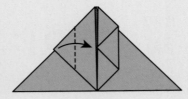

8. Fold the left point to match the right side.

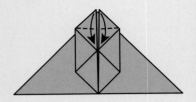

9. Fold the two top points down.

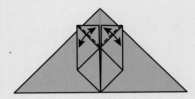

10. Fold the two top points diagonally down and unfold.

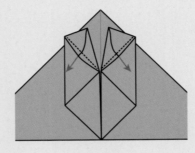

11. Insert the two top flaps down inside the pockets of the flaps underneath.

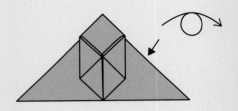

12. Flip the model over and repeat the same process on the other side.

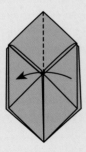

13. Fold the right side over to the left, flip the model over, and repeat on the back so that the model becomes three-dimensional.

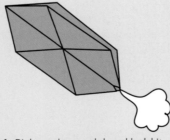

14. Pick up the model and hold it loosely. Blow into the end that has a little opening.

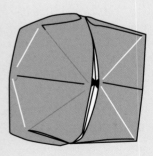

15. While blowing into the model, gently shape the sides into a cube.

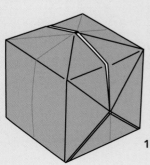

16. You can straighten the edges now if you like.

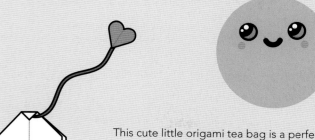

Tea Bag

This cute little origami tea bag is a perfect gift tag! Or you can use it as a greeting card by writing your message on the tea bag. You can then make a special tea bag envelope (page 25) to send them in. It's best to use white paper or the white side of your paper for this tea bag. The colored side of the paper in the instructions is the back (unseen) side of the paper.

OPTIONAL HEART MATERIALS: 1 × 1–inch (3 × 3–cm) paper + 2 inches (5 cm) of string

DIFFICULTY:

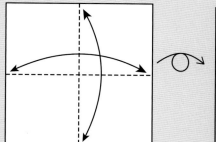

1. Fold the paper in half from top to bottom and unfold, then fold the paper in half from left to right and unfold.

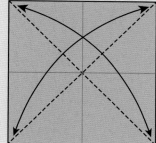

2. Flip the paper over to the other side. Fold the paper diagonally in half in one direction and unfold, then repeat in the other direction.

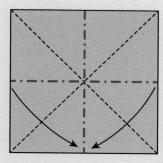

3. Bring the left and right folds diagonally down and in while folding the top section down as well.

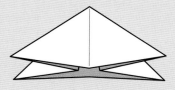

4. This is an origami water bomb base. Flatten the paper.

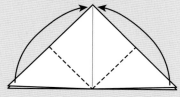

5. Fold the left and right lower points diagonally up to the top point.

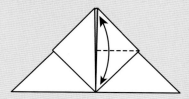

6. Make a horizontal crease on the right flap by folding the top point down to the bottom and unfolding it.

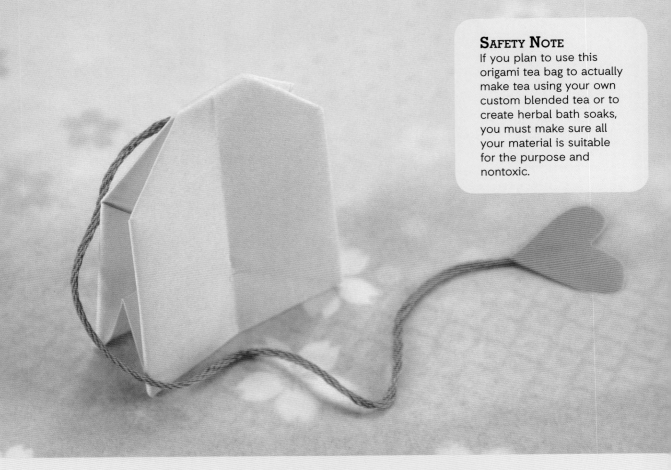

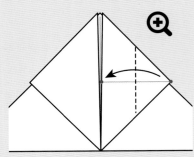

7. Fold the right point to meet the left edge of the crease you made in the previous step.

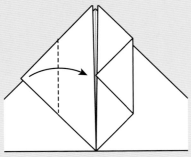

8. Fold the left point to match the right side.

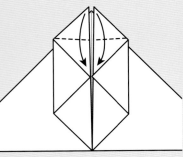

9. Fold the two top points down.

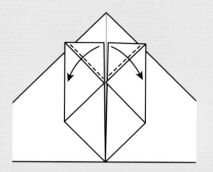

10. Fold the two top points diagonally down.

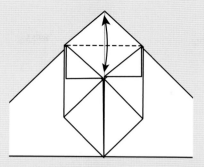

11. Fold the top point down, make a strong crease, and unfold.

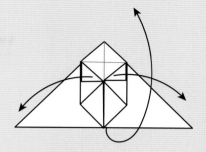

12. Open the paper completely.

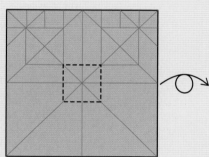

13. With the back of the paper (the colored side in this diagram) facing up, refold the central square shape.

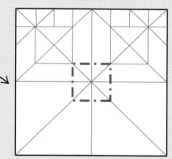

14. Flip the paper over to the front (the white side in this diagram).

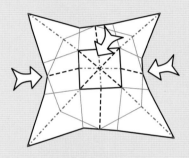

15. Sink fold the small square down inside while reforming the water bomb base.

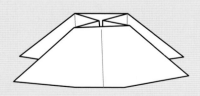

16. Find the two sides of the model that have no extra creases and work with them facing up.

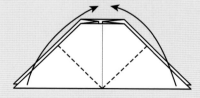

17. Fold the bottom left and right points diagonally up.

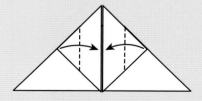

18. Fold the left and right points in to the center.

Tea Bag   23

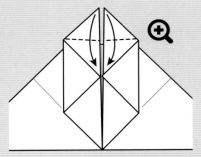
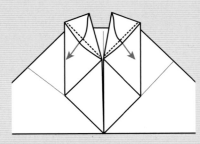
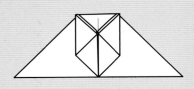

19. Fold the two top points down.

20. Fold the two top points diagonally down and insert them into the pockets of the flaps underneath.

21. Repeat the process on the other side.

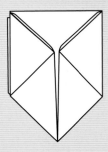
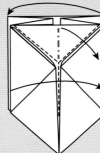
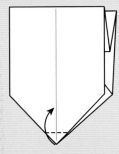

22. Your model should now look like this.

23. Fold the left side over to the right while squashing the upper triangle down. Repeat on the back.

24. Fold the bottom point up a little.

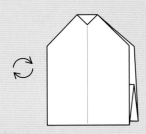
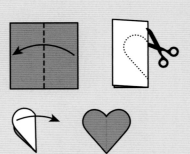
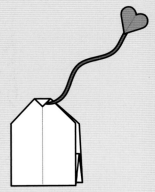

25. Rotate the model.

26. To make a little heart for the tag, fold a little square in half, cut out a half-heart shape. Open the paper back up to reveal a perfect heart.

27. You can attach a string to the heart and the tea bag using a dab of glue.

Tea Bag Envelopes

These origami envelopes just happen to be the right size to keep your little origami tea bags in! They also make great envelopes in general. Here are two versions of this easy-to-make envelope, the first is the basic version and the second is a more secure version.

DIFFICULTY:

BASIC VERSION

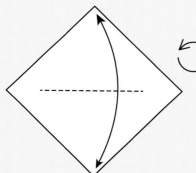

1. Make a horizontal crease by folding the bottom point up to the top point and then unfolding it. Avoid creasing the left and right ends for a cleaner result.

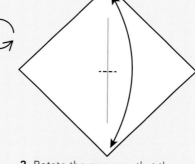

2. Rotate the paper so that the crease you made in the previous step is now vertical. Bring the bottom point up to the top point, make a small crease in the center, and unfold.

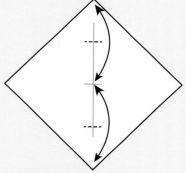

3. Bring the top point and the bottom point to the center, make two small creases, and then unfold.

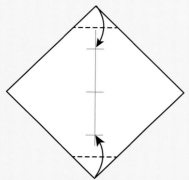

4. Fold the top point and the bottom point to the creases you made in the previous step.

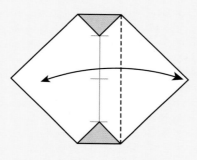

5. Fold the right point over to the left, aligning the diagonal edges to the triangular flaps, and unfold.

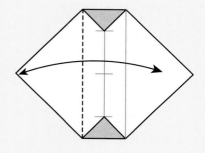

6. Repeat the previous step on the left side.

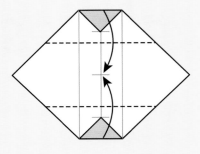

7. Fold the top and bottom edges to the middle.

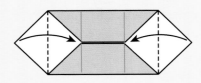

8. Fold the left and right points to align with the top and bottom sections.

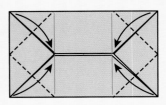

9. Fold all four corners diagonally inward.

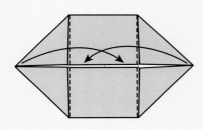

10. Fold the left and right points inward so one overlaps the other.

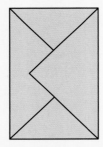

11. Here's your very own basic origami envelope!

12. You can use ribbon to secure the envelope shut.

SECURE VERSION

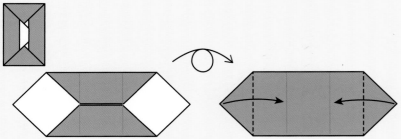

1. Unfold the envelope back to step 8, or fold a new envelope up to step 8.

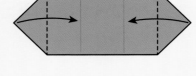

2. Flip the paper over and fold the left and right points inward.

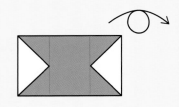

3. Flip the paper back over.

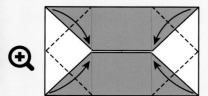

4. Fold all four corners diagonally inward.

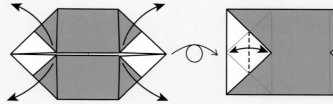

5. Unfold the previous step.

6. Flip the paper over. Make a vertical crease on the left and right triangular flaps as indicated.

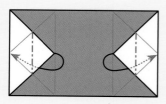 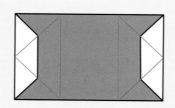 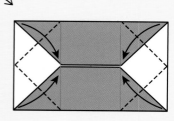

19. Tuck the two creases you created in the previous step behind.

20. Here's how your model should look now.

21. Flip the paper over and refold all four corners diagonally inward.

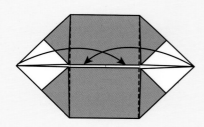 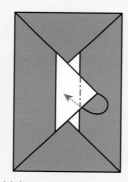 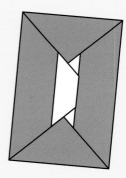

22. Fold the left and the right points inward, so one overlaps the other.

23. Fold the point on the top layer behind and underneath the pocket on the layer behind it.

24. Here's your super-secure origami envelope!

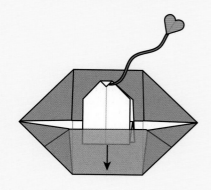 

25. You can open your envelope and place an origami tea bag inside the lower pocket, or open the envelope's top section as well to completely secure it inside.

Love Knots

These adorable, little love knots are sure to put a smile on anyone's face! You can use thin origami paper or thicker paper to make these sweet woven paper hearts. You can also use plastic ribbon or drinking straws. If you are using thicker paper or plastic, skip steps 1 and 2.

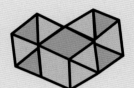

THIN PAPER SIZE: 2 strips, 11.5 × 1.5 inches (29 × 4 cm)
THICK PAPER SIZE: 2 strips, 11.5 × .5 to .75 inches (29 × 1 to 2 cm)

DIFFICULTY:

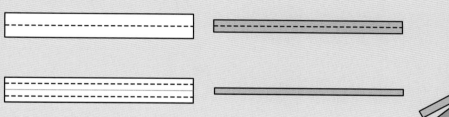
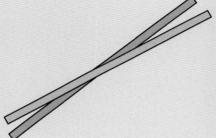

1. (a) Fold the bottom edge of the paper up to the top and unfold. (b) Fold the top and bottom edges to the middle.

2. Fold the bottom edge up to the top.

3. Repeat the process on a second strip. Use different colors to make it easier to follow the instructions.

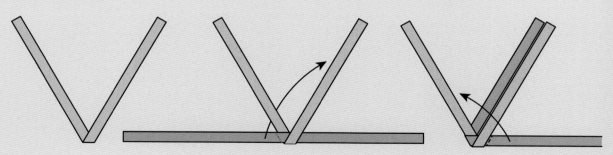

4. Take the first strip and bring the left end of it behind and up, creating a V shape.

5. Position the second strip in the bottom of the V. The left end of the strip should be slightly longer. Bring the left end of the second strip diagonally up and behind the V.

6. Next bring the right end of the second strip diagonally up along the edge of the first strip.

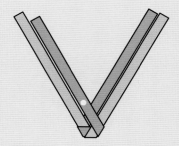

7. Tuck the strip indicated by the white dot behind the one underneath it.

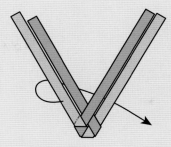

8. Fold the left-most strip diagonally down behind and to the right.

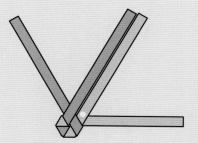

9. Tuck the strip indicated by the white dot behind the one underneath it.

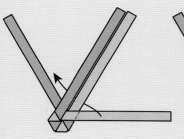

10. Fold the right-most strip diagonally up and behind to the left.

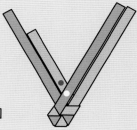

11. Bring the strip indicated by the white dot underneath the strip with the red dot.

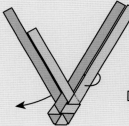

12. Bring the right-most strip diagonally behind to the left.

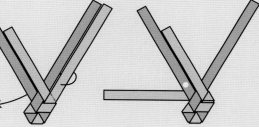

13. Tuck the strip indicated by the white dot behind the one underneath it.

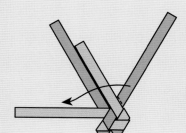

14. Fold the right-most strip diagonally over the top and to the left.

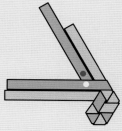

15. Tuck the strip indicated by the white dot behind the one indicated by the red dot.

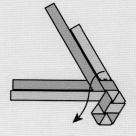

16. Fold the top right strip diagonally down to the left.

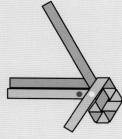

17. Tuck the strip indicated by the white dot behind the one indicated by the red dot.

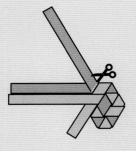

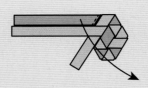

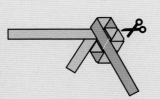

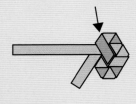

18. Trim the top diagonal strip as indicated.

19. Fold the top strip diagonally down and to the right.

20. Trim the strip as indicated.

21. Slot the trimmed strip inside the heart.

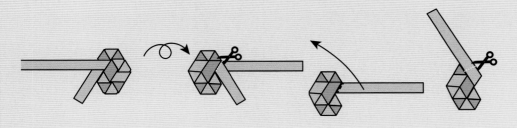

22. This is how your model should look. Now flip it over to the other side.

23. Trim the lower strip as indicated.

24. Fold the last remaining strip diagonally up and to the left.

25. Trim the strip.

26. Slot the strip underneath the top right triangular flap.

27. Love!

KAWAII TIP
To attach the love knot to a key chain, make a small hole at the top of the heart using a pushpin. Now you can attach a jump ring. You can also cover the heart in one or more layers of clear varnish to make it water resistant.

Dustpan & Scoop

Here are two origami models that can actually be used to clean up! The first is a simple dustpan which only takes a minute to make! The second one is a scoop, which is a continuation of the dustpan. Once you have mastered this bigger version, try making a mini dustpan to go with the mini origami trash bin on page 75!

MINI DUSTPAN VARIATION PAPER SIZE: 3 × 3 inches (7.5 × 7.5 cm)

DUSTPAN

DIFFICULTY:

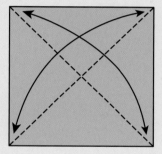

1. Start with the color side of your paper facing up. Fold the paper in half diagonally and unfold, then repeat in the other direction.

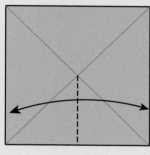

2. Fold the right edge over to the left edge, crease only the lower half, and unfold.

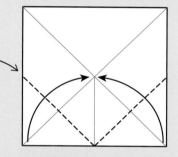

3. Flip the paper over to the other side from left to right. Fold the bottom left and right corners diagonally in to the center.

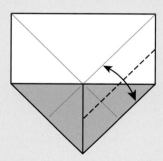

4. Take the bottom right diagonal edge and fold it diagonally up to meet the diagonal crease above and unfold. Do not fold the lower part of the paper; only make a crease where indicated by the dotted line.

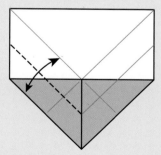

5. Repeat the previous step on the left side.

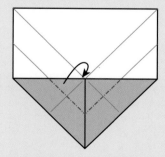

6. Fold the points of the two lower flaps behind, along the creases you created in the previous two steps.

Look how much it holds!

7. Here is what your model should now look like.

8. Flip the paper over to the other side and rotate it.

9. Using the existing creases, push the right section while pinching the left section and pushing it toward the right.

10. Your simple origami dustpan is complete! You can now use it to create the scoop if you like.

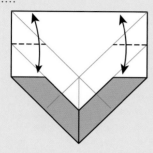

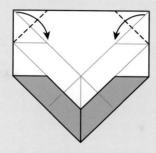

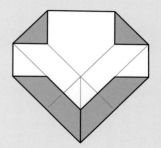

11. Open the paper back out to step 7 (or start with a new paper and fold up to step 7). Fold the top edge down as indicated, only folding on left and the right sides. Unfold.

12. Fold the top left and right corners diagonally inward.

13. Here is what your model should now look like.

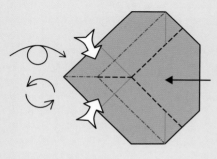

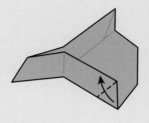

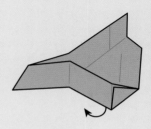

14. Flip the paper over and rotate it. Once again, push the left and right sections toward each other to make the scoop three-dimensional.

15. With your dustpan positioned as shown, fold the front-most corner flap diagonally up along the crease.

16. Open the edge of the dustpan a little.

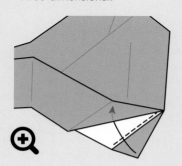

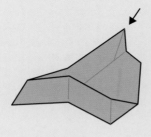

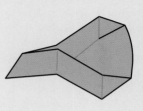

17. Refold the corner underneath the flap you just opened.

18. Repeat steps 15 to 17 on the other side of the scoop.

19. Voila! You're ready for tiny messes.

Rectangular Masu Box

This variation of the masu box on page 8 ends up being rectangular when finished.

Not only is this masu box cute as a gift box, but it also makes a great organization container.

Use a larger, thicker paper or cardstock to make a steady box to store pens or makeup brushes.

PAPER SIZE: 7 × 7 inches (17.5 × 17.5 cm)

DIFFICULTY:

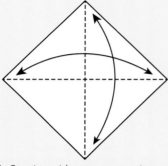

1. Starting with your paper orientated as shown, fold and unfold the paper in half in both directions.

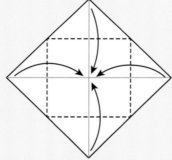

2. Fold each corner to the center.

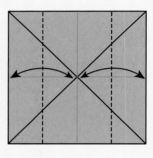

3. Fold the left and right edges to the middle and unfold.

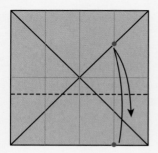

4. Fold the bottom edge up to the point indicated and unfold.

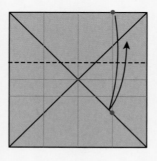

5. Fold the top edge to the point indicated and unfold.

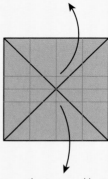

6. Open up the top and bottom sections.

They can also hold paper clips!

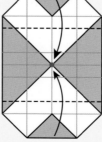

7. Fold the top and bottom points inward as indicated.

8. Fold the top and bottom edges to the middle.

9. Using the existing creases that are underneath the front flaps, refold the indicated horizontal creases.

Rectangular Masu Box   37

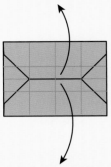

10. Open up the top and bottom sections.

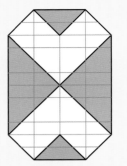

11. This is what your model should now look like. Flip the paper over to the other side.

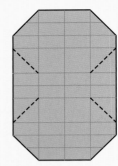

12. Fold and unfold to create the diagonal creases that are indicated.

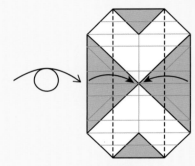

13. Flip the paper over again and fold the left and right edges inward, making the box three-dimensional.

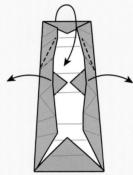

14. Using the diagonal creases you created in step 12, bring the back section up and over, inside the box.

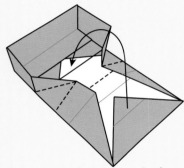

15. Repeat the last step on the front section to complete the box.

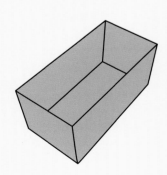

My desk is going to be so organized now!

Cute Purse

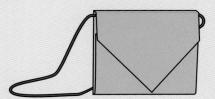

This origami purse is based on the same folding method used for the Kawaii envelopes on page 15. You can use this purse as an envelope too. What makes this one appealing is that it becomes a pouch that can be opened up and will hold items securely. You can make a real purse with this project if you use fabric that is ironed into place at each step!

DIFFICULTY:

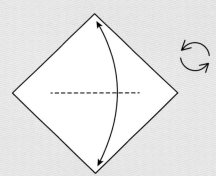

1. Create a horizontal crease by folding the top point down to the bottom point and unfolding it. For a clean finish, avoid creasing the left and right ends.

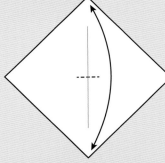

2. Rotate the paper and create a small horizontal crease in the middle using the same method from step 1.

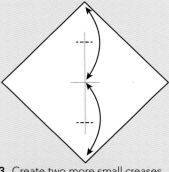

3. Create two more small creases by bringing the top and bottom points to the crease made in the previous step and unfolding them.

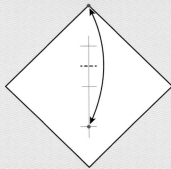

4. Make another small crease by bringing the top point down to the lowest small crease and then unfolding it.

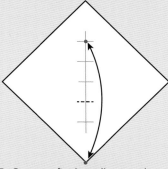

5. Create a final small crease by bringing the bottom point up to the topmost small crease and then unfolding it.

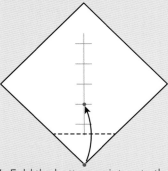

6. Fold the bottom point up to the second crease from the bottom.

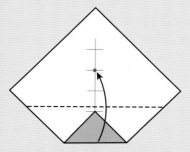

7. Fold the bottom edge up to the second crease from the top.

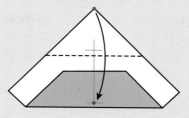

8. Fold the top point down to the small crease at the bottom.

9. Fold the bottom left and right sides diagonally up to meet the edges of the top triangle.

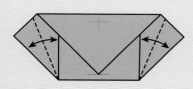

10. Create diagonal creases on the left and right sides by folding and unfolding the right and left edges.

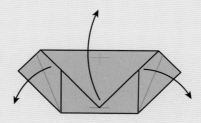

11. Unfold the top section and then unfold the left and right flaps.

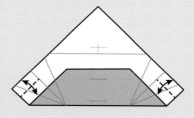

12. Create a diagonal crease where indicated on the left and right sides by folding and unfolding the right and left edges.

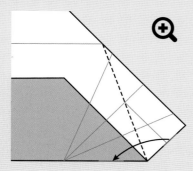

13. Create a diagonal crease where indicated on the right side of the paper by folding the right edge . . .

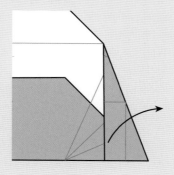

14. . . . and unfolding it.

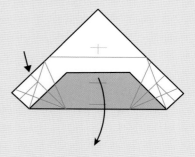

15. Repeat the previous two steps on the left side. Unfold the bottom section downward.

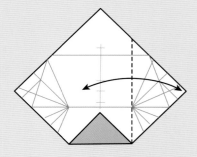

16. Fold the right section over to the left, aligning its diagonal edge to the diagonal edge of the bottom triangle. Unfold.

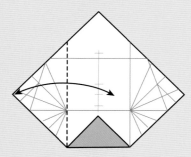

17. Repeat the previous step on the left side.

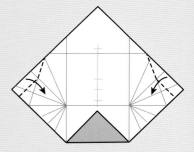

18. Refold the creases indicated on the left and right.

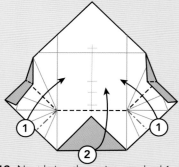

19. Next bring the points marked 1 up and diagonally in, followed by the lower edge, which is marked 2.

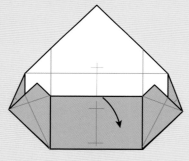

20. Flatten the paper and then open the bottom section so that you can get to the flaps underneath.

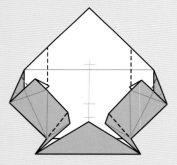

21. Use the existing creases that are indicated here . . .

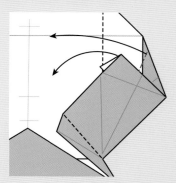

22. . . . and bring the right section to the left while using the crease indicated by the red dot as a mountain fold as indicated.

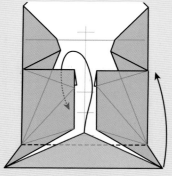

23. Repeat on the left side, then bring the bottom section back up and slot the triangular flap down inside the pocket.

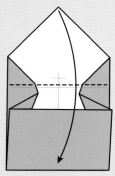

24. Now you can fold the top point down to the bottom, creating a new horizontal crease . . .

25. . . . and your purse will look like this.

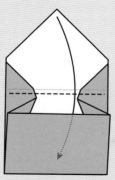

26. Or you can slot the point inside the envelope to secure it.

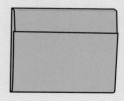

27. Then your purse will look like this.

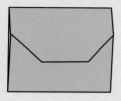

28. You could even fold the point underneath to make the flap look more rounded.

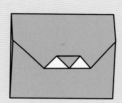

29. Or fold the flap up a little, then fold it down to make a little design. No matter what you do, it'll be cute!

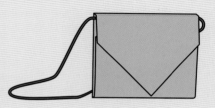

30. To use this model as a purse, you can glue or sew some ribbon underneath the flap.

This purse will go perfectly with my outfit!

Woven Bracelet

You can use thin origami paper or thicker paper to make this pretty bracelet! It makes for a thoughtful friendship bracelet too! Try different color combinations that will really make it pop! It's better to use paper that has a white side so that you get a contrasting pattern.

PAPER SIZE: 2 strips, 11.5 × .5 inches (29 × 1 cm)

DIFFICULTY:

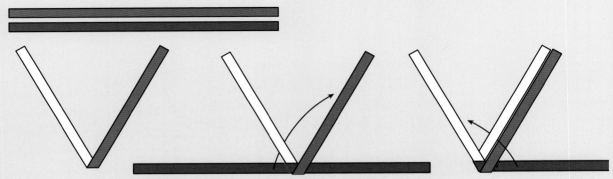

1. Start by bringing the left end of your first strip behind and up to the left, forming a V shape.

2. Place your second strip in the bottom of the V, with the left end slightly longer. Bring the left end of the strip diagonally up, behind, and to the right.

3. Fold the right end of the second strip diagonally up to the left and slot it behind the strip that is indicated.

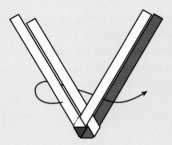

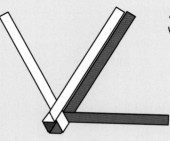

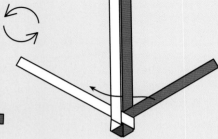

4. Bring the leftmost strip diagonally behind and to the right, slotting in front of the strip that is indicated.

5. Here is what your model should now look like.

6. Rotate the strips so that the two central strips are vertical. Fold the rightmost strip diagonally up to the left behind the next strip and then in front of the left vertical strip.

Purple and pink would also look great!

7. Bring the lower left strip diagonally up to the right, in front of the first two strips and then behind the right vertical strip.

8–9. Continue to weave the strips as indicated until you have run out of paper.

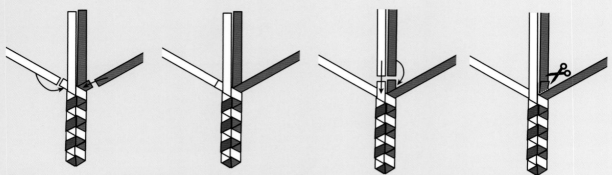

10–12. To make the bracelet longer, slot more strips into the weaving as indicated.

13. Trim off any excess paper that sticks out of the center.

14. Once you have the length you need, trim off the paper that sticks out on the left and right.

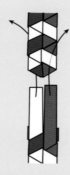

15. Bring the other end of your bracelet around so that you can slot the remaining center strips through the weave as indicated to secure the bracelet.

16. Trim off any excess paper.

17–18. This is the final pattern when using strips that are different colors and have white backs.

19. This is the final pattern when the two strips are the same color with white as the background.

20. This is the final pattern when using strips of two different colors, with a color on both sides of the paper (1 white, 1 blue).

21. This is the final pattern when you use two strips of the same colored paper that have white on the back, but in step 2, you flip the second lower strip so that the white side is facing up.

Woven Bookmark

Not only will you never lose your place again when reading your favorite book, this pretty woven-paper bookmark is a perfect gift for all occasions! Use three differently colored strips of paper for the best result. You can use paper that is the same color on each side, or paper that has a white side too!

PAPER SIZE: 3 strips, 7.75 × .75 inches (20 × 2 cm)

DIFFICULTY:

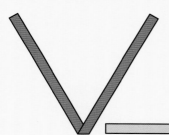

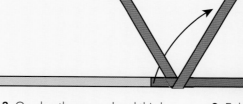

1. Create a V shape with the first strip by bringing the left end up behind.

2. Overlap the second and third strip to make one long strip and position it in the bottom of the V. (The right strip should be on top of the left strip.)

3. Fold the left end of the long bottom strip diagonally up to the right behind the left of the V.

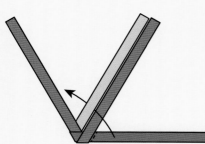

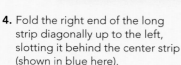

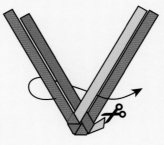

4. Fold the right end of the long strip diagonally up to the left, slotting it behind the center strip (shown in blue here).

5. Trim off the excess paper on the right side. Fold the leftmost strip diagonally up, back, and to the right, and then slot it in front of the rightmost strip.

6. Rotate the model so that the two central strips are vertical.

TIP
If you want your bookmark to be thicker, use strips of paper that are 1.5 inches (4 cm) wide and fold them in half.

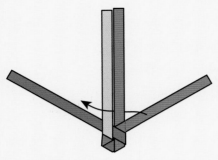

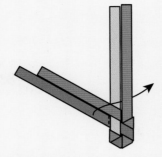

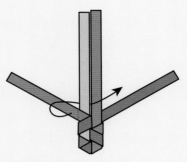

7. Fold the right strip diagonally up to the left, behind the right vertical strip and then in front of the left vertical strip.

8. Fold the leftmost strip diagonally up to the right, in front of the two left strips and then behind the right vertical strip.

9. Continue to weave the strips until . . .

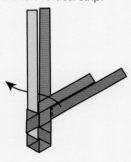

10. . . . you have the length you want. (If you'd like to make a longer bookmark, attach more strips like in the woven bracelet on page 44).

11. Trim off the excess paper from the right diagonal strip.

12. Fold the right vertical strip diagonally down to the left.

13. Trim the paper as indicated.

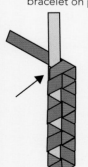

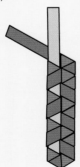

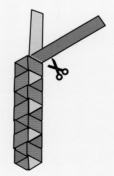

14. Insert the right vertical strip underneath the left vertical strip (shown here in blue).

15. This is what your model should now look like.

16. Flip the bookmark over to the other side. Trim the right diagonal strip.

17. Repeat steps 12 to 15 on the final strip.

18. Here is your beautiful bookmark!

Woven Bookmark   49

Cat & Dog Hearts

Perfect for either the cat or dog lover in your life, these adorable little pets can be decorated with all kinds of cute Kawaii faces. They are perfect for a peek-a-boo "Hello!" token. Try using complementary colors for the heart to go with their faces.

DIFFICULTY:

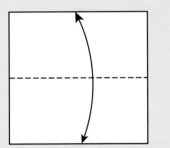

1. Starting with your paper white side up, fold the paper in half vertically and unfold.

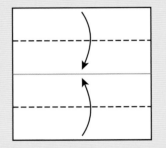

2. Fold the top and bottom edges to meet the crease you made in the previous step.

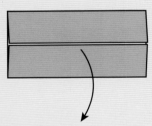

3. Open the lower section.

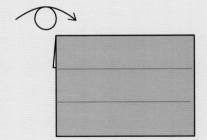

4. Flip the paper over to the other side from left to right.

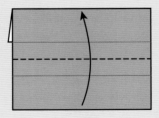

5. Fold the bottom edge up to the top edge.

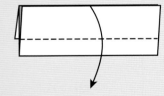

6. Fold the top edge back down along the existing crease as indicated.

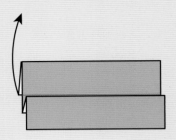

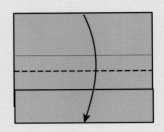

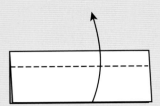

7. Unfold the top section back up from behind.

8. Fold the top edge down to the bottom edge.

9. Fold the flap back up along the existing crease.

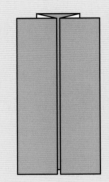

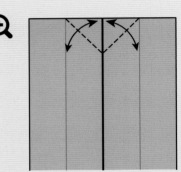

10. Rotate the paper.

11. Here is what your model should now look like.

12. Create diagonal creases on the inner corners of the top left and right sections.

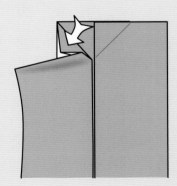

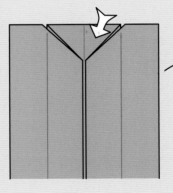

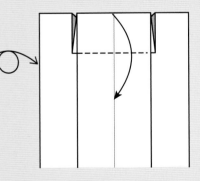

13. Reverse fold the left diagonal crease.

14. Reverse fold the right diagonal crease.

15. Flip the model over to the other side. Fold the top central section down, leaving the left and right sections in place.

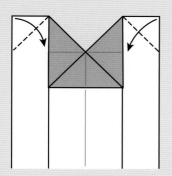

16. Fold the top left and right corners down diagonally.

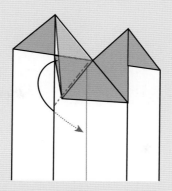

17. You can fold the inner corner down inside the central section, but only if your paper allows it.

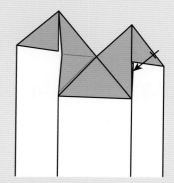

18. Repeat on the right.

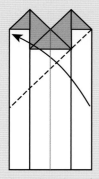

19. Bring the right edge of the paper diagonally up to the left, aligning it with the top left horizontal edge of the top triangular flap.

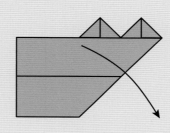

20. Unfold.

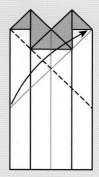

21. Repeat step 19 on the left side.

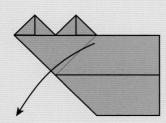

22. Unfold.

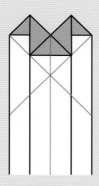

23. Here is what your model should now look like.

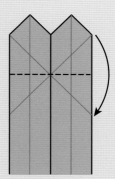

24. Flip the paper over to the other side. Fold the top section down, so that the two diagonal creases meet each other.

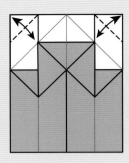

25. Fold and unfold to create diagonal creases on the top left and right corners.

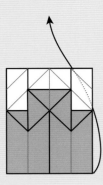

26. Bring the bottom flap up from behind.

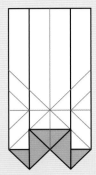

27. This is what your model should now look like. Focus on the lower section.

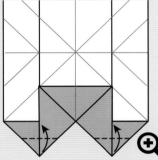

28. Fold the bottom left and right points up.

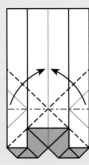

29. Bring the left and right edges up, collapsing the lower section up at the same time.

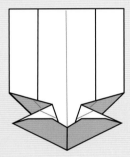

30. This is what your model should now look like.

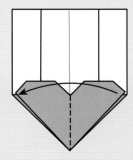

31. Flip the right section of the emerging heart shape over to the left.

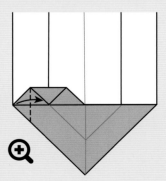

32. Fold the far-left point over to the right.

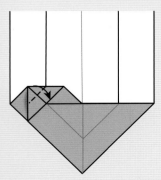

33. Fold the top left point diagonally down to complete the left side of the heart shape.

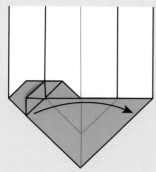

34. Fold the section back over to the right.

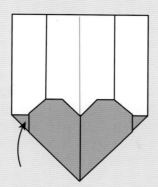

35. Repeat steps 31 to 34 on the left section of the heart.

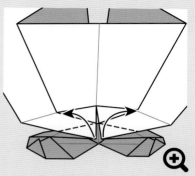

36. Look inside the heart and fold the two inner points behind, along the existing creases.

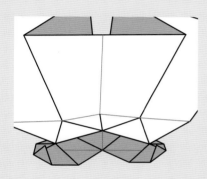

37. This is what your model should now look like inside.

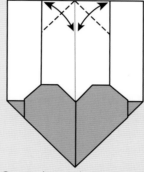

38. Create diagonal creases on the left and right corners of the central section as indicated.

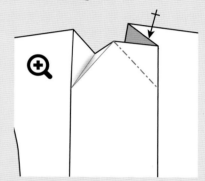

39. Reverse fold the creases you made in the previous step.

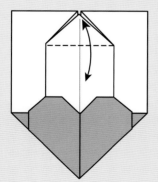

40. Fold the top point of the top central section down and back up again to create a crease.

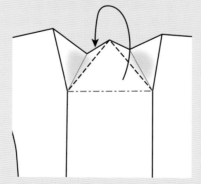

41. Open the top section a little, fold the central point down inside, and close it again.

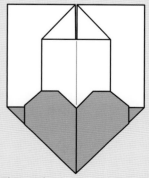

42. This is what your model should now look like.

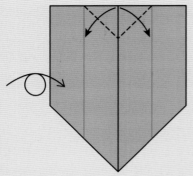

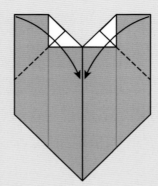

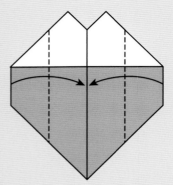

43. Flip the model over to the other side. Diagonally fold the left and right corners of the central section as indicated.

44. Diagonally fold the left and right edges inward to meet the vertical crease.

45. Fold the left and right edges in for a final time.

DOG VERSION

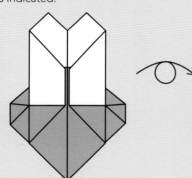

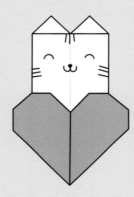

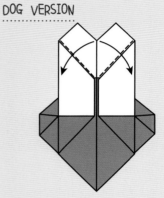

46. This is what your model should now look like.

47. Flip the model over to the other side, and draw an adorable kitty face! Or . . .

1. On the back of the heart, fold the two "ears" down diagonally.

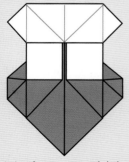

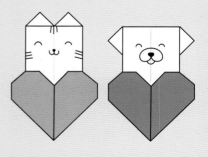

2. This is what your model should now look like.

3. Flip the model back over to the other side and draw the face of a real cute pooch!

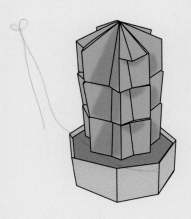

Cactus

This fun origami project is not sharp and is a perfect gift for your friend who cannot take care of a real plant—no watering is necessary! You can even make a couple of these origami cacti and stack them on top of each other to create different heights! Try different greens as well to give depth and variety.

DIFFICULTY:

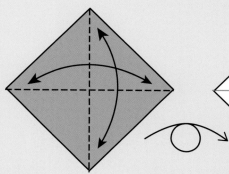

1. Starting with your paper color side up, create vertical and horizontal creases by folding and unfolding the paper in half top to bottom and then left to right.

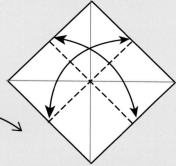

2. Flip the paper over. Create diagonal creases by folding and unfolding the paper in half diagonally in both directions.

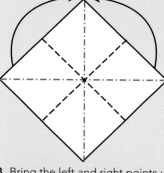

3. Bring the left and right points up, collapsing the paper into what's known as an origami square base.

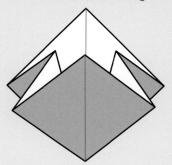

4. Flatten the paper, making sure that the open end is at the top.

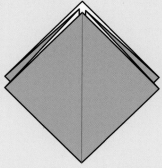

5. This is what your model should now look like.

6. Fold the left and right lower diagonal edges to the central vertical crease and unfold. Repeat this on the back.

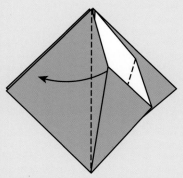

7. Open one of the flaps and squash the paper as indicated. Repeat this on all of the other flaps.

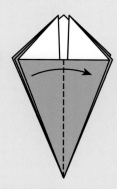

8. Fold one of the sections over so that you are viewing a solid kite shape.

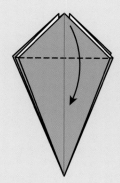

9. Fold the top point down. Repeat on all sides.

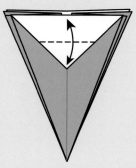

10. Fold the bottom point of the top triangular flap up to the top edge and unfold.

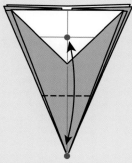

11. Bring the bottom point up to meet the point indicated by the red dot, crease well, and unfold.

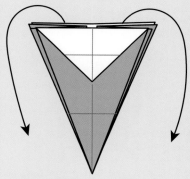

12. Open up the paper completely to the white side.

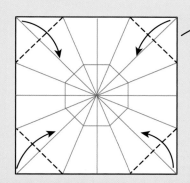

13. Fold all four points inward along the existing creases.

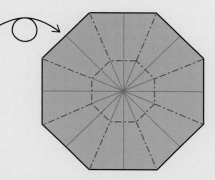

14. Flip the paper over to the other side. Make all of the creases indicated in red into mountain folds.

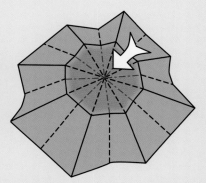

15. Pick up the paper and carefully sink fold the octagon shape down inside.

Cactus   59

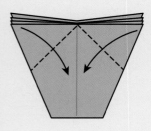

16. This is what your model should now look like.

17. Rotate and flatten the paper. Make sure that a triangular flap is behind the top layer you are working on.

18. Fold the top left and top right points diagonally down to align with the central vertical crease.

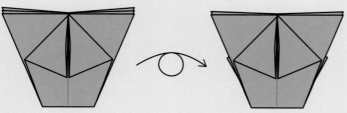

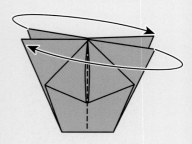

19. This is what your model should now look like.

20. Flip the paper over and repeat on the back, making sure you have equal flaps on each side.

21. Flip the sections so that you can repeat step 18 on the remaining flaps.

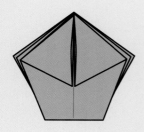

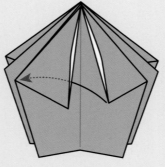

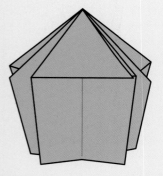

22. This is what your model should now look like.

23. Insert the right flap inside the left flap, making the model three-dimensional.

24. Repeat the previous step on all the sides.

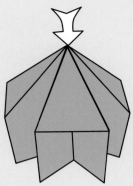

25. You can push the top point down to give the cactus a four-leaf clover shape.

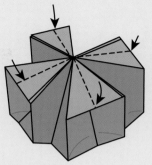

26. You can push the top flaps down, creating valley folds, and squash them, giving the cactus a pointier look.

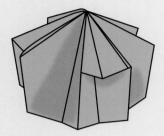

27. If you are using small paper, you may want to use a dab of glue to secure the cactus sections together once you make more of them.

We don't need to water these!

Round Pot

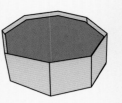

This octagonal pot is perfect to use as a base for our cactus project on page 57. We will use two sheets of paper, one for the outside of the pot and one for the inside. The paper for the inside part needs to be a tiny bit smaller than the paper used for the outside. This project uses the same method as the traditional masu box on page 8. If you are using 6 × 6–inch (15 × 15–cm) paper for the pot, then:

SOIL PAPER SIZE: 5.7 × 5.7 (14.5 × 14.5 cm)

DIFFICULTY:

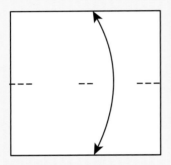

1. Start by creating horizontal creases where indicated by folding and unfolding the paper.

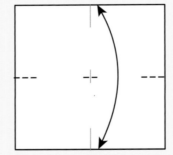

2. Rotate the paper and make the same horizontal creases.

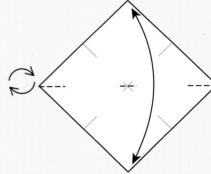

3. Rotate the paper so that it is oriented as shown and create the same horizontal creases.

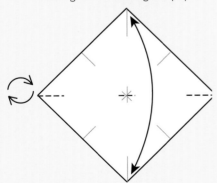

4. Again rotate the paper and create a final set of horizontal creases.

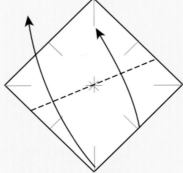

5. Fold the bottom right diagonal edge up so that the creases match as shown here.

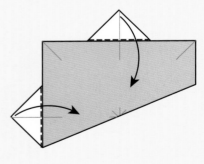

6. Fold the bottom left and top points over the front flap.

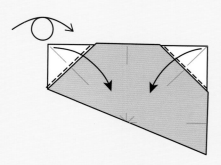

7. Flip the paper over from left to right, and fold the top left and right points forward.

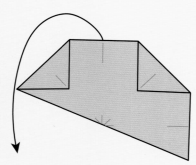

8. Open the paper, but leave the corners folded.

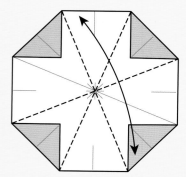

9. You should now have an octagonal shape. One of the diagonal creases is already completed; now create matching folds where indicated.

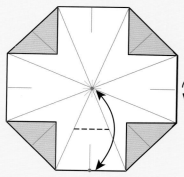

10. Bring the bottom edge to the center point and make a crease where indicated.

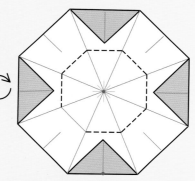

11. Rotate the paper and repeat the previous step on all eight sides.

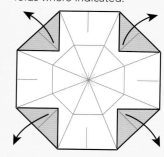

12. Rotate the paper and open up the four corner flaps.

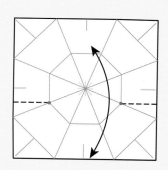

13. Make horizontal creases where indicated, avoiding the middle.

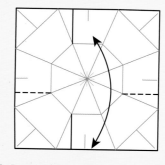

14. Rotate the paper and repeat the creases on the other three sides.

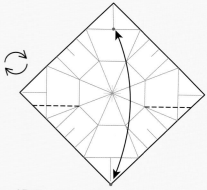

15. Rotate the paper. Bring the bottom point up to the point indicated by the red dot and unfold, creating the horizontal creases indicated. Keep avoiding the middle.

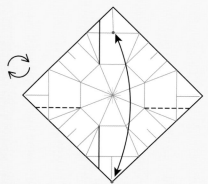

16. Rotate the paper and repeat the previous step on the other three sides.

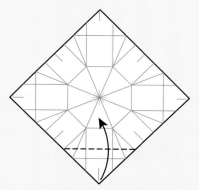

17. Using the existing creases as a guide, fold the bottom corner up.

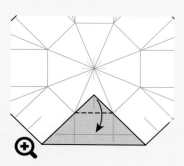

18. Fold the top point of the triangular flap down as indicated.

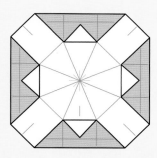

19. Repeat the last two steps on the other three points.

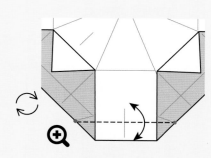

20. Rotate the paper and fold the bottom edge up from the points indicated by the red dots.

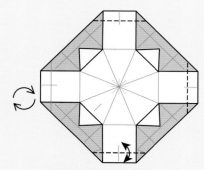

21. Rotate the paper and repeat the previous step on the other three edges.

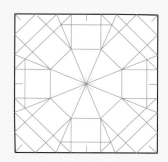

22. Open up the paper all the way.

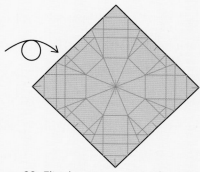

23. Flip the paper over to the color side and rotate it as indicated.

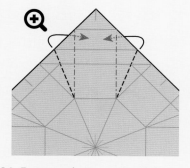

24. Focus on the top point. Pick up the paper and fold along the creases as indicated, making the pot three-dimensional.

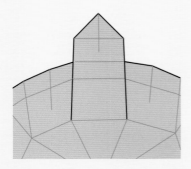

25. This is what the point should now look like. Repeat on the other three points.

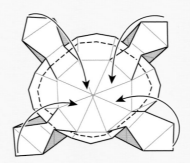

26. Looking at the pot from above, collapse all four points over and into the pot.

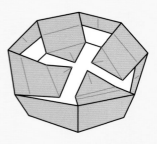

27. Straighten out the flaps inside the pot.

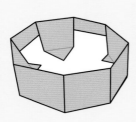

28. This is what your finished outside pot will look like.

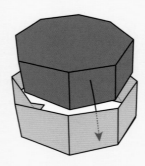

29. Create a second pot from slightly smaller paper and insert it upside down inside the larger pot.

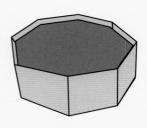

30. Here is your completed pot!

We don't have to fertliize this soil!

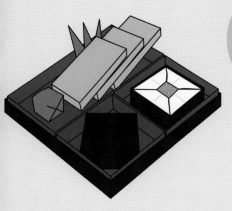

Bento Box

A showcase of your origami skills, this bento box is sure to be a display piece. It can also be used to organize your stationery, jewelry, and more! You can create a super-cute origami bento lunch with the origami sushi roll boxes (page 99), sashimi (page 73), and even a little wasabi (page 73)!

DIFFICULTY:

INNER RECTANGULAR BOX

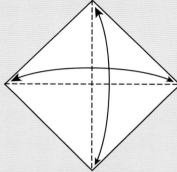

1. Create horizontal and vertical creases by folding and unfolding the paper in half from top to bottom and then left to right.

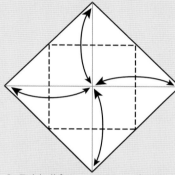

2. Fold all four corners to the middle and then unfold.

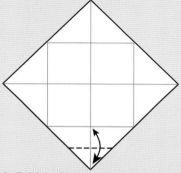

3. Fold the bottom corner up to the crease just above it and then unfold.

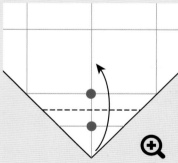

4. Fold the bottom corner up again, this time creating a crease halfway between the two existing creases, using the red dots as reference points.

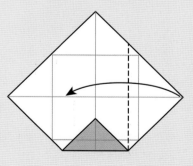

5. Fold the right point over to the left, aligning its diagonal edge against that of the lower flap you created in the previous step.

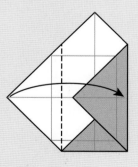

6. Repeat the same for the left point.

Bento Box   67

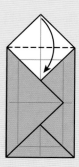

7. Bring the top point down to align with the diagonal edges of the left and right flaps.

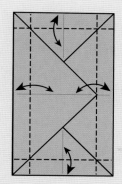

8. Using the existing creases, fold all the edges inward and unfold.

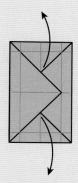

9. Open the top and bottom sections.

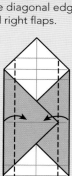

10. Refold the left and right edges inward.

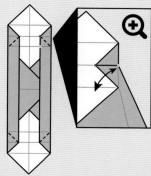

11. Create diagonal folds where indicated on all four sides. You can pick the model up to make this easier to do.

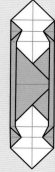

12. This is what your model should now look like.

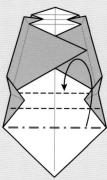

13. Focusing on the lower section, fold the bottom point over the diagonal folds you created and secure it inside the box.

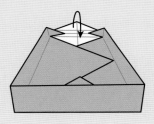

14. Repeat the last step on the opposite end.

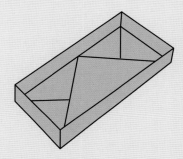

15. Now you've got yourself the inner rectangular box!

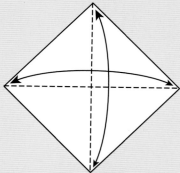

1. Create horizontal and vertical creases by folding and unfolding the paper in half from top to bottom and then left to right.

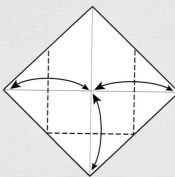

2. Fold the bottom, left, and right corners to the center, and then unfold them.

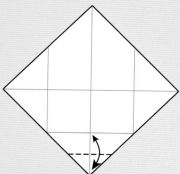

3. Fold the bottom corner up to the crease just above it and unfold.

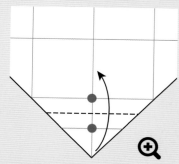

4. Fold the bottom corner up again, this time creating a crease half way between the two existing creases. Use the red dots to help guide you.

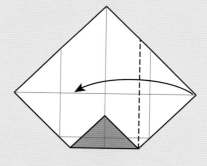

5. Fold the right point over to the left, aligning its diagonal edge against that of the edge of the lower flap you created in the previous step.

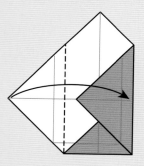

6. Repeat the same for the left point.

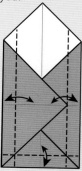

7. Using the existing creases, fold the left, right, and bottom edges inward and then unfold them.

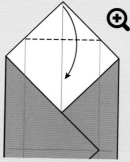

8. Fold the top point down, using the tops of the existing vertical creases as guides.

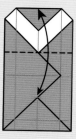

9. Fold the top edge down to meet the top point of the lower triangular flap. Unfold.

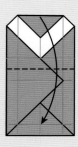

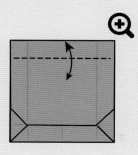

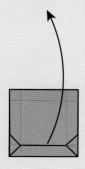

10. Fold the top edge down to lowest horizontal crease.

11. Using the existing crease, refold the top section down and unfold.

12. Unfold the top flap back up.

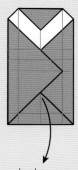

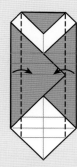

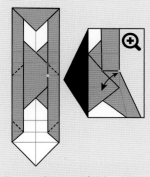

13. Open up the lower section.

14. Refold the left and right edges inward.

15. Create diagonal folds where indicated. You can pick the model up to make this easier to do.

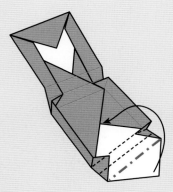

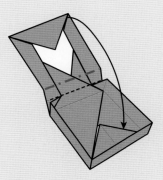

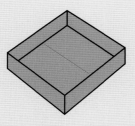

16. Focusing on the lower section, fold the bottom point over the diagonal folds you created and secure it inside the box.

17. Repeat the last step on the opposite end.

18. Here's your inner square box! You'll need two of them to make the bento box.

1. We need to fold in one-seventh of each edge. To work out sevenths, simply take the width of the paper and divide by 7. If you're using 6 × 6–inch paper, this measurement will be .85 inches.

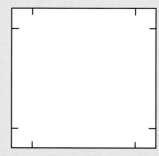

2. Mark a seventh from the left and right on all four edges of the paper.

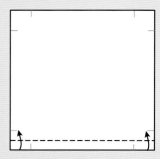

3. Fold the bottom edge up to meet the marks on the left and right edges.

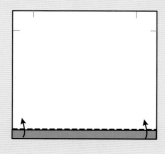

4. Fold the bottom edge up along the top edge of the flap.

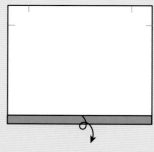

5. Unfold the paper completely.

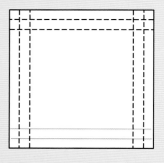

6. Repeat steps 3 to 5 on the other edges.

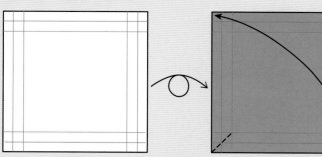

7. Here's what your paper should look like.

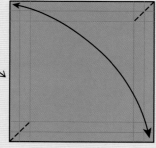

8. Flip the paper over to the other side. Take the lower right corner up to the top left corner and create diagonal creases on the top right and lower left sections only.

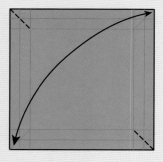

9. Repeat the last step on the opposite side.

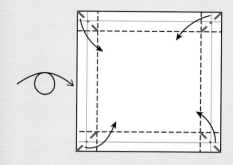

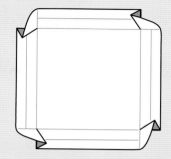

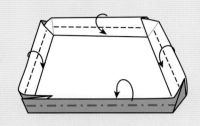

10. Flip the paper back over to the other side. Bring all four corners inward.

11. Make sure the points inside are all pointing in the same direction.

12. Fold all four edges over along with the inner triangular corners to finish the outer box.

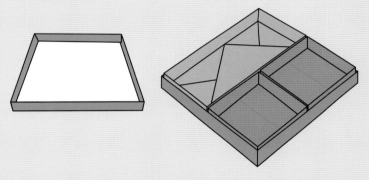

13. This box is not stable on its own, but once you put the inner boxes inside, the whole thing will be strong.

MAKE A BENTO LUNCH!

Bento boxes usually come in a deep red color with black on the outside.

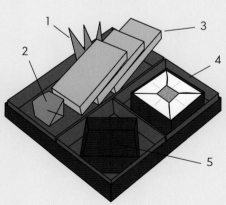

1. Lettuce: Cut some simple jagged shapes from green paper.
2. Wasabi: Make an origami water balloon with or without blowing it up (page 19) using 3 × 3–inch (7.5 × 7.5–cm) paper.
3. Sashimi: Make another rectangular box, this time using paper that is 4 × 4 inches (10 × 10 cm).
4. Sushi Roll Box: Make this by using the instructions on (page 99) using standard 6 × 6–inch (15 × 15–cm) paper.
5. Soy Sauce Dish: Make another square box (page 71) this time using 4 × 4–inch (10 × 10–cm) paper.

Mini Trash Bin

Whether used to store pencil shavings or candy wrappers, this mini trash bin is both practical and decorative, as the flap swings back and forth. It can also serve as a secret hiding place for notes and other items people would never think to look for in the trash!

PAPER SIZE & ADDITIONAL MATERIALS: 7 × 7 inches (17.5 × 17.5 cm), pencil, ruler, calculator

TRASH BIN BOX

DIFFICULTY:

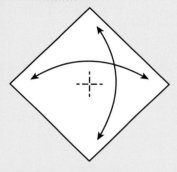

1. Fold your paper in half, top point to the bottom point, only creasing the middle point. Repeat from left to right.

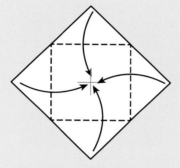

2. Fold all four points to the middle of the cross-shaped crease you created in the previous step.

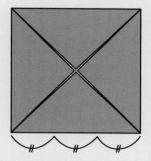

3. We need to fold this into thirds. Use your ruler to measure the width of an edge. Take that number and divide it by 3. Keep a note of this measurement, as you'll need it later on.

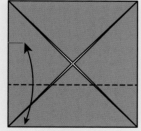

4. Measure from the bottom left edge of the paper, using the measurement you got in step 3, and mark the spot. Rotate the paper clockwise so that the mark is on the top left. Fold the bottom edge up to the mark and unfold.

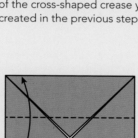

5. Fold the top edge down to meet the previous crease and unfold.

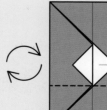

6. Rotate the paper clockwise. Fold the bottom edge up to where the previous crease intersects with the diagonal edges of the left and right flaps. Use the pink dots to help guide you.

Mini Trash Bin   75

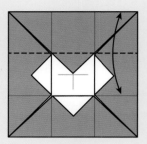

7. Fold the top edge down to the previous crease.

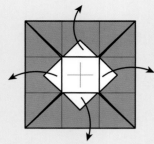

8. Unfold the paper completely.

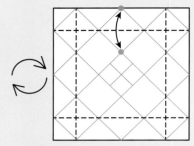

9. Rotate the paper and fold the top edge down to the point indicated and unfold. Repeat on the other three edges.

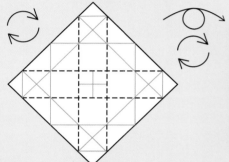

10. Rotate the paper and refold the indicated creases as valley folds.

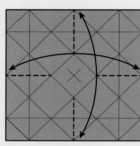

11. Flip the paper over and rotate it so it is oriented as shown. Fold the paper in half and unfold, avoiding the central diamond. Repeat with the opposite edges.

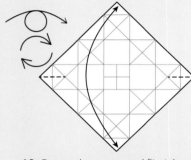

12. Rotate the paper and flip it back over to the white side. Bring the bottom point up to the top point and crease only the left and right points.

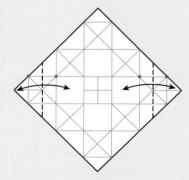

13. Fold the left and right points inward as indicated by the red dots, then unfold.

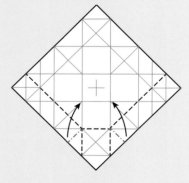

14. Fold the bottom left and right diagonal edges up, and at the same time fold the bottom point up on top.

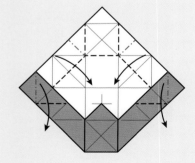

15. Repeat the same process on the top section, this time folding the left and right points down first.

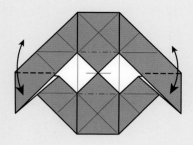

16. Refold the left and right triangles up and back down. Fold the points of the top and bottom section underneath.

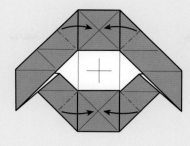

17. Using the existing diagonal creases as mountain folds, make the model three-dimensional by folding these inward.

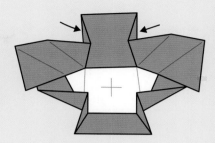

18. Starting on one end, slot the diagonal flaps in behind the back wall of the box. You need to open the back flap a little to do this.

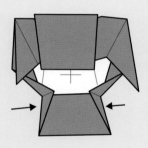

19. Repeat the same on the opposite side.

TRASH BIN FLAP

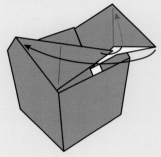

20. Slot one of the inner triangular flaps inside the other, bringing them to the middle.

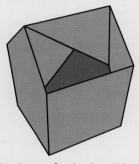

21. Here's your finished trash bin box!

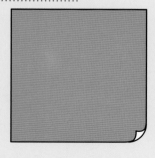

1. On another sheet of paper . . .

2. . . . take the measurement you noted earlier and multiply it by 2.

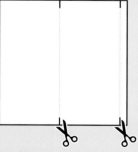

3. Using this new measurement, measure and mark it twice along the top and bottom edges. Use a ruler to connect the marks and cut along the lines. Discard the small excess strip.

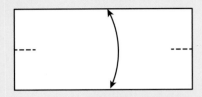

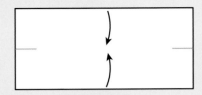

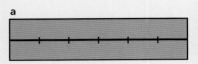

4. Take one of the paper strips and fold it in half from top to bottom, creasing only a little on the left and right sides.

5. Fold the top and bottom edges to the creases you created in the previous step. Unfold.

6a. Divide the paper into sixths using a ruler, calculator, and pencil (measure the length and divide by six). Mark the sixths along the inner edge of the top flap.

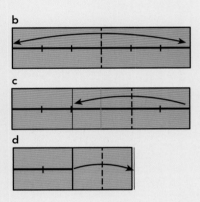

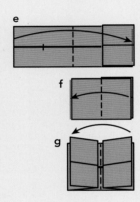

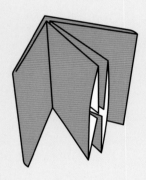

6b. Fold the paper in half side to side and unfold.

6c. Fold the right edge almost to the second mark from the left, leaving a tiny gap so that you can still see the mark.

6d. Fold the flap you created in the last step over to the right, extending it a tiny bit farther than the edge, so that you can see the central crease you made in step 6b.

6e. Fold the left edge over almost to the right edge, leaving a tiny gap.

6f. Fold the flap you created in the previous step to the left, extending it a tiny bit farther than the edge so that you can see the central crease you made in step 6b.

6g. Fold the paper in half side to side.

7. Here's how your trash bin flap should now look.

It's cute and helpful, just like me!

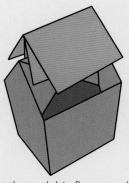

8. Slot the trash bin flap onto the top of the trash bin box. The two lower flaps should go over the horizontal top edge of the trash bin box.

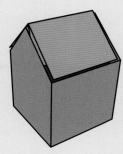

9. You should be able to push one side of the flap and the other side will raise, just like the real swinging top of a trash bin! If it is not swinging, you may need to adjust the folds you made in step 6.

INNER SUPPORT SQUARE

If you like, you can make a little square of paper to fit inside the bottom of the box to give it a little extra structural support—and a pop of color! You could also cut out a little cardboard square instead of folding the square, but it's not as fun.

1. Take the second strip of paper that you created in step 3 of the trash bin flap and fold it in half, top to bottom, only creasing the left and right edges. Unfold.

2. Fold the top and bottom edges to the marks you made in the previous step.

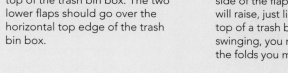

3. Fold the bottom right corner diagonally up to the top edge and unfold.

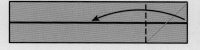

4. Using the diagonal crease you made in the previous step as a guide, fold the right edge over to the left.

5. Again, fold the right edge over to the left.

6. Fold the right edge over to the left a third time.

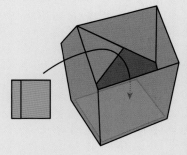

9. Now you can put the inner square facedown inside the box, which will prevent the sides from springing open.

7. Fold the excess paper on the left over to the right so that it lays on top of the right section.

8. This is your inner square.

Mini Drawer

This adorable little origami drawer makes a perfect gift box, or you can use it to store your jewelry. Make as many as you like and stack them to make a chest of drawers. To make a drawer, you need two sheets of paper, with one slightly smaller than the other. To work out what size the smaller sheet should be, all you need to do is measure an edge of the larger sheet and divide it by 1.25. So if you are using a 6 x 6–inch (15 x 15–cm) sheet of paper, your smaller sheet would need to be 4.72 × 4.72 inches (12 x 12 cm). It's easy to mark 4.72 inches (12 cm) with a ruler and pencil and trim the paper down.

PAPER SIZES: 7 × 7 inches (17.5 × 17.5 cm), 5.5 × 5.5 inches (14 × 14 cm)

DIFFICULTY:

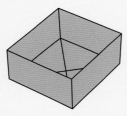

1. Make a masu box using the instructions on page 8 using your smaller sheet of paper. In our example, it's 4.72 × 4.72 inches (12 × 12 cm).

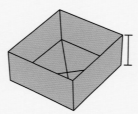

2. Measure the height of the box. Our example is 0.84 inch (2.14 cm) tall.

3. Using a ruler and pencil, mark that measurement along from the right edge of your larger sheet of paper.

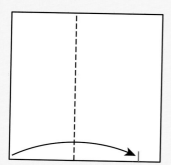

4. Fold the left edge over to the mark you made.

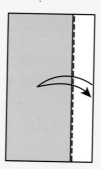

5. Fold the right edge over the top of the left section.

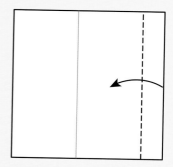

6. Unfold the previous steps and refold the right flap.

TIP
For the mini origami drawers, it's a good idea to use larger paper to start with. Example sizes would be: 7.5 × 7.5 inches (19 × 19 cm) and 6 × 6 inches (15 × 15 cm) papers, or 11 × 11 inches (28 × 28 cm) and 8.8 × 8.8 inches (22 × 22 cm).

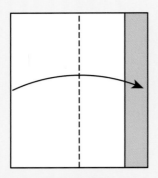

7. Refold the left edge over to the right edge.

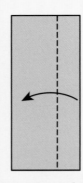

8. Fold the top layer of the right edge to the left, using the layer underneath as a guide.

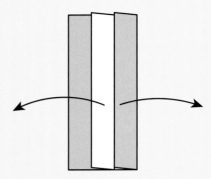

9. Unfold the paper completely.

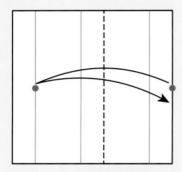

10. Take the right edge and fold it to the leftmost crease and unfold.

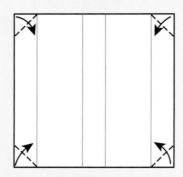

11. Fold all four corners diagonally inward, using the creases as guides.

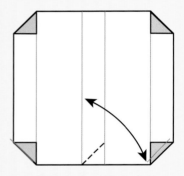

12. Make a diagonal fold on the bottom middle section by bringing the bottom right edge up to align with the vertical crease indicated.

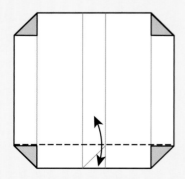

13. Fold the bottom edge up using the bottom left and right diagonal flaps as guides. Unfold.

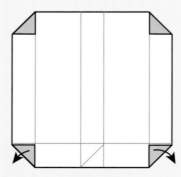

14. Unfold the bottom left and right diagonal flaps.

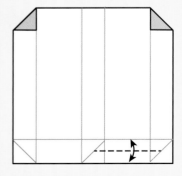

15. Make a horizontal crease on the bottom right section where indicated.

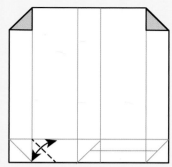

16. Make a diagonal crease on the bottom left as indicated.

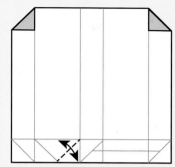

17. Make another small diagonal crease in the opposite direction as indicated.

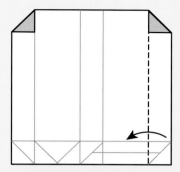

18. Refold the right edge along the rightmost crease.

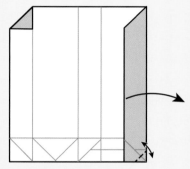

19. Make a small diagonal crease on the bottom right corner. This crease should align with the crease you made in step 15. Unfold the flap to the right.

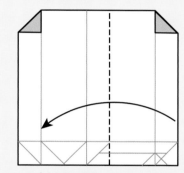

20. Refold the right edge over to the left along the crease that is indicated.

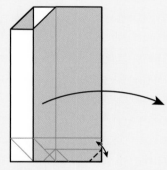

21. Make a little diagonal crease on the bottom right corner to match the one you made in step 19. Unfold the right section.

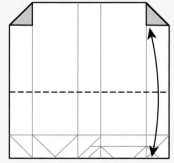

22. Take the bottom edge and fold it up to the horizontal edges of the top left and right diagonal flaps. Unfold.

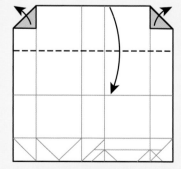

23. Unfold the top left and right diagonal flaps. Fold the top edge down to the crease you made in the previous step.

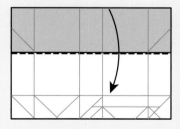

24. Fold the top edge down along the crease you made in step 22.

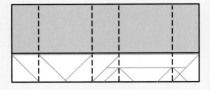

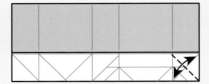

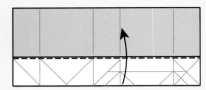

25. Refold and unfold all of the vertical creases so that they are all valley folds.

26. Make a diagonal crease on the bottom right section as indicated.

27. Refold the bottom section upward.

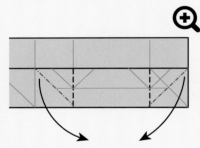

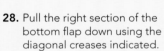

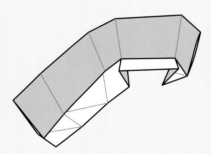

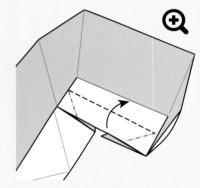

28. Pull the right section of the bottom flap down using the diagonal creases indicated.

29. The box should now start to become three-dimensional.

30. Fold the bottom flap of the box up, at the same time squash the two ends using the diagonal creases.

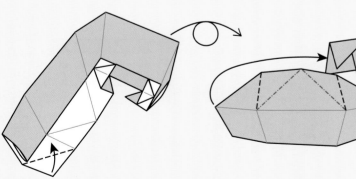

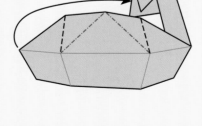

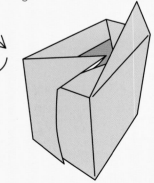

31. Refold the diagonal flap at the left end of the box.

32. Flip the box over so that you are looking at its base. Continue to close the box.

33. Slot the flap inside the open end of the box.

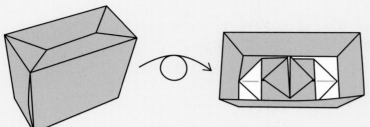
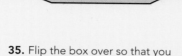
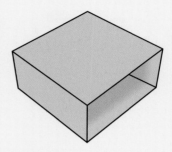

34. Fold the top triangular flap over and inside the gap.

35. Flip the box over so that you can press the flaps down inside the box.

36. Here is the outer box of your drawer.

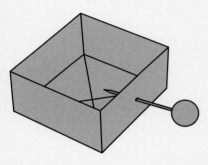

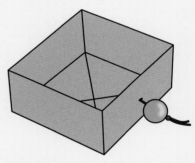

37. Take the masu box and make a small hole in one of the sides using a pin.

38. Using some thread or twine, make a small loop. You can thread it through a bead, knotting the end, if you want to add some extra cute.

39. Thread the closed end of the loop through the small hole in the masu box and then make a final knot.

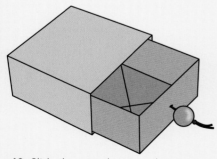
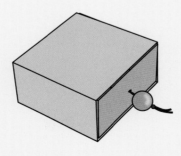

40. Slide the masu box into the outer box, and your drawer is complete!

41. Put whatever you like inside and close the drawer for safekeeping.

I'm going to hide my secret notes!

Stationery Boxes

Organize your envelopes and papers with these stationery boxes! There are many ways to arrange these boxes together to create your own customized stationery organizer. Sturdy paper is recommended. In addition to experimenting with square and rectangular paper for different heights, try using bold colors to make the drawers stand out, or similar colors for a subtle desktop décor.

PAPER SIZE: 7 × 7 inches (17.5 × 17.5 cm), cut in half

DIFFICULTY:

TIP
For best results, use thick paper or card stock for these stationery boxes.

BASIC FORM

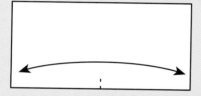

1. Bring the left edge to the right edge and make a small crease on the bottom edge. Unfold.

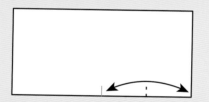

2. Fold the right edge to the crease you created in the previous step and make a small crease along the bottom. Unfold

3. Fold the right edge of the paper to the crease you created in the previous step.

4. Next fold the left edge to the right edge.

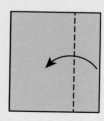

5. Using the layer underneath as a guide, fold the right edge to the left.

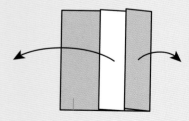

6. Open up the paper completely.

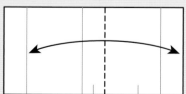

7. Fold the right edge to the leftmost crease and unfold.

8. Fold the bottom left and right corners diagonally inward.

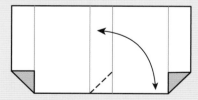

9. Create a small diagonal crease where indicated by folding the bottom right section up to the crease indicated and then unfolding.

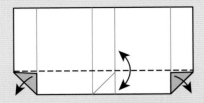

10. Fold the bottom edge up along the horizontal edge of the triangular flaps and unfold. Then unfold the triangular flaps.

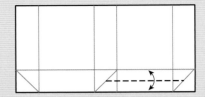

11. Create a small horizontal crease on the right side of the lower section as indicated.

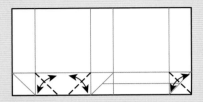

12. Create three more small diagonal folds where indicated. This is the basic form you need to create all the components of your stationery box. The following instructions will show you how to turn this into all the different components you will need.

LID

1. Fold the top edge down to the crease that is indicated.

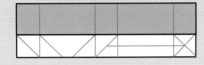

2. Close the box in the same manner as the mini origami drawer on page 84, starting on step 27.

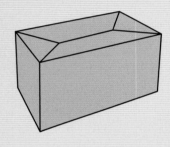

BOX

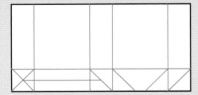

1. To create a matching box that is a bit taller than the lid, use paper that is a tiny bit smaller than what you used for the lid and fold the basic form of this project. If you would like a clean finish, all of the creases from steps 9 to 12 should be completed in the opposite manner, as if the creases are mirrored. The result of doing this is shown here. (This is optional.)

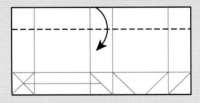

2. Fold the top edge down about ⅓ of the way.

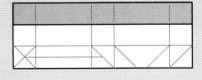

3. Continue closing the box in the same manner as the mini origami drawer on page 84, starting on step 27.

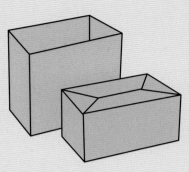

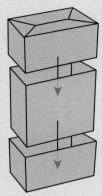

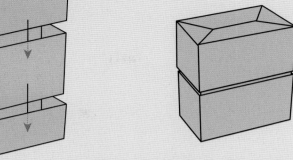

4. Here is a completed lid and box.

If you make two lids using the same size paper and make one box using paper that is a tiny bit shorter, you can slot the bottom of the box into the lids, creating a unique origami gift box.

MAKING A TALLER BOX

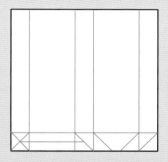

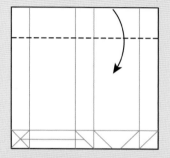

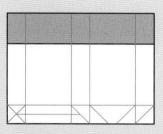

1. Start with square paper, instead of rectangular paper, and fold the box in the same manner as the basic form and box.

2. You can fold the top edge down as much or as little as you like.

3. Close the box in the manner described for the mini origami drawer on page 84, starting on step 27.

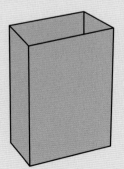

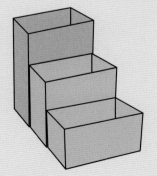

4. You can create boxes of different heights and secure them together using glue, ribbon, or washi tape!

TIP
These boxes can be made with square or rectangular paper for different results.

Ice Cream

This pretty, three-dimensional origami ice-cream cone almost looks like the real thing! You can use one or two colors of paper for the ice cream, depending on if you want one "flavor" or two.

ICE CREAM PAPER: 3 to 4 sheets of 6 × 6 inches (15 × 15 cm)

OPTIONAL ICE CREAM STAND PAPER SIZE: 2 × 2 inches (5 × 5 cm)

DIFFICULTY: ⭐⭐⭐⭐

OUTER CONE

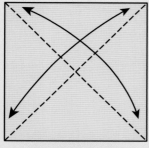

1. With the color side up, fold and unfold the paper in half diagonally in both directions.

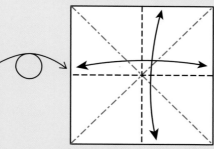

2. Flip the paper over and fold and unfold the paper in half top to bottom and left to right.

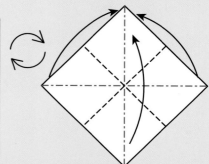

3. Rotate the paper. Bring the left, right, and bottom points up using the creases made in the previous steps.

4. Flatten the paper into an origami square base with the open end at the top.

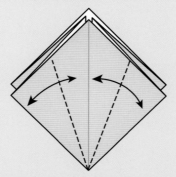

5. Fold the left and right diagonal edges to the central vertical crease and unfold. Repeat on the back.

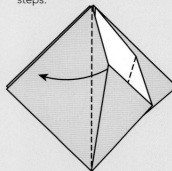

6. Open one of the flaps to the left, squashing the center. Repeat on all of the other sides.

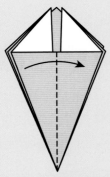

7. Fold one of the flaps to the right so that you are looking at a kite shape.

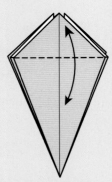

8. Fold the top point down and back up again. Repeat this step on all of the other sides.

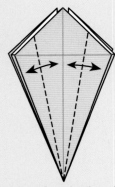

9. Fold the left and right sides to the central vertical crease and unfold. Repeat on all sides.

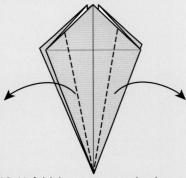

10. Unfold the paper completely, laying it down with the colored side up.

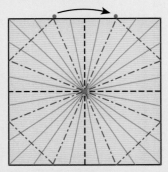

11. Reinforce all of the creases using mountain and valley folds as indicated. Pick up the paper and bring the left point indicated over to the right point indicated.

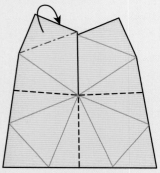

12. Fold the top left point over and behind. Repeat steps 11 and 12 on the other points until you have a closed cone.

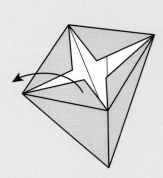

13. Holding the cone, open one of the flaps.

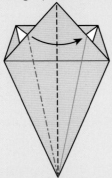

14. Using the existing crease on the left as a mountain fold, bring it over to the right crease that is indicated.

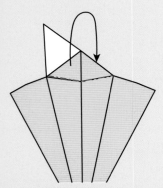

15. Fold the top flap over and down inside the cone along the indicated crease.

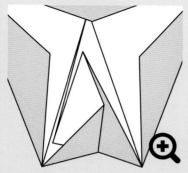

16. If you look inside the cone, this is what you should have.

17. Here's your yummy cone!

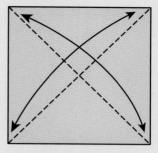

1. With the color side facing up, fold and unfold the paper diagonally in both directions.

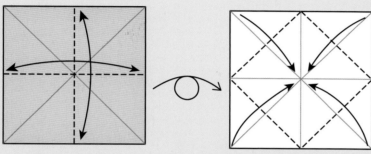

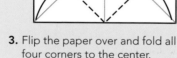

2. Fold and unfold the paper in half top to bottom and left to right.

3. Flip the paper over and fold all four corners to the center.

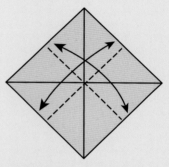

4. Fold and unfold the paper diagonally in half in both directions.

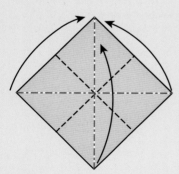

5. Bring the left, right, and bottom points up to the top.

6. Flatten the paper into an origami square base with the open end at the top.

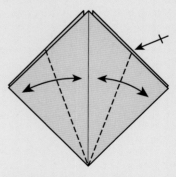

7. Fold the lower left and right diagonal edges to the central vertical crease and unfold. Repeat on the back.

Ice Cream 93

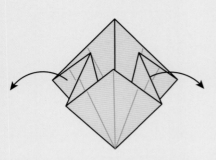

8. Open the paper back up to step 4.

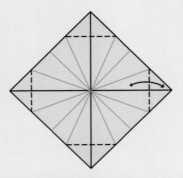

9. Using the existing creases as a guide, fold all four corners inward and unfold.

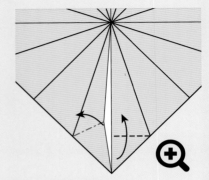

10. Focus on the bottom point of the paper. Using the existing fold, open the left side of the corner while pushing the right side of the corner up.

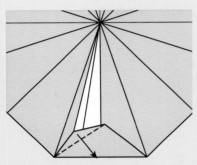

11. Push the left side of the flap back down on top.

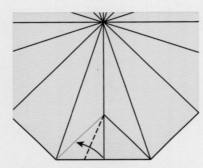

12. Make the indicated diagonal crease on the left section.

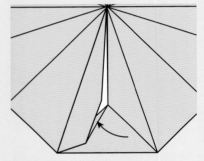

13. Reverse the fold you created in the previous step so it sits inside. Repeat steps 10 to 13 on all the other corners.

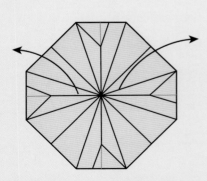

14. Open the paper up completely with the colored side facing up.

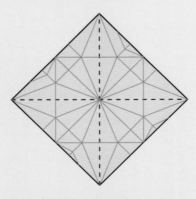

15. Refold the indicated creases.

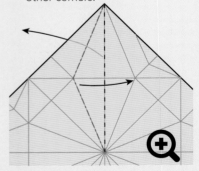

16. Focusing on the top corner, bring the indicated mountain folds over to the right in a similar manner to the outer cone.

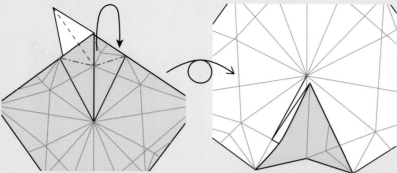

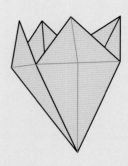

17. Fold the top section down and behind along the indicated creases.

18. Flip the paper over to make sure that it is folded correctly (it should look like this).

19. Repeat steps 16–18 on the other three corners. Here is how your inner cone should now look.

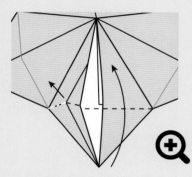

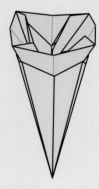

20. Refold steps 10 to 13 on each point of the cone.

21. Apply a dab of glue on the lower part of the inner cone.

22. Slot the inner cone into the outer cone. Allow the glue time to dry.

ICE CREAM

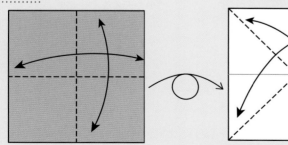

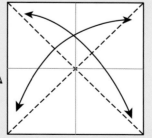

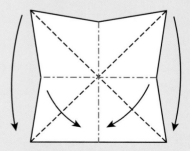

1. With the color side up, fold and unfold the paper in half top to bottom and left to right.

2. Flip the paper over and fold and unfold it in half diagonally in both directions.

3. Bring the top left and right points down while pushing the left and right central points inward.

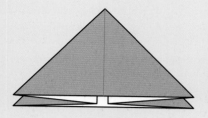

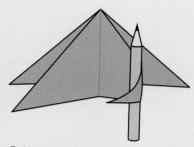

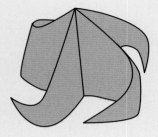

4. Now you have an origami water bomb base.

5. Use something cylindrical, such as a pencil, to curl a flap in a clockwise direction.

6. Continue to curl each of the flaps clockwise.

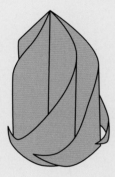

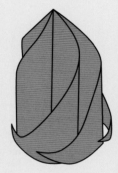

FLAVOR TIP
For a fuller-looking ice cream, use another sheet of paper that is the same color. Or for ice cream that is two "flavors," use another sheet of a different color.

7. You've got some great ice cream! You can slot this into the inner flaps of the cone (see step 10) and enjoy it just as it is, or . . .

8. . . . if you are having two "flavors," repeat steps 1 to 6 using your second sheet of paper.

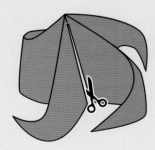

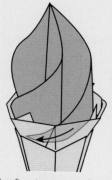

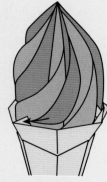

9. Open the second ice cream up a bit and cut slots as indicated on each side without cutting all the way to the top.

10. Slot the first ice cream flavor into the inner flaps of the cone.

11. Slot the second flavor (if using) over the top, in between each section of the first flavor, and into the small flaps you created in step 20 of the inner cone.

STAND

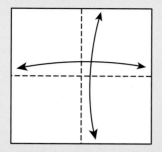

1. Fold and unfold your paper in half top to bottom and left to right.

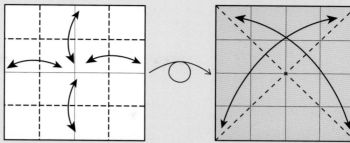

2. Fold each edge of the paper to the middle and unfold.

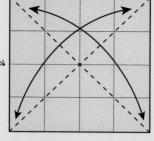

3. Flip the paper over and fold and unfold the paper in half diagonally in both directions.

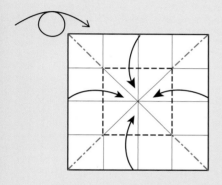

4. Flip the paper back over and bring the left, right, top, and bottom edges inward while also bringing each corner to the center.

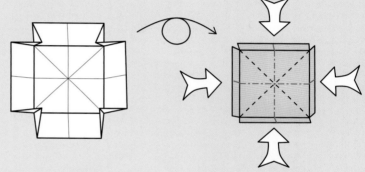

5. Here is what your model should now look like.

6. Flip the paper over and push all of the sides inward.

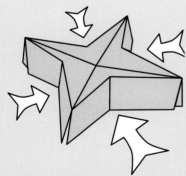

7. Continue pushing the sides until you have an X shape.

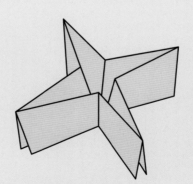

8. Here is the stand for your delicious ice-cream cone!

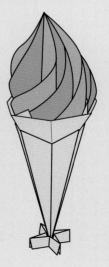

Sushi Roll Boxes

These cute little boxes look like sliced sushi rolls! You can make a few of them and line them up in a row for a fun Japanese snack display, or they can be added to your bento box on page 67.

SUSHI ROLL BOX PAPER SIZE: 6 × 6 inches (15 × 15 cm)

OUTER MASU BOX PAPER SIZE: 4 × 4 inches (10 × 10 cm)

SUSHI ROLL BOX LID

DIFFICULTY: ⭐⭐⭐⭐

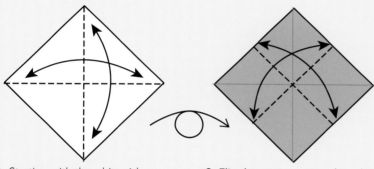
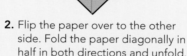

1. Starting with the white side up, fold the paper in half in both directions and unfold.

2. Flip the paper over to the other side. Fold the paper diagonally in half in both directions and unfold.

3. Bring the left, right, and bottom points up to the top.

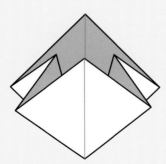
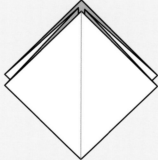
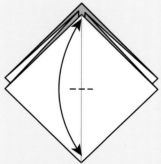

4. Flatten the paper to form an origami square base.

5. Make sure the open end is at the top.

6. Create a small horizontal crease by folding the top point down to the bottom point and unfolding it.

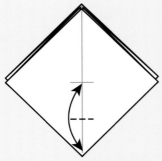

7. Fold the bottom point up to the crease you created in the previous step, make a small crease, and unfold.

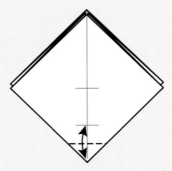

8. Fold the bottom point up to the crease you made in the previous step, crease well, and unfold.

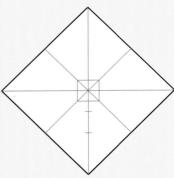

9. Open up the paper completely.

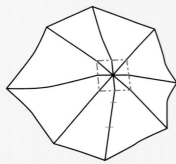

10. Pick up the paper and refold the small square shape in the middle as mountain folds.

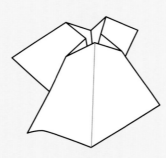

11. Sink fold the small square down inside while reforming the square base.

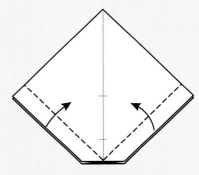

12. Flatten the paper and rotate. Fold the top layer of the lower left and right diagonal edges up as indicated.

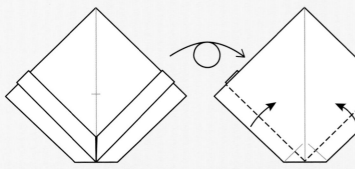

13. This is how your model should now look.

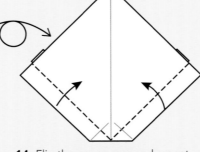

14. Flip the paper over and repeat step 12 on this side.

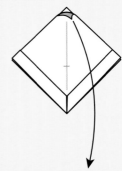

15. Carefully pull the topmost layer down while keeping the diagonal flaps folded.

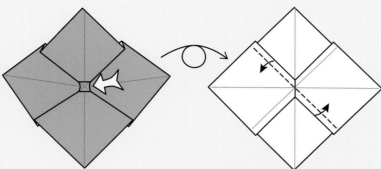

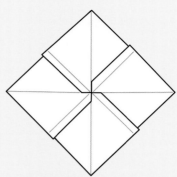

16. Fold out the paper carefully and flatten the central square shape.

17. Flip the paper over from left to right. Fold the top left diagonal flap and bottom right diagonal flap as indicated.

18. Here's what your model should now look like.

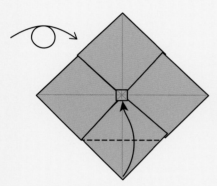

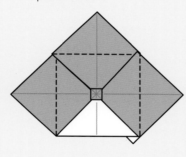

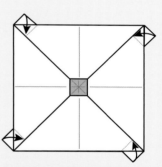

19. Flip the model over from left to right and fold the bottom point up and underneath the square shape, making sure the edges are aligned.

20. Here's how your model should look. Rotate the paper and repeat the previous step on all the sides. You can glue these flaps down if you like.

21. Tuck the small corners in and slot them underneath.

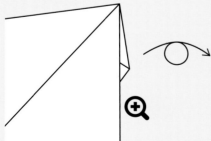

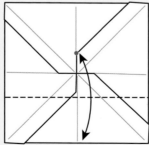

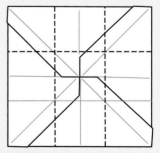

22. Here's a close-up of what the corners should look like.

23. Flip the paper over to the other side. Fold the bottom edge up to the point indicated and unfold.

24. Rotate the paper and repeat the previous step on the other three sides.

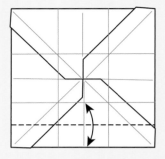

25. Fold the bottom edge up to the horizontal crease that is indicated and unfold.

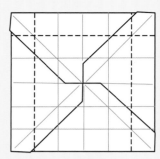

26. Repeat the previous step on the other three sides.

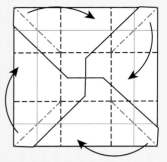

27. Lift all four points up and rotate them clockwise, making the box three-dimensional.

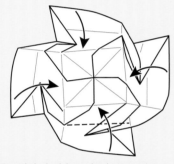

28. While holding the box in shape, fold the lower edges over and inside the box.

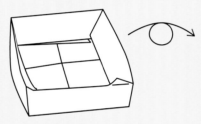

29. Here's how your box should look.

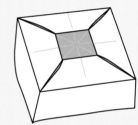

30. Flip the box over.

31. Next make a masu box (page 8) using paper that is two-thirds the size of the paper you used for the sushi roll box lid. Put the sushi roll box lid inside the masu box and enjoy!

VARIATION

For a more advanced, cleaner version, use paper with white on both sides.

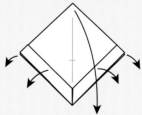

1. Fold up to step 14 of the sushi roll box lid, except this time unfold the paper completely.

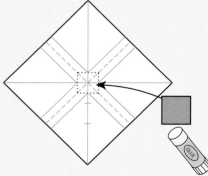

2. There is a small square shape in the center of the paper. Glue on a square of colored paper here . . .

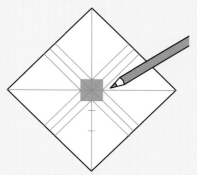

. . . or you could use a pencil to color the square in.

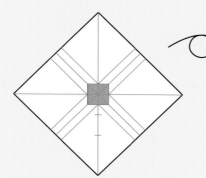

3. Here is your paper.

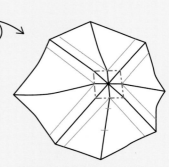

4. Flip the paper over to the other side and sink fold the small square.

5. Here is what your model should now look like.

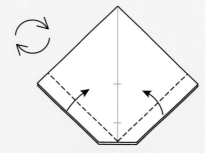

6. Flatten and rotate the paper so that the opening is at the top and refold the lower diagonal creases on the front and back.

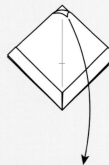

7. Carefully pull the top layer down while keeping the diagonal flaps in place.

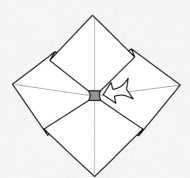

8. Carefully flatten the paper including the little square in the middle.

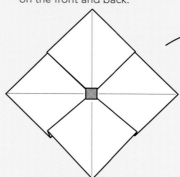

9. Here is what your model should now look like.

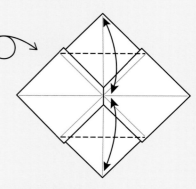

10. Flip the paper over and fold the top and bottom points to the middle and unfold.

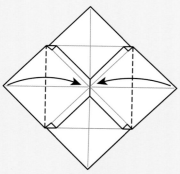

11. Fold the left and right points to the center.

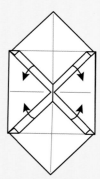

12. Fold the four inner diagonal flaps as indicated.

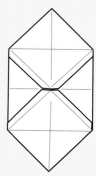

13. Here is what your model should now look like.

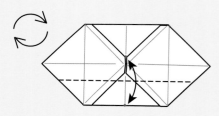

14. Rotate the paper. Fold the bottom edge to the point indicated by the red dot and unfold.

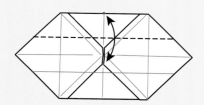

15. Fold the top edge to the point indicated by the red dot and unfold.

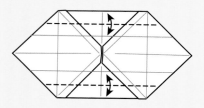

16. Fold the top and bottom edges to the two creases you just made and unfold.

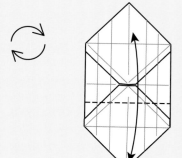

17. Rotate the paper. Create a new horizontal crease that runs through the points indicated by the red dots.

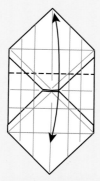

18. Create another new horizontal crease that runs through the points indicated by the red dots.

19. Create two more horizontal creases where indicated by the red dots.

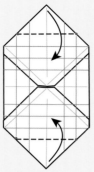

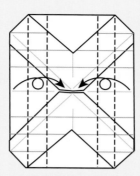

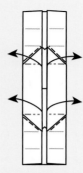

20. Using the two outermost vertical creases as a guide, fold the top and bottom points inward.

21. Using the existing creases, fold the left and right edges in twice to the middle.

22. Create diagonal folds where indicated, with the same method used for closing the traditional masu box on page 8. Open up the left and right flaps in the center, making the box three-dimensional.

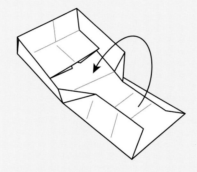

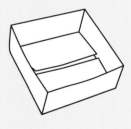

23. Close the top of the box by bringing the top flap down and inside the box.

24. Insert the lower section into the inside of the box.

25. You can use a dab of glue to secure the flaps inside if you like.

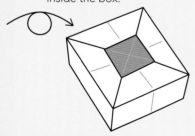

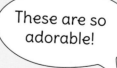

These are so adorable!

26. Flip the box over.

27. Make a masu box (page 8) using paper that is two-thirds the size of the paper you used to create this variation of the sushi roll box lid. Put the sushi roll box lid inside the masu box and give yourself a pat on the back!

Nigiri Sushi Boxes

This trio of cute nigiri sushi boxes goes perfectly with the origami sushi roll boxes! We have tamago (egg), salmon, and ebi (shrimp). Each one starts with the same thirteen steps and can be made with or without the "seaweed" wrap.

PAPER SIZE: 7 × 7 inches (17.5 × 17.5 cm) or larger

DIFFICULTY:

BASIC NIGIRI SUSHI BOX

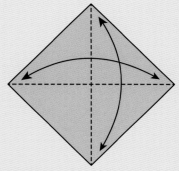

1. Starting with your paper color side up, fold and unfold it in half diagonally in both directions.

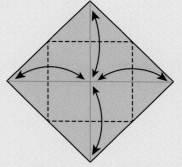

2. Fold all four corners to the middle and unfold.

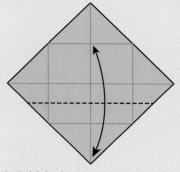

3. Fold the bottom point up to the topmost horizontal crease and unfold.

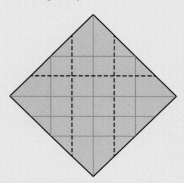

4. Repeat the last step on the other three points by rotating the paper.

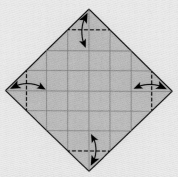

5. Fold all four points inward as indicated and unfold.

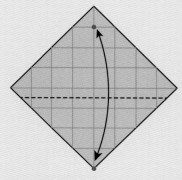

6. Fold the bottom point up to the point indicated by the red dot and unfold.

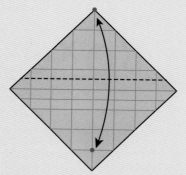

7. Fold the top point down to the bottom point indicated by the red dot and unfold.

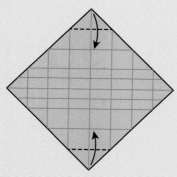

8. Fold the top point and bottom point inward.

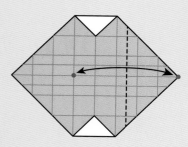

9. Fold the right point to the point indicated by the red dot and unfold.

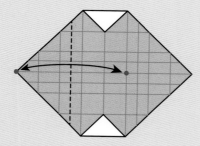

10. Fold the left point to the point indicated by the red dot and unfold.

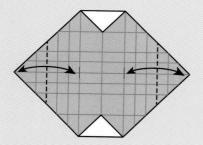

11. Fold the left and the right points to the indicated creases and unfold.

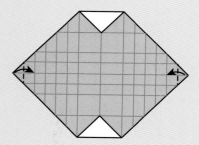

12. Fold the left and the right points inward to the creases indicated.

TAMAGO NIGIRI SUSHI BOX

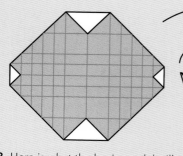

13. Here is what the basic model will look like for all of your nigiri sushi boxes.

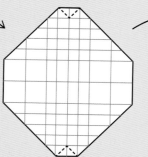

14. Flip the paper over and rotate it. Create diagonal creases on the top and bottom where indicated.

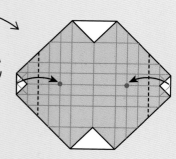

15. Flip the paper over and rotate it. Using the existing creases, fold the left and right edges inward to the points indicated by the red dots.

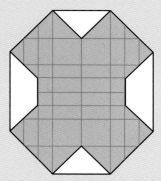

16. Here is what your model should now look like.

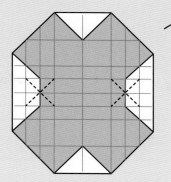

17. Create X-shaped diagonal creases where indicated.

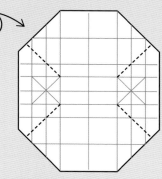

18. Flip the paper over and create the indicated diagonal creases.

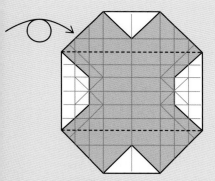

19. Flip the paper over and create the top and bottom horizontal creases as indicated.

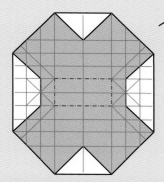

20. Refold the central rectangular shape as mountain folds.

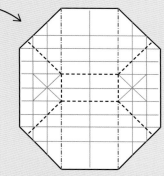

21. Turn the paper over and reinforce the indicated diagonal creases as valley folds and the indicated vertical creases as mountain folds.

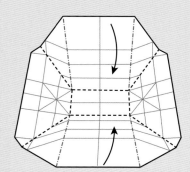

22. Bring the top and bottom edges forward, making the model three-dimensional.

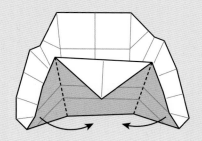

23. Repeat on the back.

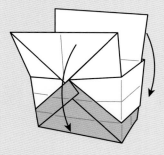

24. Fold the top flaps of the box over and down.

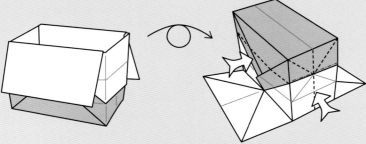

25. This is how your model should now look.

26. Flip it over so the base is at the top. Push where the arrows indicate to collapse the model's sides together.

27. Your model should now look like this.

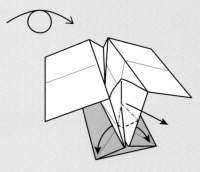

28. Turn the model back over and use your finger to pull open the front of the model, forming one end of the box while squashing the sides down.

29. Repeat the previous step on the other end of the model.

30. Squash the model so that it is no longer springy.

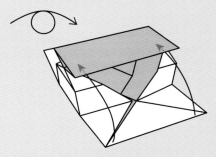

31. Turn the model over and insert the points of the flap inside the slot on the underside of the colored section.

32. Repeat the previous step on the other side.

33. Enjoy your tamago nigiri sushi!

SALMON NIGIRI SUSHI BOX

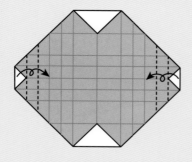 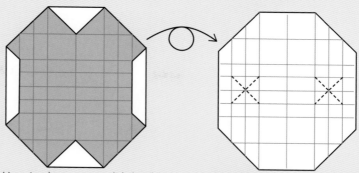

1. Unfold the tamago sushi box to step 13, or start again and fold up to step 13. Fold the right and left sides in twice as indicated.

2. Here is what your model should look like.

3. Flip the paper over to the other side and create diagonal-shaped creases as indicated.

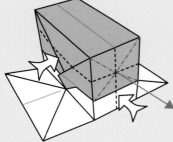 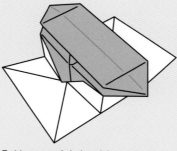 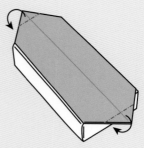

4. Continue folding the tamago nigiri sushi box from step 18 to step 25. Then, instead of pushing in the end of the box, use your finger to pull the ends to create points while collapsing the sides of the box together.

5. Your model should now look like this. Continue folding the salmon nigiri sushi box in the same manner as the tamago nigiri sushi box.

6. You can fold the points of the top under to make your salmon more rounded.

SHRIMP NIGIRI SUSHI BOX

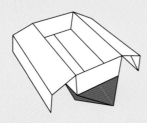 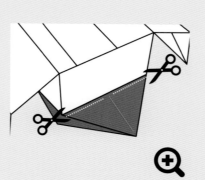 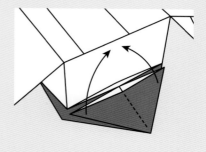

1. After completing a salmon nigiri sushi box, open up the sides of the box.

2. Using scissors, make small cuts where indicated on the top layer only.

3. Fold the two flaps up toward each other.

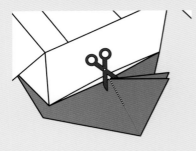

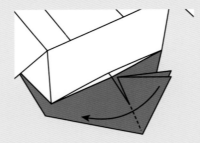

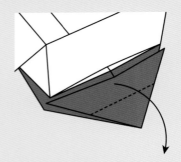

4. Use the scissors to cut where indicated. Be careful not to cut to the end.

5. Fold the flaps back down.

6. Fold the triangular flap away from the box, taking the layers underneath with it.

SEAWEED STRIP

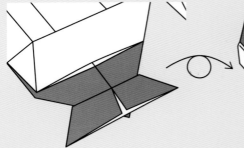

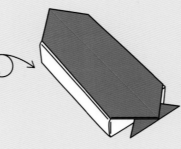

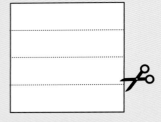

7. You model should now look like this.

8. Flip it over, and you've got one cute shrimp nigiri sushi box!

1. Taking the same size paper you used for the nigiri sushi box, fold in half and then fold it in half again. Unfold it and cut along the creases so that you have four equal strips of paper.

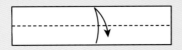

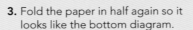

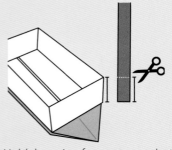

2. Fold the bottom edge of the paper up to top edge and unfold. Fold the top and bottom edges of the paper to the central crease.

3. Fold the paper in half again so it looks like the bottom diagram.

4. Hold the strip of paper up against the side of a completed nigiri sushi box and trim an amount equal to its height off of your strip of paper.

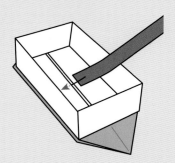

5. Insert the strip of paper into the slot on the inside of the lid.

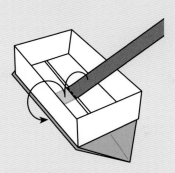

6. Fold the strip of paper in the opposite direction and flatten it against the inside of the box.

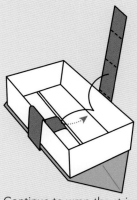

7. Continue to wrap the strip of paper around the outside of the box.

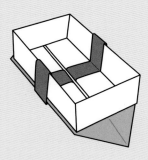

8. Fold the strip of paper inside the other side of the box, and slot the end of the paper into the inside pocket of the box.

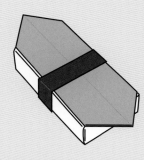

9. Here's your seaweed-wrapped nigiri sushi box! To make a lower box for the sushi lids, use the tutorial on page 36 for the rectangular masu box. You can use the same size paper (or a tiny bit smaller) to make the lower box.

I love ebi!

I love tamago!

Flower Bowl

This origami flower bowl is one of the more complex origami models included in this book. You can use it to decorate during spring, and it is sturdy enough to hold jewelry or makeup. I recommend using a large piece of paper, such as 8 × 8 inches (20 × 20 cm) the first time you try to make this model.

DIFFICULTY:

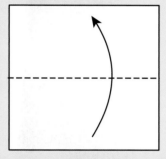

1. Start by folding the bottom edge of the paper up to the top edge.

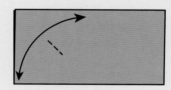

2. Fold the bottom left corner diagonally up to the right, make a small crease, and unfold.

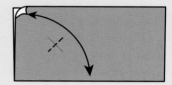

3. Fold the top left corner of the paper diagonally down, make another small crease, and unfold.

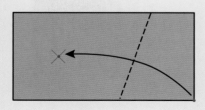

4. Bring the bottom right point over to the center of the small creases you made in the previous steps.

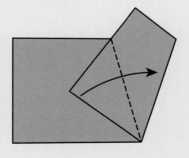

5. Fold the diagonal left edge of the front flap over to the right edge.

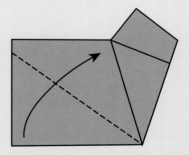

6. Fold the bottom left edge of the paper diagonally up to meet the diagonal edge of the right section.

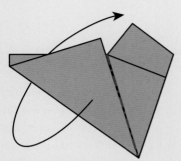

7. Fold the left section behind.

8. Use scissors to trim the top section of the paper along the top edge of the front section.

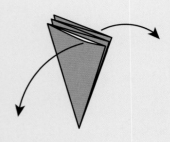

9. Open up the paper.

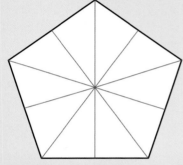

10. Position the pentagon as shown.

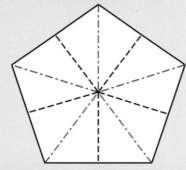

11. Refold the mountain and valley creases as indicated.

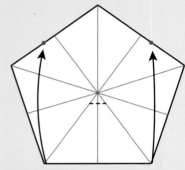

12. Bring the bottom edge of the paper up to the points indicated by the red dots and make a small crease in the center section only.

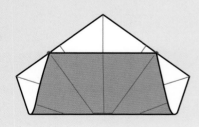

13. This is how your model should look. Unfold it.

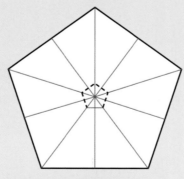

14. Repeat steps 12 and 13 on all of the other edges by rotating the paper.

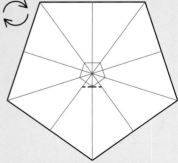

15. Rotate the paper so that one of the points is pointing downward. Create a small crease in the center section that intersects with the point of the small upside-down pentagon in the middle.

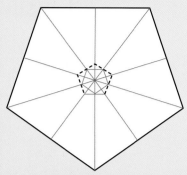

16. Repeat the last step on all of the other sides.

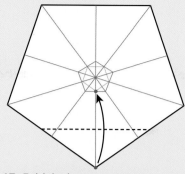

17. Fold the bottom point up to the bottom edge of the larger pentagon in the middle.

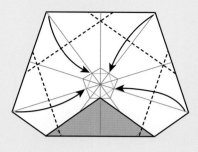

18. Rotate the paper and repeat the previous step on all of the other points.

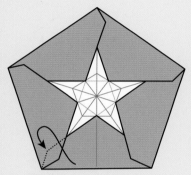

19. On the last section, open the first point that you folded up and insert the last point underneath it.

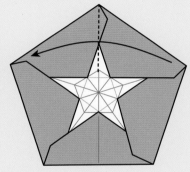

20. Fold the right point over to the left using the existing crease and then unfold.

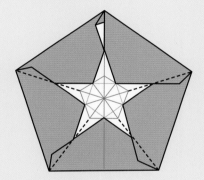

21. Rotate the paper and repeat the previous step on all of the other points.

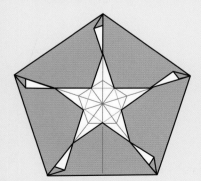

22. Fold all of the little flaps backward, making sure they are all well-formed. This is what your model should now look like.

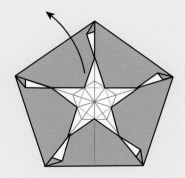

23. Open one of the flaps.

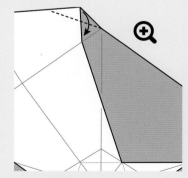

24. Fold down the little flap that you made in steps 20–22.

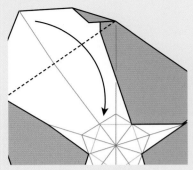

25. Refold the flap that you opened in step 23. Repeat this process on all of the points.

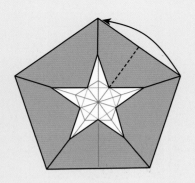

26. Refold the right section diagonally up to the top point.

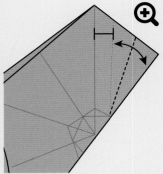

27. Create a diagonal crease by folding the right diagonal edge to meet what you would imagine to be a vertical line running parallel to the existing vertical line. Unfold and repeat this step on all of the sides.

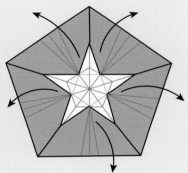

28. Open up the paper completely.

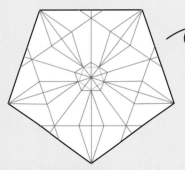

29. This is what your paper should now look like.

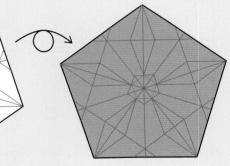

30. Flip the paper over and position it as shown.

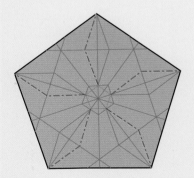

31. Reinforce the creases indicated as mountain folds.

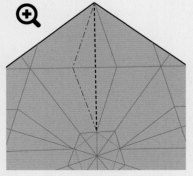

32. Focusing on the top section, make a valley fold where indicated and bring the left diagonal mountain folds over to the right.

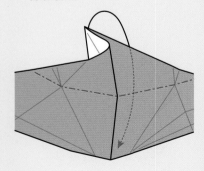

33. Fold the top section over and behind.

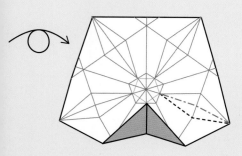

34. Flip the paper over and start the same process on the next section.

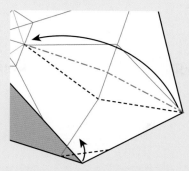

35. As you go through each section, fold the small flap that is indicated here first.

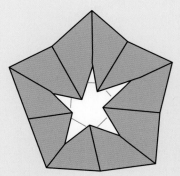

36. This is what your model should now look like.

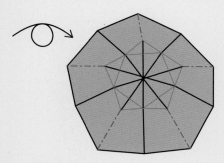

37. Flip the model over and reinforce all the creases indicated as mountain folds

38. Push the inside of the model inward.

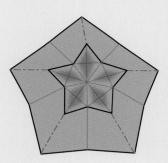

39. Continue pushing until . . .

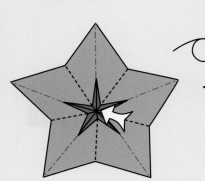

40. . . . you have a star-shaped hollow.

41. Flip the model over to the other side and continue pushing the sides inward while making sure that the flaps inside are behind the small three-dimensional star in the middle.

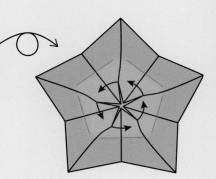

42. Flip the model back over and flatten the flaps while rotating them all in one direction.

Flower Bowl   119

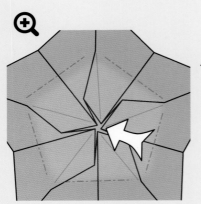

43. Flatten the inside.

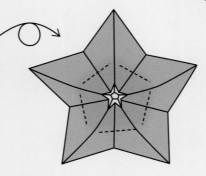

44. Flip the model over, and it should look like this.

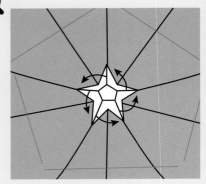

45. You can flatten the star in the center if if you like by rotating all its edges and pressing down gently.

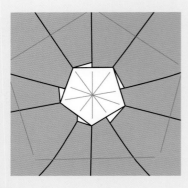

46. The star will become a pentagon if you flatten it.

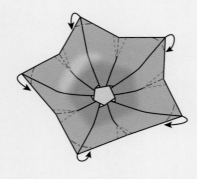

47. You can now shape the flower by folding all of the points over to round the petals.

48. You can also make little crimps between the petals to give the model a more flowery shape.

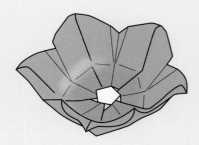

49. Your pretty flower bowl is now complete!

Try a combination of colors!

Star Bowl

This variation from the flower bowl on page 115 uses the same beginning steps, but then differs to make a star bowl. When placed together, the pair looks so sweet as a tabletop arrangement.

DIFFICULTY:

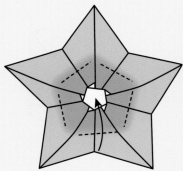

1. Starting from step 46 after flattening the star in the center, fold the lower central point to the middle of the star

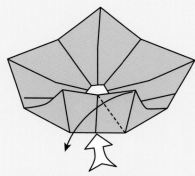

2. Make a diagonal fold, bringing the top right point down to the left.

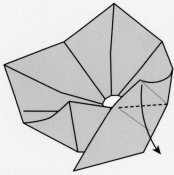

3. Rotate the paper and continue folding the points diagonally to the left.

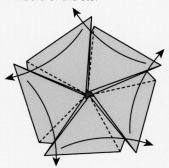

4. Fold all of the points back in the other direction.

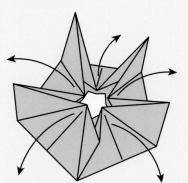

5. Open all of the sides to complete the star bowl.

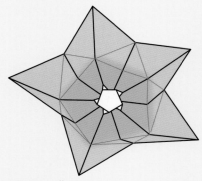

6. It's stellar!

Too cute!

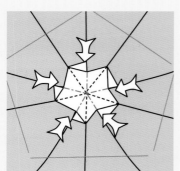

7. You can push in the edges of the inner star if you like.

8. Now you've got lots of stars!

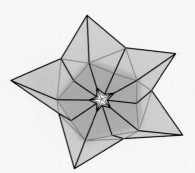

Twinkle Star

This cute, puffy origami star makes a great decoration. If you use yellow or gold paper, it is perfect for Christmas or Tanabata, the Japanese star festival—or try different colors for a bright design arrangement!

RECOMMENDED PAPER SIZE: 7 × 7 inches (17.5 × 17.5 cm)

DIFFICULTY:

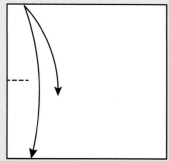

1. Bring the bottom edge of the paper up to the top edge, make a small crease on the left side, and unfold.

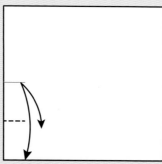

2. Bring the bottom edge up to the crease you made in the previous step, make another small crease on the left side, and unfold.

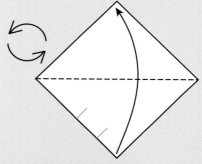

3. Rotate the paper counterclockwise so that the little creases are on the lower left diagonal edge. Fold the bottom point up to the top point.

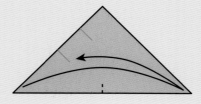

4. Make a small crease along the bottom edge at the vertical center of the paper.

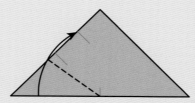

5. Using the crease you made in the previous step, bring the left point up to meet the topmost mark on the left diagonal edge.

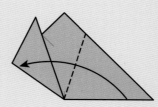

6. Fold the right point over to the lower left diagonal edge.

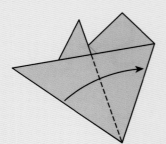 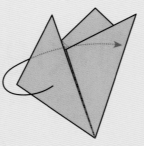 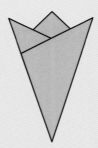 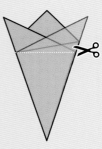

7. Fold the left side of the top layer over to the right diagonal edge.

8. Fold the left section behind and to the right so all of the edges align.

9. This is what your model should now look like.

10. Mark the points that are the lowest parts of the folds on both sides and draw a line connecting the two marks. Now trim off the top along the line.

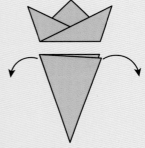

11. Open up the paper completely. You now have a decagon.

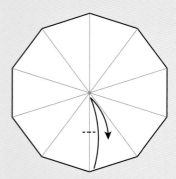

12. Making sure that one of the points of the decagon is pointing up, fold the lower point up to the center and make a small crease.

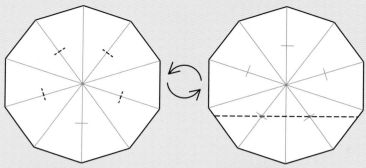

13. Repeat the previous step on alternating points as indicated.

14. Rotate the paper so that the little creases are now in the positions indicated. Using the two lower creases as guides, create a crease that runs through the center of them.

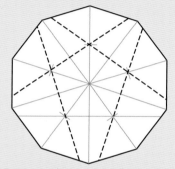

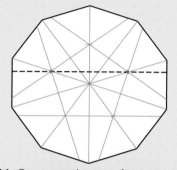

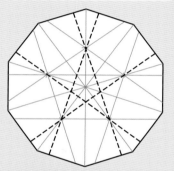

15. Rotate the paper and create the creases on the other angles.

16. Create another set of creases that run from the two intersecting creases indicated by the red dots.

17. Rotate the paper, creating creases on the other angles indicated.

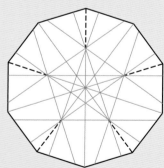

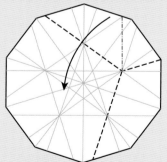

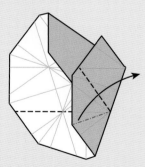

18. Make sure that all five of the creases indicated are valley folds.

19. Fold the top right section down along the crease indicated while you fold the lower right section of the paper on top. A new mountain fold will be created as you squash the paper into place.

20. Fold the lower section of the front flap over to the right along the crease indicated. As you do this, fold the lower section underneath and up to the right.

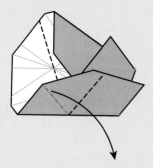

21. Repeat the same process on the lower left of the topmost flap.

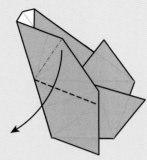

22. The last flap needs a little extra attention. Bring the top left flap down to the left and hold it open.

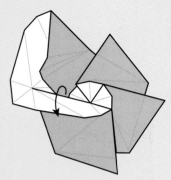

23. While the top left section is open, bring the little inner flap over the top of the topmost layer.

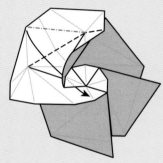

24. Complete the shape by folding the top left section down and to the right, underneath that little flap you worked on in the previous step.

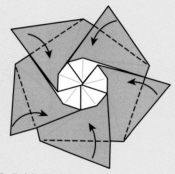

25. Fold all of the points inward using the existing creases.

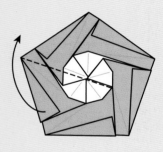

26. Focusing on the bottom left section, open it upward so that you can see underneath.

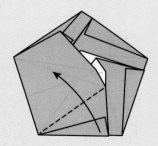

27. Fold the bottom right section diagonally up to the left, using the existing crease.

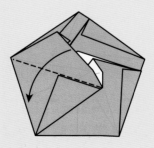

28. Fold the left section back down.

FOLDING TIP

If your star looks misaligned, it's probably because some creases were not properly formed earlier on. One slight misalignment will not affect the final model, but things can get wonky if you're not careful.